Going Viral

Going Viral

Zombies, Viruses, and the End of the World

DAHLIA SCHWEITZER

Rutgers University Press

New Brunswick, Newark, and Camden, New Jersey, and London

Library of Congress Cataloging-in-Publication Data
Names: Schweitzer, Dahlia, author.
Title: Going viral : zombies, viruses, and the end of the world / Dahlia Schweitzer.
Description: New Brunswick : Rutgers University Press, 2018. | Includes bibliographical references and index.
Identifiers: LCCN 2017014954 (print) | LCCN 2017057488 (ebook) | ISBN 9780813593166 (E-pub) | ISBN 9780813593180 (Web PDF) | ISBN 9780813593159 (hardback) | ISBN 9780813593142 (paperback) | ISBN 9780813593166 (ebook)
Subjects: LCSH: Epidemics in mass media. | Apocalypse in mass media. | Mass media—Social aspects—United States. | BISAC: PERFORMING ARTS / Film & Video / History & Criticism. | SOCIAL SCIENCE / Disease & Health Issues. | SOCIAL SCIENCE / Media Studies.
Classification: LCC P96.E632 (ebook) | LCC P96.E632 U673 2018 (print) | DDC 791.43/615—dc23
LC record available at https://lccn.loc.gov/2017014954

A British Cataloging-in-Publication record for this book is available from the British Library.

∞ The paper used in this publication meets the requirements of the American National Standard for Information Sciences—Permanence of Paper for Printed Library Materials, ANSI Z39.48–1992.

www.rutgersuniversitypress.org

Manufactured in the United States of America

Contents

Preface

In 1995, I saw a movie called *Safe* at an art house theater in downtown Washington, DC. Written and directed by Todd Haynes, the film left me speechless. As the enigmatic Carol White, the normally luminous Julianne Moore's radiant beauty becomes whiter and fainter as the film progresses; she is the victim of a disease no one can diagnose, much less cure. There is no question that *Safe* is significant not only as a work of cinema but also as an accurate reflection of a particular moment in American history and a prophetic statement about how, in an identity-based culture, diseases would, in the subsequent decades, become another middle-class way to categorize ourselves, manage our problems, file our grievances, and find our communities.

As the years passed and AIDS shared the media spotlight with SARS, Ebola, and avian influenza, I grew fascinated not only with the fear that these viruses could stir up but also with the ways that they changed fundamental social interaction. Suddenly, "personal space" could mean the difference between life and death—or so the media headlines would have you believe. The healthy-looking person beside you could kill you. The plane you are about to board could be flying hundreds of viruses around the world.

It is not just that viruses impact, but that they impact our understanding of the world; they are talking points for politicians as much as box office fodder for Hollywood. Why do we fear these viruses so? And why, over the last few years, have we become so preoccupied with visualizing our demise?

Zombies in a postapocalyptic dystopia have become a meal ticket for publishers and producers alike, with readers and viewers hungry for the next visualization of what our world may become or what we, as humans, can become.

The outbreak narrative has become a parable for our fears, evolving to depict our horrors of contagion, of the world, of monsters, and of becoming monsters. It is a template that adapts with changing cultural and social anxieties, as well as a guidepost that tells us where we are going and where we have been. How provincial we were back in 1995, when a deadly virus from Africa only threatened the small town of Cedar Creek, when viruses could forge romances and bring lovers together! In 2011, the world was a much colder place, full of isolation while still, perversely, heavily interconnected—a virus was capable of crossing the world in the blink of an eye. Now, *The Walking Dead* one of the highest-rated basic cable shows of all time, visualizes for its viewers week after week just how brutal the future can look and how quickly we can get there.

The biggest question is why. Why are we so drawn to these narratives? Why is a film cycle launched in the mid-1990s continuing to reap box office rewards and gain television ratings? Why are we so afraid of viruses halfway around the world? Why are we obsessed with zombies? And how does the outbreak narrative reflect anxieties about globalization, risk society, and neoliberal capitalism?

This book attempts to answer these questions and more by tracking the permutations of the outbreak narrative as it moves into the twenty-first century and by studying the intersections between fields of medicine, politics, media, and representation. This book attempts to understand why we fear the things we do, how film and television feed those fears, and why we cannot stop watching.

Going Viral

Introduction

⎯⎯⎯⎯⎯⎯⎯⎯⎯⎯⎯⎯⎯⎯⎯⎯⎯⎯⎯●

> Plague remains a virulent metaphor: a
> powerful and historically lethal way of
> labeling enemies and outsiders, a dis-
> turbing vector for our fears surrounding
> the fragility of the social bond, and a
> puissant figuration of the conceptual
> and psychic infectiousness at work
> within psychoanalytic thinking and its
> reception.
> —Jennifer Cooke, *Legacies of Plague in
> Literature, Theory, and Film*

American film and television outbreak narratives surround us, even if we are unaware of their presence, repeating particular characters, images, and story lines in service of a formulaic narrative that both reflects and shapes paradigms of disease and fear. The "outbreak narrative" generally begins with the discovery of an emerging infection and follows it as it spreads, documenting the journey to contain or neutralize it. Some versions incorporate terrorism, while others use zombies. Some destroy the world, while others save it. Many dwell on corporate and government conspiracies, while still others reflect upon what the world would look like if most of us—including those corporations and governments—were dead. All variations of this template reflect various real-life anxieties about emerging infections and potential pandemics, occasionally relieving these anxieties in the neatly removed world of the Hollywood screen, but often feeding them as well. It is with this feeding of the fear that I am most intrigued.

The outbreak narrative reveals anxieties related to three types of increasingly ineffective boundaries: first, between the personal body and the body politic; second, between individual nations; and third, between "ordinary" people and potentially dangerous disenfranchised groups. Significantly, the outbreak narrative also reveals various ways these anxieties have been constructed and commodified. While fears of viral outbreaks can be valid responses to actual threats, they also reflect latent and/or hyperbolic anxieties triggered by changes in how the world now works. It is not as simple as "disease has impacted our understanding of globalization," or "globalization has impacted our understanding of disease." It is that these outbreak narratives—and the anxieties they reflect—feed into larger narratives constructed by government organizations, journalists, and Hollywood to fuel an ever-expanding relationship between fear, power, and money. Fear requires a multiplier in order to spread, whether it be word-of-mouth rumor, print media, radio, film, or television.[1] While it is true that fear may be a result of a particular situation, it is also a product of social construction, shaped by cultural scripts that instruct people how and of what to be afraid. In order to understand fear in a contemporary society, one must assess that society's culture and the ways fear is shaped and expressed within it.[2]

For example, during the 1950s, the language of bodily invasion and immune system failure pervaded film: in *Invasion of the Body Snatchers* (Siegel, 1956), emotionless alien duplicates slowly replace the population of the fictional California town of Santa Mira, and in *Invaders from Mars* (Menzies, 1953), a young boy realizes that residents of his town are being taken over by aliens. This acted as a metaphor for the imagined threat to the American body politic at the hands of Communism. However, starting in the 1990s, the outbreak narrative turned these metaphors literal. The threat was no longer from the outside but from the inside, not so much a threat to the body from aliens or monsters or Bolsheviks, but the body literally acting as a threat. Significantly enlarged microscopic views of deadly germs attacking bodily cells became visualizations of this new kind of invasion. Outer space was replaced with inner space, the body "simultaneously an uncontrollable mutineer and a vulnerable victim."[3]

This idea—that one's own body cannot be trusted or protected—is illustrated in Todd Haynes's film *Safe* (1995). Carol White (Julianne Moore) is an ordinary housewife in the affluent suburbs of Los Angeles who develops multiple chemical sensitivity (MCS). MCS often begins as allergic reactions to chemicals and synthetic products but can spread to include almost everything, including one's own body. When Carol starts to show symptoms (nosebleeds, weakness, coughing, vomiting, and convulsions), no one takes her seriously, including her husband, doctor, and psychiatrist. *Safe* plays with both the metaphorical and the literal, leaving it unclear whether Carol's symptoms are psychological or physical. The film acts as a transition of sorts from an era when such fears were metaphorical to now, when these fears feel alarmingly literal.

Safe is also an eerily prescient film that predicted just how much we would become obsessed with our own immunities and how little that obsession could save us. In 2014, Haynes emphasized that the themes of *Safe* still remained relevant, that we are a culture struggling with a sense that our immunity is in peril.[4] Haynes has also acknowledged that *Safe* is an analogy for the AIDS crisis, with MCS acting as a surrogate virus for the human immunodeficiency virus (HIV). While MCS forces the immune system into overdrive, making almost everything potentially hazardous, HIV makes it harder for the infected person's immune system to fight off infections and diseases—literally rendering the immune system deficient—which also makes almost everything hazardous to those infected. In other words, while MCS reduces the body's ability to defend itself because the immune system is in overdrive, HIV reduces the body's ability to defend itself because the immune system has been weakened.

During the 1980s, not only did HIV/AIDS heighten awareness of the immune system—how it works as well as how it fails to work—but it also exacerbated the failure of the scientific community to rid the world of infectious diseases. Following World War II, many thought the scientific community had done exactly that. Antibiotics had basically eradicated contagious diseases like tuberculosis and syphilis, and during the 1960s, infectious disease was seen as such a declining specialty that medical students were told to concentrate instead on "real problems" like cancer and heart disease.[5] But then AIDS hit, with its mounting death tolls, and no one could stop it.

The threat of highly contagious disease often creates fear, and much like contagious disease, this fear can spread like wildfire. AIDS acted both as a reminder of that fear and as an indicator of other emerging viruses to come AIDS reinforced concerns that all boundaries—but especially bodily ones—are porous and that there is no real protection against microbial invasions. Government organizations like the Centers for Disease Control and Prevention (CDC), journalists, and Hollywood capitalized on these fears for attention, power, and money. For example, in "The Killers All Around," published in *Time* magazine in September 1994, Michael Lemonick writes,

> Protozoans, bacteria, viruses—a whole menagerie of microscopic pests constantly assaults every part of our body, looking for a way inside. Many are harmless or easy to fight off. Others—as we are now so often reminded— are merciless killers . . . The danger is greatest, of course, in the underdeveloped world, where epidemics of cholera, dysentery and malaria are spawned by war, poverty, overcrowding and poor sanitation. But the microbial world knows no boundaries. For all the vaunted power of modern medicine, deadly infections are a growing threat to everyone, everywhere.[6]

This kind of hyperbolic language is not unusual. Articles about viruses often sensationalize in order to sell magazines under the guise of providing information. However, while it is true that the danger is great in the "underdeveloped world," this article uses that danger to set up the "us versus them" trope that will persist within the outbreak narrative, stigmatizing the "primitive and dangerous" other so threatening to those in the developed world. The article also exaggerates the fear of death "to everyone, everywhere." Many dangerous viruses, including Ebola, are not actually deadly when proper medical care is available. Nonetheless, hyperbolic language continues to be a common accompaniment to information about emerging viruses. Even though concerns about microbial enemies are not new, it was in the 1990s that they—often described with the term "emerging viruses"—appeared both as a coherent concept and as a deadly threat.

The notion of "emerging viruses" is generally credited to Stephen S. Morse, professor of epidemiology at Columbia University, who chaired the 1989 conference "Emerging Viruses: The Evolution of Viruses and Viral Disease." In 1993, Oxford University Press published his book *Emerging Viruses*, which was selected by *American Scientist* as one of the top science books of the twentieth century. Morse also coined the phrase "instant-distant infections," referencing the idea that we are only "a plane ride away" from a "chain of lethal transmission."[7] Morse was also credited, as well, for establishing links between the largest and smallest scalar extremes. For example, he drew attention to the ways large-scale events like urbanization, globalization, environmental destruction, and war would have a direct impact on the microbial level.[8] This meant that, in turn, altering local behavior could then have global repercussions. For instance, an outbreak in a small African or Asian village could have a global impact.

In 1991, the National Academy of Sciences (NAS) convened a committee of scientists and health experts, including Morse and his colleague Joshua Lederberg—geneticist, microbiologist, and winner of the 1958 Nobel Prize in Physiology or Medicine—to put together a report on the effects of global change on American health and security. Lederberg is the one whose quote ("The single biggest threat to man's continued dominance on the planet is a virus") opens one of the most successful and influential outbreak narratives, the film *Outbreak* (Petersen, 1995). In his article "The Scale Politics of Emerging Diseases," Nicholas B. King argues that this report transformed Morse's ideas "into a civic advocacy campaign, distilling a complex constellation of ideas into a coherent yet flexible discourse intended to convince policy makers of the national consequences of global change." Significantly, King observes, this report was written at a time when the public health community, and infectious disease researchers in particular, was reeling from decades of budget cuts.[9] The public health community desperately needed to remind the public (and the government) of its importance.

Right on cue, Richard Preston's article "Crisis in the Hot Zone" was published in the *New Yorker* in 1992. It detailed what transpired when a strain of Ebola broke out at a primate quarantine facility in Reston, Virginia, not far from Washington, DC, and the efforts of two virologists from the US Army Medical Research Institute of Infectious Disease (USAMRIID) to contain the outbreak. The strain was an airborne version of Ebola, which, if humans had been susceptible to it, could have been extremely dangerous. (Human-to-human transmission of the Ebola virus is not airborne but rather spreads via direct contact with infected bodily fluids.) However, the virus was only lethal to monkeys, and so the outbreak was eventually stopped, but only after all the monkeys had been killed. While Lederberg is not quoted in the article, it was Lederberg who initially told Preston about the outbreak, encouraging him to look into it.[10]

Appropriately, Preston references the report commissioned by the NAS in the article (calling it a "frightening report") and quotes its description of the Reston event (a "classic example of 'the potential of foreign disease agents to enter the United States'"), adding that the incident had "scared a lot of epidemiologists." Preston goes on to frighten his readers further by summarizing that the report warns that "not only emerging viruses but also mutant bacteria . . . have become major and growing threats to the American population . . . We lack the forces to deal with a monster, at the very time that a monster could appear." Additionally, and here Preston quotes from the NAS report directly, "'We can also be confident that new diseases will emerge, although it is impossible to predict their individual emergence in time and place.'" He ends his article with an interview with Stephen S. Morse, asking him if an emergent virus "could wipe out our species." Morse replies that HIV "might actually do the job," offering up the possibility of an aerosolized form of HIV that "would circle the globe in a flash," conceivably killing "one in three people on earth."[11] The article proved such a success that Preston was offered both book and movie deals based on the events in Reston.

Not only did Preston draw connections among Ebola, HIV, and other emerging viruses, but he cast the scale of what would otherwise have been a small, successfully contained outbreak upward, transforming an anticlimactic story in one primate facility into "a narrowly averted disaster and harbinger of pandemics to come."[12] Not only does this transference, from local to global, mirror Morse's link between scalar extremes, but it is also what journalists would later mirror when writing about these new hot-button topics (emerging diseases! pandemics! viral outbreaks!). For example, as Stephen S. Hall writes in the *New York Times* in October of 1994,

> Ebola is a virus to which the adjective "deadly" clings like spandex . . . It can kill up to 90 percent of the people it infects . . . First people would develop fevers and then they would begin to bleed from every orifice—suffering nosebleeds, bleeding gums, bloody diarrhea, bloody vomit, bleeding eyes—until, in a viral end game, they would be reduced to a feverish slush of blood, a single soggy imploding hemorrhage (thus the name "hemorrhagic" virus). Once it was loose in the camps, the Ebola virus would hop from refugee to refugee, then to aid workers, U.N. peacekeepers, and the volunteer doctors and nurses who minister to the dying. In less than two weeks, carried far and wide by

soldiers and relief workers returning home, Ebola virus would disembark on three continents. Pandemic, panic, public health disaster.

In the blink of an eye, according to this article, Ebola could hop between patients and doctors, and "in less than two weeks" go global. Hall goes on to offer the disclaimer that this scenario had not yet happened, that it was merely a scenario concocted by infectious disease experts during an annual meeting, but his disclaimer falls far short when it is followed by the unsettling declaration that if this worst-case scenario *were* to come true, "no national or international agency (not even the World Health Organization or the Centers for Disease Control and Prevention) would be equipped to do much about it."[13]

Screenwriter James V. Hart, hired by producer Lynda Obst to write the script for the *Hot Zone* film adaptation, did extensive research for the project, including going to USAMRIID and speaking with the virologists who had been involved with the Ebola outbreak. He recounts that "the biggest problem they had with the Ebola outbreak at the monkey house was the fact that no human being died." If one human being had died, they would have been able to "get government funding to begin work on a vaccine, on anti-serums, on controls about people coming in to this country with infectious diseases . . . All they wanted was to scare the shit out of people, so they'd have some more juice to go back to Congress and get more funding for virology research, for virology protocols, for infectious diseases—how they're diagnosed—for immigration controls, checks at airports."[14] Since monkeys were the only casualties, it was easier for everyone to look the other way.

In the 1991 report prepared for the NAS, there were also threats that justified funding, as well as recommendations for how those funds should be spent on a national scale. Specifically, the report targeted American policy makers and framed its arguments in terms of American public health and national security. The report emphasized how emerging diseases—defined as "clinically distinct conditions whose incidence in humans has increased"—provided multiple potential threats to the United States "because of global interdependence, modern transportation, trade, and changing social and cultural patterns," as well as population growth and migration, changes in sexual behavior, new medical treatments and technologies, breakdowns of public health measures such as sanitation, and immunization, among others. Recommendations revolved around surveillance, training and research, vaccine and drug development, and behavioral change, fusing national self-interest with global humanitarianism, and national security with international health.[15] Disease surveillance, a core part of Morse's plan, involves gathering and tracking information, and analyzing and interpreting large volumes of data originating from a variety of sources—primarily hospitals—in order to enable doctors and scientists to keep track of what might be new and emerging diseases.

Alexander D. Langmuir, who had consulted with the Armed Forces Epidemiological Board before acting as the director of the epidemiology branch of the CDC from 1949 to 1970, initially popularized the term "surveillance," with its overtones "of military or intelligence activities" (at odds with the dull bureaucratic paperwork more traditional disease reporting entails) in order to support his argument that epidemiology was a defense expenditure.[16] By associating the CDC with national defense priorities, Langmuir managed to capitalize on fears of biological warfare during and after the Korean War in order to reinvigorate funding for the CDC. Langmuir later recalled that the "emotional hysteria"[17] about biological warfare at the time "was unbelievable and worse the higher one reached into the establishment." Recognizing the power of this fear, Langmuir used it to get a detailed plan and budget for the CDC through military intelligence, accompanied by "a plain unvarnished statement of the potentialities of BW [biological warfare]."[18] Langmuir, who had originally become involved with biological warfare when he was a member (and then chair) of the Department of Defense's Committee on Biological Warfare, warned that the nation was vulnerable to "sabotage of food and water supplies" and that epidemiologists needed to provide "the first line of national defense."[19]

In December 1950, just a few short months after the war with Korea began, several key publications were released regarding biological warfare, explaining to the public what they needed to know. The executive office of the president, with input from Langmuir, published a report that detailed how easily America could be a target for biological warfare. The Federal Civil Defense Administration and the US Army also published pamphlets to inform the general public. These pamphlets warned that ventilation systems, as well as food and water supplies, could be used to spread plague, typhus, cholera, smallpox, anthrax, and a host of other biological agents. According to Elizabeth Fee, chief of the history of medicine division at the National Library of Medicine, and Theodore M. Brown, professor of public health and policy at the University of Rochester, "These official pamphlets communicated a curious mix of anxiety, information, and reassurance," discounting some rumors while also feeding others with the assertion that "an invisible biological warfare attack could come at any time, without warning."[20]

In April 1951, Langmuir even starred in a television program produced by the Department of Defense and the US Federal Civil Defense Administration—*What You Should Know about Biological Warfare*—that argued for the importance of the public health system as the country's best defense against biological warfare.[21] In the program, Langmuir gave several demonstrations using everyday tools to display how easily a city could be contaminated with infectious material. For example, he demonstrated how easily a pathogen could be aerosolized using a dry ice and a blender or spread via a city's water supply. The only recourse? To build a "complete biological warfare defense system" that would be based on the existing public health system but with more effective tools and facilities. His vision would, in many ways, shape the future development of the CDC.[22]

Though President Truman was scaling down all nondefense budgets in order to fund the war with Korea, "epidemiologic intelligence" was listed as a defense expenditure and therefore remained protected.[23] By 1951, it was the CDC, rather than the National Institutes of Health (NIH), that assumed responsibility for protecting the nation against an attack involving biological weapons.[24]

Ironically, Fee and Brown found it "very difficult, if not impossible, to discover much evidence for any real threat of biological aggression against the United States around the time of the Korean War."[25] The arguments they found were based purely on hypothetical scenarios rather than actual facts. In a perverse twist, the nation with the most fully developed commitment to biological warfare was the United States; research into biowarfare had begun during World War II and expanded in the decades that followed.

It is worth noting that Langmuir's Epidemic Intelligence Service (EIS), a practical training program for young epidemiologists, was created using military funds. A two-year applied training program with an emphasis on fieldwork, the EIS was developed to prepare trained field investigators to deal with biological warfare. These young epidemiologists later went on to act as directors of the CDC and the National Heart Institute, assistant director general of the World Health Organization, executive director of the National Foundation for Infectious Diseases, Surgeon General, and many more high-level positions, further spreading Langmuir's ideas to influential places.

Concerns about biological warfare persisted throughout the latter half of the twentieth century. Richard Preston, the author of "Crisis in the Hot Zone," also became interested in bioterrorism a few years after his article appeared in the *New Yorker*, and in 1998, he published *The Cobra Event* (Random House), a fictional account of bioterrorist attacks in Washington, DC, and New York City. In fact, Preston testified in front of the Senate that same year during hearings on American preparedness for biological warfare. *The Cobra Event* had such an impact on President Clinton that he not only passed the book along to Defense Secretary William Cohen and House Speaker Newt Gingrich but also subsequently announced the development of a series of antibioterrorism initiatives for which he requested an additional $294 million from Congress in his budget request for the 1999 fiscal year. Furthermore, Secretary of Health and Human Services Donna Shalala would open her article "Bioterrorism: How Prepared Are We?" for the CDC's *Emerging Infectious Diseases* journal with an outline of *The Cobra Event*, writing that the thought-provoking novel raises this question: "How do we successfully contain and combat the threat of bioterrorism?"[26] Shalala overlooks the book's fictional status. Stephen S. Morse—the man who may have coined "emerging disease" as a coherent concept and who told Preston in the "Crisis in the Hot Zone" article that HIV might kill one in three of the world's population—left his university position in 1996 to join the Defense Advanced Research Projects Agency (DARPA) as manager of the Unconventional Pathogen Countermeasures program.[27] Much as the line between fact and fiction would prove blurry, so, too, would the line between the scientific community and the military industry.

Given this carefully cultivated fear, it should be no surprise that in 1999, Congress allocated $121 million in funding to the CDC's newly created bioterrorism preparedness and response program to begin enhancing the nation's epidemiology and laboratory systems. This funding would increase to approximately $194 million in fiscal year (FY) 2001.[28] President Obama's proposed budget for FY 2015 included $1.5 billion for programs solely devoted to civilian biodefense ($211 million less than biodefense appropriations in FY 2014) and $948 million to pandemic influenza and emerging infectious disease programs. Biodefense programs were defined as "federal programs focused on prevention, preparedness, and response to attacks on civilians with biological agents and accidental releases of biological material," and pandemic influenza and emerging infectious disease programs were defined as "federal programs focused on preparedness and response to large, naturally occurring, and potentially destabilizing epidemics."[29]

The rhetoric of biological threat also spawned a flurry of biodefense legislation in the United States: The Bioterrorism Act, Project Bioshield, the Biosurveillance Project, The National Electronic Disease Surveillance System (NEDSS), the National Pharmaceutical Stockpile, as well as a host of classified bioweapons projects.[30] The 2014 federal budget for civilian biodefense would total $6.69 billion. Of that total, $5.86 billion (88 percent) was budgeted for programs that had both biodefense and nonbiodefense goals and applications, and $835 million (12 percent) was budgeted for programs that had objectives solely related to biodefense.[31]

Bioterrorism was a very real fear by the start of the twenty-first century; the presence of "agents suitable for biological weapons development" was one of the justifications for going to war with Iraq in 2002.[32] Ruth Mayer writes that the debates around the second Iraq War in particular demonstrate the power of this fear: "While, obviously, the large-scale bioweapons programs . . . did not exist . . . the rhetoric of biological threat on its own proved powerful enough to override important objections and to legitimate the war for many."[33] The well-publicized outbreaks of Ebola and HIV during the 1980s and 1990s, followed a few years later by September 11, 2001 and the anthrax attacks, served as a reminder of America's vulnerabilities to viruses, biowarfare, and terrorism. All three could threaten large-scale attacks seemingly anywhere at any time.

Released in 2002, John Murlowski's *Contagion* (not to be confused with Soderbergh's later film) revolves around the aftermath of an attack upon the American president, shot in the neck with an Ebola-infused dart. The choice of Ebola was deliberate, Murlowski explains, precisely because it would tap into a fear that most viewers would recognize: "The producers wanted to keep it simple and primal." The hospital is quarantined and the terrorist tries to use the cure as leverage. While Murlowski admits the timing—so soon after both the anthrax and the 9/11 attacks—was coincidental, the film's production team was "well aware of terrorist threats, both homegrown and foreign," figuring that it was only a matter of time until the United States would suffer a terrorist threat: "One just had to look at the politics at the time in the Middle East and see the collision course we were on."[34]

The persistent appearance of bioweapons in the news only intensified these fears. On October 5, 2014, at the height of an Ebola outbreak, the retired captain Al Shimkus, then a professor of national security affairs at the US Naval War College, told *Forbes* that in the context of terrorist activity "it doesn't take much sophistication to go to that next step to use a human being as a carrier." Terrorists would not even have to isolate the virus. They could find an Ebola outbreak and intentionally expose themselves.[35]

A couple weeks later, on October 17, 2014, the *Fox News* website published an article entitled "Could Ebola Virus Become 'Bioterrorist Threat'?" The article quickly abandons the ambiguity of the title, quoting Amanda Teckman—then an administrative assistant at Seton Hall University, who had written about the dangers of ignoring Ebola in a 2013 *Global Policy Journal* article—in the second paragraph, where she declares that "the government should be concerned about [weaponization], because if it does happen it could be devastating." By the fourth paragraph, the article tells us how easily it could happen, this time quoting Dr. Ryan Hall, a forensic psychologist who has written about psychological trauma associated with bioterrorism. Dr. Hall declares, "If you want to do the equivalent of a dirty bomb all you need is a bag of [vomit]." The article also quotes Scott Gotlieb, a physician and former Food and Drug Administration official during the George W. Bush administration, who confirms that turning Ebola into a bioweapon would not take a lot of sophistication.[36] On that same day in October 2014, the *Blaze* published an article entitled "GOP Congressman: Ebola as a Terrorism Tool 'Should Be on the Radar Screen.'" The second paragraph of the article quotes North Carolina Congressman Robert Pittenger, who agrees that Ebola "could be a place for terrorists to engage . . . They are unrelenting. If they could get infected with the virus, they could try to pass it on to others."[37]

Given this discourse of fear, is it any wonder that people are terrified of a virus that is relatively difficult to transmit? As of January 2017, there were only four laboratory-confirmed cases of Ebola diagnosed in humans in all of US history. Only two of those people had contracted the virus in the United States—both nurses, treating an infected patient—and they recovered. And yet security agencies, journalists, and politicians continue to parrot the same talking points, in part to draw attention to their agendas and in part, perhaps, to justify their existence, their actions, and their funding.

Much as Langmuir had a few decades before, many involved with public health during the 1990s would capitalize on the newly energized fear of emerging viruses post-AIDS in order to shift attention and funding back to them. Following the release of the 1991 NAS report, the CDC and the cabinet-level National Science and Technology Council (NSTC) issued their own reports repeating the NAS's initial findings with "little modification." In 1995, the CDC launched an online journal entitled *Emerging Infectious Diseases*, and the World Health Organization (WHO) established the Division of Emerging and Other Communicable Diseases Surveillance and Control. In October of that same year, during a US Senate hearing on the topic, Joshua Lederberg, clearly given to dramatic sound bites, referenced Morse's concept of instant-distant infections with his warning that "the microbe which felled one child in a distant continent yesterday can reach your child today and seed a global pandemic tomorrow."[38] Emerging viruses had become terrifying possibilities, rich with the potential for death and destruction—perhaps even that of the entire world. To make matters worse, experts kept insisting that America was unprepared and public health departments underfunded.

In a May 1994 column for the *New York Times* entitled "The Doctor's World," Dr. Lawrence Altman, the first doctor to work full time for a daily newspaper, wrote that "not so long ago, Government officials and medical leaders all but pronounced the end of infectious diseases as a major public health problem," but new and emerging diseases like AIDS, Lyme disease, Lassa fever, Ebola, and Marburg had proved that prediction wrong. Altman argued that "overconfidence about infectious diseases has weakened public health systems in this country and elsewhere, jeopardizing their ability to detect and prevent new and old ones." Citing a "new Federal report, from the Centers for Disease Control and Prevention," Altman proposed that the United States needed "an infusion of up to $125 million a year to carry out a plan to provide the vigilance and rapid response needed to contain infections."[39]

While Altman did not specify which federal report from the CDC encouraged this funding, it is likely to have been the one largely repurposed from the 1991 NAS report. Altman also argued for increased "surveillance," a key element in Morse's disease agenda. Using Morse's style of language, Altman declared, "The single most important weapon in any country's defense against infections is its disease surveillance system." Altman also mentioned that the CDC needed more Federal resources to support the national disease reporting system, warning that the surveillance systems had been so weakened by budget cuts that there was no national system in place to monitor or defend against current and future problems.[40]

Ironically, in a *Time* magazine article written by Michael Lemonick and Bruce Crumley during the 1995 Ebola outbreak, Dr. Peter Piot, who had investigated the first Ebola outbreak in 1976 and headed the United Nations AIDS program, explained that, even though it was "theoretically feasible that an inflicted person from Kikwit could go to Kinhasa, get on an airplane to New York, fall ill and present a transmission risk there," the outbreak would still likely stop at that point.[41] Piot's argument was that "the Ebola virus is ill-suited to sustaining an epidemic: it kills victims so quickly that they don't have much chance to infect others." He also emphasized that "the virus is not all that easy to pass along. Unlike the most highly contagious illnesses—tuberculosis or influenza, for example—Ebola can't be transmitted with a sneeze or cough." He reassured his readers that "most people, especially those outside Zaire, have little to fear from Ebola."[42]

But reassurances will not sell magazines. And so the article still has the alarming title "Return to the Hot Zone: The Gruesome Ebola Virus, Dormant for 16 Years, Has Arisen to Kill Again in Zaire. Will It Spread?," and it concludes with the question "haunting" public health officials: "Suppose we get a virus that is both deadly to man and transmitted in the air?" The article reminds readers of the sobering fact that the virus does not even need to be a new organism. An existing virus could turn deadly, "since viruses undergo mutations" that sometimes make them more virulent, much like what Morse warned Preston might happen with HIV—creating an aerosolized form of HIV that "would circle the globe in a flash"—or as did happen in Reston, Virginia. The final warning of the article by Lemonick and Crumley is that "the next time the Ebola virus emerges from the jungle, it might be much harder to control."[43] And just like that, the article cancels out any calming reassurances that Piot may have made. Significantly, the coauthor is the same Michael Lemonick whose article "The Killers All Around" contained such dramatic statements as this: "For all the vaunted power of modern medicine, deadly infections are a growing threat to everyone, everywhere"; "It's getting harder to enjoy a meal, make love or even take a walk in the woods without a bit of fear in the back of the mind"; and "By now nearly every disease organism known to medicine has become resistant to at least one antibiotic, and several are immune to more than one."[44]

Reassurances will also not yield increased funding for health initiatives. It should come as no surprise that even articles like Lemonick's for *Time* magazine push Morse's agenda, using virtually the same talking points as Altman did for the *New York Times*. After building up reasons to be afraid, Lemonick advocates increased vigilance by public health authorities, a strengthening of surveillance and information-gathering networks, improvement of health conditions around the world, and the development of new drugs. While all these will be "enormously expensive," Lemonick argues that the price of doing nothing "may be measured in millions of lost lives."[45] Funding requires support, so is it any wonder that, in 1996, thirty-six medical journals in twenty-one countries focused all or part of their issues on the topic of emerging viruses?[46] The concept had taken hold, as a marketable idea, a political agenda, and a source of fear.

Writers rushed to capitalize on consumers' renewed interest. For instance, journalist Laurie Garrett, who had been working on her own book, *The Coming Plague: Newly Emerging Diseases in a World Out of Balance*, accelerated production so that it would come out before Preston's book version of his "Crisis in the Hot Zone" article. *The Coming Plague* was released on January 1, 1994, and it was a *New York Times* bestseller for nineteen weeks. Her focus, unlike Preston's global view, was on how years of declining public health, combined with economic inequality, were to blame for the rise in emerging diseases. She declared that "humanity will have to change its perspective on its place in Earth's ecology if the species hopes to stave off or survive the next plague."[47]

In his review of Laurie Garrett's book for the March 1995 issue of *Public Health Reports*, Stephen A. Morse, director of the Sexually Transmitted Diseases Laboratory at the CDC (not to be confused with the aforementioned Stephen S. Morse of DARPA), warns that "advances in medicine, such as antibiotics and vaccines, have caused many people to become complacent, believing that infectious diseases are no longer a major domestic problem. As a result, resources for infectious diseases have dwindled." Morse describes Garrett's book as "a wakeup call." His review would dramatically be titled "The Year 2000: Only a Plane Flight Away from Disaster?"[48]

Since drama sells copy—and movies, and books, and even public policy—this kind of dramatic language would continue to be embraced and the idea of a global threat perpetuated and carefully groomed. Published in September of 1994, Richard Preston's book, *The Hot Zone: The Terrifying True Story of the Origins of the Ebola Virus* (Random House), spent almost two years on the hardcover and paperback bestseller lists. Part of its appeal was, unquestionably, that it was a "true story." Preston thanks both Stephen S. Morse and Joshua Lederberg in the credits for the book, grateful to them for "philosophical guidance," for bringing world attention to the concerns expressed in the book, and for "decades of thinking and commentary by Lederberg."[49] The book, like the original article, emphasizes the threat of global annihilation at the hands of microbes. Page sixteen of the book, for example, contains a warning that is reiterated throughout: "A hot virus from the rain forest lives within a twenty-four hour plane flight from every city on earth."[50] In his blurb for the book, Stephen King describes *The Hot Zone* as one of the most horrifying things he has ever read, while a review in the *British Medical Journal* concludes with the promise that the book "is likely to leave you wondering when and where this enigmatic agent will appear next and what other disasters may await."[51]

The success of these two books, combined with the previous *New Yorker* article and the books and television shows they would inspire, directly contributed to the frequency of television news reports about emerging viruses. The fear spread further as real life fueled viral-related fears all the more. Ebola would hit the major African town of Kikwit, Zaire (now known as the Democratic Republic of Congo) in 1995, intensifying fears of a worldwide epidemic. The outbreak was heavily featured by American news media, with "virtually every major news organization [drawn] to the hitherto unknown city of Kikwit."[52] Weekly magazines published cover stories on the virus, and network news programs such as ABC's *Nightline* and PBS's *Nova* devoted special episodes to the outbreak. Even CNN aired a special report, "The Apocalypse Bug," on May 14, 1995. Not only did the May 22, 1995, issue of *Newsweek* focus on this new fear of viruses, but it even had a graphic cover with the words "Killer Virus" in large bold lettering and the subheading "Beyond the Ebola Scare—What Else Is Out There?" The issue also included numerous articles exploring different aspects of viral panic, including "Why Viruses Push Our Hot Buttons," "Outbreak of Fear," and "A World of Viruses." Suddenly, small stories about a few sick people could be big news, because a few sick people could now kill the world. Dr. Robert J. Howard, director of strategic communication at the CDC from 1991 to 2000, describes the front lawn of the CDC during the spring of 1995 as

> the scene of an ever growing constantly expanding number of reporters, satellite trucks, cameras, and literally miles of cable associated with radio, television, and newspaper coverage. Live programmes, taped programmes, hourly updates, and every aspect of the epidemiology, recognition, treatment and control of a severe viral hemorrhagic illness most Americans had never even heard of, played itself out in the homes of Americans. News programmes and newspapers seen and heard by Americans detailed countless perspectives and angles of this tragedy. Internet homepages were created to update the latest case counts and deaths, and videocrews from around the world were dispatched to a small village in Zaire. Thanks to modern satellite media, Ebola hemorrhagic fever had arrived.[53]

All this, despite the fact that not a single American had died from the virus.

While it is no surprise that journalists and Hollywood would embrace this new topic, it would also be no accident. For example, Brigitte Nerlich and Christopher Halliday analyzed media coverage of the avian flu outbreak in the United Kingdom in 2004. They found that the initial surge in UK media coverage—before the virus had even been detected in the UK—was not triggered by any of the typical reasons certain risks are embraced (e.g., easy-to-write human interest stories), but rather due to an increasing amount of activity by pressure groups, professional bodies and politicians, and the WHO, in particular.[54] Nerlich and Halliday go on to argue that the "underlying motive of heightening awareness for an impending pandemic was probably to use the scientific status of experts to cause a shift in public policy, e.g. to increase national and global resource allocation for public health."[55] Contrary to the usual knee-jerk reaction of blaming media for stoking the fire of fear, distorting and hyperbolizing the truth in order to gain readership and viewership, Nerlich and Halliday write that, in this case, the media are actually more of a "direct conduit of scientific information," not so much distorting a message as heating it up by presenting it to the public in easily digestible bundles.[56] And these easily digestible bundles could then be used to justify increased national and global resource allocation for public health.

In August of 1996, Turner Publishing released *Level 4: Virus Hunters of the CDC: Tracking Ebola and the World's Deadliest Viruses*. It was written by Joseph B. McCormick, former chief of the CDC's special pathogens branch in Atlanta and mentioned extensively in both Preston's *The Hot Zone* and Garrett's *The Coming Plague*, with his former colleague at the CDC (and wife) Susan Fisher Hoch, along with medical thriller writer Leslie Horvitz. The book capitalized on the "Ebola craze" by providing personal accounts of people who had spent decades fighting and researching Ebola, as well as other less known outbreaks. "Level 4" is a reference to the biohazard unit in the CDC where scientists examine some of the most lethal pathogens known to man. HIV, by comparison, is most often handled in a Level 2 environment. The publication of this book, following Preston's and Garrett's literary success, is not surprising but provided more fuel for fears of Ebola and other exotic viruses.

American sociologist Dorothy Nelkin, who has written extensively about the relationship between science and society, frequently focuses on the consequences of unchecked scientific progress and its unquestioning acceptance by the public. She explains the mutually beneficial relationship between science and mass media as follows:

> The quest for publicity is increasingly prevalent in the medical and biomedical communities. Those working on the costly frontiers of modern medicine must maintain their legitimacy and their sources of public support. Many researchers believe that scholarly communication is no longer sufficient to maintain their enterprise, that national visibility through the mass media is strategically necessary to assure a favorable public image and adequate research support . . . They employ sophisticated public relations techniques and communication controls to manage the news. The press is receptive to their efforts. Promising therapeutic advances and dramatic medical interventions are front-page news.[57]

To help scientists "manage" media, Robert J. Howard from the CDC published a guide in 2000 entitled "Getting It Right in Prime Time." Currently included on the CDC's website as part of its *Emerging Infectious Diseases* journal, Howard makes suggestions on how to develop a communication strategy and objectives with an emphasis on maintaining proper perspective. He concludes with the following message, clearly inspired by Morse's emphasis on scalar extremes: "Even though cases of Ebola virus infection had not yet reached the shores of the United States . . . what happens in Zaire or the Sudan today may well be a U.S. problem tomorrow. 'We live in a global village' and 'diseases are only a plane flight away' are messages that everyone can understand."[58] After all, if we live in a global village and, as Lederberg declared, a microbe in a distant continent "can reach your child today and seed a global pandemic tomorrow," no one and nowhere are safe. While it is true that these *are* messages everyone can understand, they are also messages that can inspire fear and messages that are not always accurate or productive.

In that same issue of the *Emerging Infectious Diseases* journal, Vicki Freimuth, professor of health and risk communication at the University of Georgia, and Polyxeni Potter, managing editor of *Emerging Infectious Diseases*, along with independent researcher Huan W. Linnan, published another instructional article, this one entitled "Communicating the Threat of Emerging Infections to the Public." This article emphasizes that while communicating with the public had usually been left to the press, AIDS, combined with "the emergence of new infectious organisms, microbial resistance to therapeutic drugs, and a new emphasis on prevention" had made the role of communication an important and necessary component of public health practice. The authors argue that this shift had occurred simultaneously with the rise in public interest in health information caused by aging baby boomers and the spread of electronic publishing. They emphasize, "Even the best-crafted message is useless if it fails to reach the intended audience."[59]

So how to reach that audience? Freimuth, Potter, and Linnan are quick to specify the pros and cons of various types of media, including news, entertainment, advertising, and the importance of using as many types of media as possible. For instance, the America Responds to AIDS campaign included "television and radio public service announcements, printed materials (posters, booklets, brochures, billboards, bus ads), telephone hotlines, AIDS prevention messages integrated in movies and television shows, and specific AIDS information disseminated electronically through the Internet."[60] While mass exposure is beneficial, it is popular entertainment in particular that effectively educates audiences, since behavior is often learned through modeling. Not only does entertainment media reinforce certain behaviors, but it also taps into audience's emotions. This is important because, as the article outlines, "When the audience responds emotionally, the educational message is more likely to influence their behavior than when they respond only rationally."[61]

Having witnessed the successful use of mass communication by fascist propagandists during the World War II, groups like the United Nations' Educational, Scientific, and Cultural Organization (UNESCO) began investing heavily in print, radio, and film. Nicholas B. King observes that these organizations saw film in particular as an effective way of educating the public. Knowing that the films with the greatest impact were both entertaining and informative, the United Nations contracted with commercial filmmakers and, in 1948, released an educational film devoted to the state of the world and disease control entitled *The Eternal Flight*. Over an animation of a train bearing a large skull representing cholera passing from city to city, the narrator warns, "New means of transportation brought the world tight and close together, making it one tremendous and congested city. From a disease-infected zone, the traveler now became, unwittingly, a carrier of deadly germs. Wherever he went, the germs stayed and spread." Later, over a visual montage of air travel footage and world maps, the narrator declares, "Today there are no distances . . . The people of the world are one people . . . Modern transport poses new dangers of complete, universal contagion."[62]

If modern transport posed new dangers, the media would be more than happy to exploit these new dangers for ratings and box office dollars. Peter N. Stearns, in his book *American Fear: The Causes and Consequences of High Anxiety*, points out that, "as foreign news declined on nightly telecasts during the 1990s—a fruit of the cold war's end—health news increased, catching American fear where it now seemed to live." Stearns also argues that this shift was exacerbated by the fact that "growing numbers of Americans had become accustomed to taking media presentations for reality, blurring the lines between entertainment and news and accepting an ever mounting diet of fear in the process."[63] This tendency has only increased in recent years. According to a survey conducted in 2016 by Ipsos Public Affairs, "fake news headlines fool American adults about 75% of the time." This survey was "the first large-scale public opinion research survey into the fake news phenomenon," a phenomenon that garnered widespread attention during the 2016 American presidential campaign.[64]

In a study conducted by Sheldon Ungar for the *British Journal of Sociology*, he found that, before 1994, coverage devoted to diseases like tuberculosis and cholera was "sporadic and of limited scope." However, 1994 would mark the "'coming out' ceremony for infectious diseases in the popular media." These diseases would now be placed firmly on the public agenda, possibly catapulted "ahead of nuclear war and climate change as the primordial source of apocalyptic anxieties." Annual coverage of emerging diseases also increased significantly between 1993 and 1994 and even more between 1994 and 1995. Starting almost at zero in 1989, by 1995, there would be forty stories in that year about emerging diseases on the three major American television networks. Ungar details several noteworthy occurrences that "all but guaranteed" the rise in media coverage. His first noteworthy occurrence was the publication of the reports mentioned earlier, such as those from the CDC and the NAS, as well as the publication of books such as those written by Garrett, Preston, and McCormick. Ungar states that, by using a "rhetoric of endangerment," these publications aimed to "animate the problem and convince reluctant publics of the magnitude of the crisis." This rhetoric was reinforced by two other noteworthy occurrences: the apparently "sudden onset of novel diseases that attracted short-lived bursts of attention," such as the 1993 outbreak of hantavirus carried by rodents in the American southwest (generating eight television news stories), as well as the 1994 outbreak of plague in India (generating nine in a single week). A breakout of antibiotic-resistant bacteria fueled ten stories in 1994, with four more in early 1995.[65]

What makes this change in coverage even more striking is that there was not just a shift in quantity but a shift in style as well. This new influx of stories evolved from episodic to thematic, allowing them to address the topic of emerging disease more broadly, referencing Morse's scalar approach to the ways local behavior could have global repercussions. Viruses now had mass significance. While it is difficult to argue whether the books and articles on emerging viruses fueled attention for the viral outbreaks or the viral outbreaks fueled attention for the books and articles, Unger argues that what tied everything together was a converging element: the "Hollywood factor."[66]

The way infectious viruses are appropriated by Hollywood may provide the greatest insight into the viruses themselves and the world we live in. After all, few things reflect social trends and anxieties like film and television. Cultural theorist Douglas Kellner observes that films "are an especially illuminating social indicator of the realities of a historical era, as a tremendous amount of capital is invested in researching, producing, and marketing the product. Film creators tap into the events, fears, fantasies, and hopes of an era and give cinematic expression to social experiences and realities."[67] To put it simply, Hollywood reads the zeitgeist in order to translate it into box office profits.

However, this kind of "social reflection" is not limited to film. In fact, during recent years, it has been increasingly hard to distinguish between film and television, as premium television demands larger and larger budgets and cinematic cinematography, and personnel (including directors, actors, and producers) move from big screen to small screen and back to big again. Most significant may be the fact that more and more people are watching television and film in the same place—at home. While the lines continue to blur between film and television, the outbreak narrative in particular does not rely on medium specificity. Rather, it is a rhetorical pattern that persists across media forms and platforms. I will discuss the characteristics of this pattern in greater depth in chapter 1.

Desperate to capitalize on the success of Preston's article and subsequent book, as well as the new fear of emerging disease, both Warner Bros. and Fox raced to release their outbreak movie first. Fox stuck close to the Preston original—even naming the movie *Crisis in the Hot Zone*—with Ridley Scott at the helm and Robert Redford and Jodie Foster as the leads. In contrast, Warner Bros. went for a more fictionalized take with *Outbreak*, directed by Wolfgang Petersen and starring Dustin Hoffman and Rene Russo. Initially courted by the producers of both films—even receiving the two scripts on the same day—Petersen told *Entertainment Weekly* that he decided to do *Outbreak* because "sometimes you can tell a better story with fiction."[68] Determined to be first, producer Arnold Kopelson sent Petersen and his crew to begin shooting in July 1994, before the script had even finished, announcing in the trades that production had begun.[69] Things had been rocky for *Crisis in the Hot Zone* for a while, as script rewrite after rewrite met dissatisfaction from either a star or someone on the production team, but after this announcement, things fell apart for good, and Fox pulled the plug. Petersen's version was released on March 10, 1995, and went on to gross $67,659,560 domestically and almost $200,000,000 worldwide.[70] It arguably established the template for the outbreak narrative—a template that would be followed and built upon for years to come.

Other outbreak narratives quickly followed. The television show *The X-Files* (Fox, 1993–2002, 2016–present) got on board the outbreak narrative trend, airing "F. Emasculata" on the Fox network on April 28, 1995. The episode fuses a pharmaceutical conspiracy with an Ebola-esque virus that spreads via prison inmates, killing its victims within thirty-six hours of infection. Similarly, on May 8, 1995, NBC aired *Formula for Death*, also known as *Virus*. Starring Nicolette Sheridan in the lead role as a CDC researcher, *Formula for Death* revolves around a plague outbreak in Los Angeles. Universal Studio's contribution to the outbreak narrative, *12 Monkeys*, directed by Terry Gilliam, premiered on December 27, 1995. Based on Chris Marker's short film *La Jetée* (1962), it tells the tale of a convict's journey back in time to discover the truth behind a man-made virus that has killed most of the human population. Starring Bruce Willis, Madeleine Stowe, and Brad Pitt, it earned almost $170 million worldwide.[71]

It can take years to bring a film to the screen, and the synchronicity of outbreak films around 1995, much like the synchronicity of bioterrorist narratives during the start of the twenty-first century or the current success of zombies, are examples of cultural ideas developing in parallel, drawing from the zeitgeist to explore similar themes. For Douglas Kellner, films also have "an aesthetic, philosophical, and anticipatory dimension" that provides "artistic visions of the world that might transcend the social context of the moment and articulate future possibilities."[72] For example, the shot of the notice board in *28 Days Later* (Boyle, 2002), lined with posters of people gone missing, bears an uncanny resemblance to similar flyers posted in New York following 9/11. However, the film was shot prior to 9/11, and the shot had been based on images Danny Boyle saw following an earthquake in China. The pilot episode of Fox's *24* (2001–10), which aired on November 6, 2001, and had clearly been filmed long before 9/11, features a 747 exploding over the desert near Los Angeles, with the terrorist (Mia Kirshner as Mandy) parachuting out of the plane seconds before it crashes. As a concession to the similar events that had happened on September 11, the shot of the plane exploding was cut from the episode, but the rest of the episode remained intact. Another example is Robin Cook's novel *Vector* (G. P. Putnam's Sons, 1999), in which he depicts a series of anthrax attacks by mail in New York City, two years before they would happen in real life, providing a template for how the real-life events might later unfold.

Fears of viral outbreak would eventually include West Nile fever and SARS (Severe Acute Respiratory Syndrome) and grow steadily more global in scope. By the time Steven Soderbergh tackled the outbreak narrative with the film *Contagion* in 2011, fears had shifted to include avian and swine flu. But while the viruses may have changed, the basic template of the outbreak narrative stayed the same, evolving only to reflect different modes of transmission, a heightened awareness of how easily diseases can spread around the world, and evolutions in the source of the current fear. For example, outbreak narratives released shortly after 9/11, like *Contagion* (Murlowski, 2002), *Global Effect* (Cunningham, 2002), and season 3 of *24* (Fox, 2003–2004) would reflect the vulnerability many would feel to terrorism and, specifically, growing fears of a bioterrorist outbreak. More recent outbreak narratives, such as *I Am Legend* (Lawrence, 2007) and *The Walking Dead* (AMC, 2010–present), would circumvent the initial outbreak or terrorist attack scenario, reflecting instead on what the world might look like after the virus has done its work—after the kinds of death tolls predicted by hyperbolic headlines had already ravaged the human race.

All of this is not to imply that fears of a viral outbreak are insane or implausible. Populations are large, travel is rapid and accessible, developing countries are still building proper sanitation infrastructures, and people come and go from all across the world. Viral outbreaks are to be expected. However, the way media (and here I refer to both journalistic and entertainment media) exploit and sensationalize headlines—a situation compounded by the fact that we now have access to information twenty-four hours a day, seven days a week—facilitates the spread of both correct and incorrect information and encourages the spread of fear. Americans do experience an inordinate amount of fear about things that are relatively remote to their experience (like Ebola outbreaks); as a society, it is common for Americans to exaggerate threats to our existence in ways that betray our relative safety, comfort, and hence guilt vis-à-vis the rest of the world; and the media does contribute to the problem by further exaggerating and broadly circulating these unwarranted fears. Peter N. Stearns recalls how Americans *heard* about the Pearl Harbor attacks: "They might soon see pictures of carnage in newspaper and magazines and, if they chose, could add detail in the newsreels at movie houses. But they had the news before the visuals; the visuals were far less graphic (and were in black and white, not color) and, above all, were less ubiquitous. Even if one were prone to the mesmerization of disaster, it was simply harder to engage sixty years ago."[73] Now, however, with multiple ways to watch, and more than enough full color detail, it has become much easier to engage with—and much harder to avoid—the information, however accurate or inaccurate it may be.

In particular, fear of Ebola, much like fear of terrorism, demonstrates how certain responses are disproportionately shaped and intensified by the government, the media, films, and television shows. These responses, in turn, shape government policy, journalistic coverage, and the films and television shows we watch. Many outbreak narratives opt to use variations of Ebola, a virus that has never been an actual threat on American soil but that triggers panic nonetheless whenever supposed threats of the virus arise. And that panic has political consequence. For example, the WHO acknowledges that public perception of Ebola has influenced official policy. Professor Melissa Leach, cofounder of the Ebola Response Anthropology Platform and lead social scientist in the UK and WHO Ebola scientific advisory committees, explains in an interview on the WHO's website that during the early- to mid-1990s, Ebola had been portrayed "as a global threat, a fierce predator emerging from tropical areas in Africa and spreading rapidly to the rest of the mobile and interconnected world." This portrayal was both shaped and exacerbated by films and books, all of which "created fear about Ebola hemorrhagic fever in western populations." Leach emphasizes that "the perception that the 1995 outbreak in the Democratic Republic of the Congo 'was going to spread to the rest of the world' was one of the factors that built political momentum leading to the revision of the International Health Regulations in 2005."[74]

Fear of Ebola persists. In December 2013, when Ebola resurfaced in Guinea, West Africa, before continuing for more than two years and spreading to Liberia and Sierra Leone, with a few isolated cases elsewhere, it caused widespread panic on American soil. After it was revealed that Dr. Craig Spencer rode the subway and went bowling in New York shortly before being diagnosed with Ebola, his actions met with hysteria. Despite the fact that Ebola spreads via contact with blood or other bodily fluids, not via touched surfaces or the air, the bowling alley was closed, and some New Yorkers threatened to boycott the subway.[75] Spencer was only the fourth person to be diagnosed with Ebola in the United States, and he survived.

Nonetheless, a 2014 poll conducted under the joint direction of Anderson Robbins Research and Shaw & Company Research from August 10 to 12 of 2014 found that 62 percent of Americans were concerned about Ebola reaching US soil and 30 percent of those were "very concerned." About one in four (27 percent) also felt that infected Americans should not be allowed to return to the country for treatment. Current worry over Ebola is almost identical, the survey found, to concerns over the spread of the H1N1 swine flu in 2009 (65 percent) and the H5N1 bird flu in 2006 (61 percent).[76] Similarly, according to a 2015 survey from national pollster McLaughlin & Associates, 74.2 percent of likely American voters said they fear a terrorist attack,[77] though the actual odds of dying from a terrorist attack are 1 in 3.5 million.[78]

These statistics provide a vantage point onto some of the consequences of globalization—for instance, that the world feels smaller and more interconnected, with increasingly porous and ineffective boundaries—as well as the way perceptions of risk can irrationally fuel hysteria. In their article on the social amplification and attenuation of perceptions of risk, Roger Kasperson and Jeanne Kasperson, both of whom are American risk analysts and researchers, outline the elements that shape those perceptions. First is the extent of the media coverage and, specifically, "the volume of information provided"; second, "the ways in which the risk is framed" that, in turn, shape the public's perception of that risk; third, the way the information is interpreted; and fourth, "the symbols, metaphors, and discourse enlisted in depicting and characterizing the risk."[79] What makes these viruses cause so much fear is not only the amount of coverage they get—in both print and online media, in both fictional and nonfictional formats—but also the specific information provided and the way the risk is framed (unfortunately, often in hyperbolic fashion). Additionally, this fear is fueled by the metaphors used to visualize both the risk and the associated factors, as in the scientists who may save the day if given enough funding (typically white and American), the shadowy other responsible, knowingly or unknowingly, for spreading the infection (often and interchangeably Asian, African, or Muslim), and those infected (usually innocent, frequently white).

If one understands fear of Ebola as a microcosm of cultural fears of contagion and disease, the seemingly inflated percentages from the 2014 poll make sense. Ebola—arising from the depths of Africa to threaten the world—has become the perfect disease metaphor, complete with its not-so-latent racism. Many storylines for both cinema and television continue to use variations of Ebola as a default virus, as a stand-in for AIDS, SARS, sarin gas, avian flu, anthrax, swine flu, MERS, or any others from the seemingly endless list circulating in news headlines. In marked contrast to AIDS, which may have been the first "emerging virus" to catch people's attention during the last decades of the twentieth century, Ebola progresses faster, without HIV's long latency period, and its visually horrific and dramatic symptoms lend itself more readily to film and television thrillers. It can also be cured, which is crucial for narrative resolution, and it does not tap into deep-seated homophobia. In a more cinematically egalitarian fashion, Ebola affects everyone regardless of sexual orientation or practice. The crux with these new emerging viruses is that one can catch them by doing *nothing at all*—or so the media would have you believe.

In May 2005, the editors of *Nature* magazine wrote that the threat of avian flu is "enormous" and that it was now a "plausible scenario" for "millions of people [to be] killed in highly developed countries within months" before ultimately impacting tens of millions worldwide, leaving the global economy in tatters. In fact, the editors declared, "each human case that occurs in Asia is potentially a global threat." Despite the fact that "the science and medicine of flu have advanced substantially," the editorial lamented the "remarkably little progress" made to mount an effective public health response. Ironically, the editors acknowledged that "the potential for panic is, if anything, greater given the impact of television and the Internet" without admitting any culpability in feeding that panic.[80]

This specific kind of hyperbole—warning of death tolls in the millions— shows no sign of abating, and scientists are just as prone to it as journalists. For instance, Dr. Michael Osterholm, director for the Center of Infectious Disease Research and Policy at the University of Minnesota, as well as associate director of the Department of Homeland Security's National Center for Food Protection and Defense, predicted a death toll of 180–360 million due to an imminent pandemic, possibly the avian flu, in an article that appeared the July/August 2005 issue of *Foreign Affairs* and was reprinted in the *New York Times*. In his article, Osterholm declares that the reality of a coming pandemic cannot be avoided, and that if an influenza pandemic struck today, the world would change overnight. Foreign trade and travel would shut down, global and national economies would come to an abrupt halt, international vaccine supplies and health care systems would be overwhelmed—and panic would reign![81]

Osterholm, much like Lederberg and Morse, has been preaching the pandemic threat since the mid-1990s. In November of 1997, he published an article in *Newsweek* stating that the smallpox virus was in the hands of several rogue states, possibly including Iraq. Then, at a symposium held by the Johns Hopkins Center for Civilian Biodefense, he pronounced that there was no doubt Iraq had smallpox, based on his experience as a personal advisor on bioterrorism to King Hussein of Jordan. Osterholm had significant impact in high places, according to one Bush administration official, and his claims would fuel the Bush administration's belief that Saddam Hussein's bioweapons program had illegal stores of smallpox. In 2003, Osterholm also warned of deadly mosquito-borne infections, such as Rift Valley fever, malaria, and dengue: "It's going to happen. As water runs down a hill, it's going to happen."[82]

But it still has not, and it will not, according to evolutionary epidemiologist Paul W. Ewald of the University of Louisville, for the same reasons that there has been no large-scale lethal epidemic of mosquito-borne disease since malaria was wiped out in the 1940s: window screens and air conditioning. Ewald also argues that the SARS virus is not a threat, though, through an emphasis on SARS worst-case scenarios, both the WHO and the CDC have spread fear and economic havoc worldwide. Many estimate the cost of SARS to local economies to be more than thirty million, and stigma has also been an effect, as "Toronto was cut off by the WHO travel advisory through much of April 2003," and "Chinatowns were deserted in all the major cities."[83]

Like avian flu, SARS is thought to be a disease of animals (in this case, civet cats) that, through mutation, began infecting humans in late 2002, killing about eight hundred people out of around eight thousand known to be infected. It never became a pandemic. In order for it to spread more widely, it would have needed to be more effective at transmission. This is the quandary that prevents most viruses from becoming pandemics: in order to keep its host mobile, the virus has to become less virulent. Unless great numbers of people immobilized by illness are packed into close quarters with the healthy—a disease factory that does not exist today—a pandemic is virtually impossible.[84]

Nonetheless, in September 2005, headlines in various media outlets, including *BBC News*, the *Guardian*, and the *Telegraph*, proclaimed that a new flu pandemic could kill 150 million, with David Nabarro, one of the most senior public health experts at the World Health Organization, vouching for these numbers. Science writer Michael Fumento says that these types of figures "are tantamount to wild guesses," blaming politicians, public health officials, and journalists for crossing the line between informing the public and starting a panic. He also blames journalists specifically for intentionally citing the more alarming of the "experts." Specifically, Fumento criticizes Dr. Irwin Redlener, head of the National Center for Disease Preparedness at Columbia University. During a nationally televised interview on September 15, 2005, Redlener asserted that one billion could die from avian flu, giving the television program permission to introduce the topic with the following chilling words: "It could kill a billion people worldwide, make ghost towns out of parts of major cities, and there is not enough medicine to fight it."[85]

Similarly, in October 2005, Pittsburgh microbiologist Dr. Henry Niman warned that the situation was "extremely critical," that the current strain of avian flu had an "unusually high mortality rate," and that people should stock up on antiviral medication and devise a plan to isolate themselves with "enough food and water for an extended period of time," since the government would not be able to supply "advice, assistance, or an immediate vaccine."[86] Dr. Niman and others quote figures such as a 50 percent mortality rate for those infected with avian flu. However, what these figures do not reveal is that, much like Ebola, the small number of avian flu deaths have occurred in "poor countries with substandard medical systems" and that most people who reveal symptoms are already weak.[87] Many people do not show symptoms at all, and people in urban areas rarely come into contact with birds, greatly reducing risk of exposure. Nonetheless, Klaus Stohr, former head of the World Health Organization's Global Influenza Programme, predicted seven million deaths worldwide. Shigeru Omi, regional director for the WHO Western Pacific Regional Office (WPRO) for a decade, claimed one hundred million. Dmitri Lvov, director of the Ivanovsky Research Institute of Virology at the Russian Academy of Medical Sciences, expected one billion fatalities.[88] In actuality, there were forty-one victims in 2005, twenty-seven in 2006.[89]

However overblown, these exaggerations of scale are a common feature of disease scares. In the 1990s, for example, newspaper reports predicted that, in the United Kingdom, "as many as 100,000 people would perish from an incurable brain disease due to BSE" (Bovine spongiform encephalopathy, or mad cow disease). By 2005, there had been 150 deaths due to the disease. Similarly, even though SARS led to only a couple hundred deaths, alarmist accounts continued to circulate. Rather than spread the information that the death tolls were far lower than expected, the media treats each outbreak as a prelude to new viral pandemics.[90]

Much of this is accepted without argument; overreaction is seen as safer than underreaction. Even the success of *The Hot Zone* was hardly hindered by critics who deemed it sensationalized and inaccurate. When science writer David Quammen spoke with experts like virologist Karl Johnson, a major character in *The Hot Zone*, Quammen discovered that Ebola does not have the same impact on the body as described by Preston: "People do not dissolve. Their internal organs do not liquefy. People do not shed bloody tears . . . in the majority of cases, there's no dramatic bleeding."[91] However, unlike other threats, such as global warming or gun control, with viral outbreaks, "there is no vocal opposition requiring the media to present 'balanced' stories," so critics like Quammen are in the minority. To make matters worse, many of the quotations in articles about viruses come directly from scientists and/or the CDC, making potential critics even less likely to deem the articles hysterical and inaccurate.[92]

A rare backlash incident occurred in 1976, when the CDC grossly overestimated the risk of swine flu. In response to an outbreak at Fort Dix that resulted in the death of one army recruit, the CDC launched a federal immunization campaign—the first of its kind—that would result in some forty million vaccinations.[93] President Gerald Ford, as part of a $135 million effort, made a plea on national television "to inoculate every man, woman, and child in the United States."[94] However, when the death toll held steady at one and a British study suggested "the swine flu virus is actually less virulent than other recent forms of influenza," the media critiqued Ford and the CDC for "an inflated response to a minimal danger."[95] In August 1976, a *New York Times* editorial condemned experts for "making the most pessimistic projections from . . . scanty data," pointing out that worldwide surveillance had "failed to find a single additional case of swine flu," and that other nations, such as Britain, France, and West Germany had known better than to push a comprehensive mass vaccination program.[96] In December 1976, another *New York Times* editorial opined that the public health panic had merely been a political ploy for the CDC to "increase the size of its empire and multiply its budget," as well as a "sorry debacle" that exemplifies "the misunderstandings and misconceptions that have marked Government approaches to health care during the last eight years."[97]

Similarly, John Barry, a scholar at the Center for Bioenvironmental Research, wrote in an op-ed in the August 10, 2002, *New York Times*, "the emergence and spread of any new disease is something to take seriously, but the reaction to the West Nile virus has been characterized not by seriousness but by hysteria." A few days later, on August 13, 2002, the *Chicago Tribune* labeled Dr. Julie Gerberding, the director of the CDC, "part of the problem for calling the virus 'an emerging infectious disease epidemic,' despite the fact that medical experts throughout the United States saw no reason to panic . . . By way of comparison, West Nile had killed eleven people so far that summer, whereas the flu kills thirty-six thousand per year."[98]

Wendy Orent, American anthropologist and author of *Plague: The Mysterious Past and Terrifying Future of the World's Most Dangerous Disease*, argues in her article "Chicken Little" that "evolutionary biology tells us that the worst-case scenario—a lethal, transmissible, world-destroying flu—cannot happen, any more than Ebola or Marburg can steal out of the jungle and destroy the human race."[99] If a disease has a high mortality rate, it will kill those infected before it can spread too far. If it is highly contagious but not fatal, it will spread, but those infected will recover. And thanks to window screens and air conditioning, mosquitoes have limited ability to spread disease. For these reasons, Orent continues, "We do not need a 'new Manhattan Project' . . . to protect us from pandemic flu. We need an inoculation to protect us from disease hysterics."[100] Similarly, Dr. Marc Siegel, of the New York University School of Medicine, says that the likelihood of an avian flu outbreak in 2005 had been exaggerated, and that if "anything is contagious right now, its judgment clouded by fear."[101]

However, despite these isolated criticisms, flu experts, science writers, public health officials, and Hollywood have continued to lead us down the same path, regardless of whether the threat is avian flu, swine flu, Ebola, SARS, or whatever new virus is trending. Fear sells—and brings grant money. Or, as John Munch (Richard Belzer) puts it on the *Law & Order: Special Victims Unit* episode "Savant" (NBC, Oct. 16, 2007), "Fear feeds capitalism. Panic sells gas masks."

In all forms of emerging viruses media—from articles in *Time* magazine to television shows and Hollywood blockbusters—science is used to make fear of a viral outbreak seem credible, which is why it is appropriate that the outbreak narrative would germinate in the words of science writers and scientists and in the genre of science fiction. Science fiction films and television shows intentionally create an atmosphere of credibility, depicting something we have not yet seen in our actual lives but that we might one day discover. As Vivian Sobchack describes, the tension arises from the anticipation of this potential manifestation—not if it will happen but *when*: "Science fiction is a branch of fantasy identifiable by the fact that it eases the 'willing suspension of disbelief' on the part of its readers by utilizing an atmosphere of scientific credibility for its imaginative speculations in physical science, space, time, social science, and philosophy . . . While we are invited to wonder at what we see, the films strive primarily for our belief, not our suspension of disbelief."[102]

This same premise also occurs in books and articles when predictions are made about the 180 to 360 million people who will die as a result of the next pandemic. If a scientist or doctor says it, then it must be true. If enough scientific credibility exists elsewhere in the book or article, then the hyperbolic aspects, in turn, will appear more plausible. Another way of adding credibility to a potential pandemic is to compare it to an earlier outbreak, such as the flu pandemics of 1918 and 1997. For instance, in their analysis of media coverage of the 2004 avian flu outbreak in the United Kingdom, Nerlich and Halliday found that historic outbreaks were referenced twenty-nine times in a sample of fifty-one articles.[103]

Our fears of—and fascination with—viral outbreaks have only intensified since the early 1990s as a result of several factors: one, a growing fear of viral outbreaks following the discovery of HIV in 1981; two, the continued efforts of Morse and his colleagues to draw attention to emerging viruses; and third, the increasing pervasion into daily life of disaster-driven news media that virally spreads news of impending death and catastrophe, allowing perceptions of risk to increase exponentially. Significantly, it is not that we now live with more risk than before but that we have become more *aware* of those risks. As German sociologist Ulrich Beck points out, "It is not clear whether it is the risks that have intensified or our *view* of them. Both sides converge, condition each other, and because risks are risks in *knowledge*, perceptions of risks and risks are not different things, but one and the same."[104] Current conditions of communication and information access guarantee the spread of risk perception to more people, and faster, than ever before.

The fears that manifest on the news or in our lives feel especially discomforting because, in the twenty-first century, science and technology were meant to have eradicated uncertainty and risk. At the very least, they were meant to make our lives more controlled and safe. However, it is precisely science and technology, as well as globalization, which have created a new set of risks. We cannot protect ourselves against the dangers of radioactive emissions, global warming, viral outbreaks, terrorism, or an eroding ozone layer. Significant to these risks is not only the inability to insure against them but that they are not limited to a particular geographic area, demographic, or temporal dimension.[105]

Pandemics—and specifically fear of contagion—trigger a specific kind of fear and anxiety created by events with no end point or temporal dimension. For instance, according to American sociologist Kai Erikson, a specialist in the social consequences of catastrophic events, emergencies without distinct beginnings or ends "are often harder to deal with" than events, like earthquakes, which happen and then end. In this case, "the danger one is exposed to has no duration, no natural term; and as a result one remains in a permanent state of alarm and anxiety."[106] Erikson talks specifically about toxins, but toxins work much like contagions: "They contaminate rather than merely damage; they pollute, befoul, and taint rather than just create wreckage . . . And the evidence is growing that they scare human beings in new and special ways, that they elicit an uncanny fear in us."[107] Like toxic emergencies and global terrorism, globalized contagion is open-ended and messy. There is nowhere to hide. Anyone, anywhere may fear infection, however implausible those fears may actually be.

The outbreak narrative—with its explicit depictions of viral outbreak, its portrayals of bodily failure and decay, its literalization of ineffective borders and dangerous sources of contagion, and its portrayal of changing understandings of health and disease—is uniquely suited for an investigation of these fears. After all, its fusion of science fiction and horror allows it to explore not only our darkest fears of where the world might be headed, but to do so in a way that can feel chillingly plausible, bridging the gap between fantasy and reality. How a society responds to disease, especially epidemic disease, can illuminate its relationship not only to science and medicine, but also to illness, fear, death, and identity. Studying how outbreak narratives evolve can provide a useful starting point for tracing the evolution of that response.

As I have outlined, "emerging viruses" as a concept began penetrating the cultural consciousness and public discourse in the mid-1990s. Since then, outbreak narratives have continued to be popular and to resonate with changing anxieties in the American cultural and social fabric. I will focus primarily on feature films, television series, and miniseries produced in the United States from the mid-1990s to the present. The case can be made that US audiences are still the preferred audiences for blockbuster production and distribution. They are the more lucrative audiences, and American premieres prime the engine of a franchise as it moves around the globe. Therefore, engaging with particularly American fears and desires at a narrative level is still a common practice despite the increasingly transnational nature of film and media production. Engaging with American texts also allows me to focus on American fears and American audiences.

While Peter N. Stearns, in his book *American Fear*, admits that Americans are not totally unique, an examination of American media can still provide an interesting case study for exploring the evolution and construction of contemporary American fear. As Stearns argues, American reactions to fear have "exhibited distinctive features in recent decades," and changes in American approaches to fear have made many Americans more vulnerable to fear and anxiety (despite the actual reduction of risk), with "fear as a foundation for national unity in the absence of confidence in more positive programs."[108]

Fear, in fact, would be the Republican Party's foundation for national unity during the Presidential campaign of 2016. In many ways, fear was the theme of the Republican National Convention of that year. During the convention, former Republican House speaker Newt Gingrich warned that major American cities were at risk of being lost to terrorists with weapons of mass destruction and that Hillary Clinton could have indirect links to Lucifer, a sentiment shared by Presidential candidate Ben Carson and conspiracy theorist Alex Jones. Former mayor of New York City Rudolph Giuliani declared, "The vast majority of Americans do not feel safe. They fear for their children."[109] In addition to reinforcing the legitimacy of the fear many may feel, this could make those who, in fact, did feel safe wonder what they were missing. Journalist Dylan Matthews describes Trump's convention speech as "one of the darkest, most foreboding, and aggressively fearmongering speeches in modern political memory," a description of a world "where citizens are living under constant threat of attack." Despite the fact that this is not true, and "America has more or less never been safer," fear was the capital and the Republicans were trading on it.[110]

Chapter Outline

Going Viral proceeds roughly chronologically—as well as thematically—from the mid-1990s through present day. It aims to situate the outbreak narrative in several historical trajectories: the growing anxiety fueled by emerging viruses and a shrinking, borderless world; the insertion of bio-terrorism into that initial anxiety starting in the twenty-first century; and the current fascination with manifesting the end of the world. There is no clear-cut start or stop to these trajectories. Rather, they are layers and variations upon an initial idea. Examining these texts in thematic groups, as well as individually, offers an opportunity to understand how popular culture interprets social and historical events and how Hollywood, in turn, capitalizes on these interpretations.

Chapter 1 introduces the outbreak narrative template in terms of film cycles—series of films associated with each other, much like a genre, but which maintain financial viability for a shorter length of time. This limited viability is a result of film cycles being more closely tied to current events, as well as a frequently shorter production time. This kind of repetition allows for key tropes—both visual and thematic—that are either repeated and reinforced or slightly tweaked in order to maintain cultural and social currency.

As covered in chapter 2, "The Globalization Outbreak," the original outbreak template focuses on the repercussions of globalization and the ultimate failure of national boundaries as prophylactics, as well as fears of conspiracy and government mismanagement. Films like *Outbreak* and *Contagion* depict a world reimagined as increasingly unbounded zones of containment, protection, and vulnerability, and demonstrate how our understanding of that world would shift from 1995 to 2011. Globalization is portrayed as, if not the cause of pandemics (at least partly), then their facilitator, while the networks of world health organizations often result in the discovery and distribution of the cure or vaccine. As globalization leads to the increased threat of a viral outbreak, some argue for a return to antiquated borders, but the lesson most commonly drawn here is that this would be impossible. These narratives also integrate issues of human responsibility in terms of environmental destruction, placing blame on human presence in remote locations—a result of progress and capitalistic expansion—for the emergence of the virus.

Starting in 2000, the outbreak narrative began to incorporate not only these types of concerns but also newly energized fears of terrorism and, specifically, of a bioterrorism attack. Chapter 3 looks at "The Terrorism Outbreak," featuring plots centered around the threat of biocontamination, inaugurated either by terrorists, as in the miniseries *Covert One: The Hades Factor* (CBS, 2006) or season 3 of *24* (Fox, 2003), or corporate greed, as in *Toxic Skies* (Erin, 2008), *Formula for Death*, and the *X-Files* episode "F. Emasculata." This narrative became increasingly common following 9/11, when fears of terrorism intensified, as did the idea of the terrorist as the infected (or the infected as terrorist). Government and corporate conspiracy also became frequent tropes, demonstrating an increased loss of faith in "the system" and fears of vulnerability, even in our own homes.

Most recently, the outbreak narrative has begun to explore what happens *after* the viral outbreak, in films like *I Am Legend* (Lawrence, 2007) and television shows like AMC's *The Walking Dead* (2010–present), TNT's *The Last Ship* (2014–present), or FX's *The Last Man on Earth* (2015–present). This is the subject of chapter 4: "The Postapocalypse Outbreak," where the viral outbreak has already decimated populations, as well as social and governmental infrastructures, reflecting our current fascination with portrayals of postapocalyptic wastelands and a return to a more primal society. *28 Days Later* and *I Am Legend* provide breathtaking vistas of abandoned cities, empty roads, and desolate buildings, almost romanticizing the end of the world. *The Walking Dead* shows us over and over again what a world would look like without people to maintain it, clearly fascinated with the dissolution of society and the end of life as we know it.

This chapter also includes a discussion of the contemporary zombie figure, which reflects contemporary fears of disease, especially those of a viral pandemic, demonstrating the new hybrid of science fiction/outbreak narrative. Danny Boyle, director of the film *28 Days Later*, said that he wanted to redo the traditional portrayal of zombies in order to reflect contemporary fears of disease, especially those of a viral pandemic. Boyle describes his film as "a warning for us as well as entertainment."[111] The recent proliferation of zombie narratives can also be seen, in part, as a reflection of a larger tendency to position the elite at war against the masses, the special few against the undifferentiated and perpetually hungry many. Interestingly, in certain zombie narratives—often parodies such as *Shaun of the Dead* (Wright, 2004) or *iZombie* (CW, 2015–present)—the focus is on the integration of zombies into existing social and governmental infrastructures.

Part of the pleasure of the outbreak narrative for the viewer is the way it manifests disease and information vectors, and the way it simplifies moral ambiguities, which allows the viewer to judge—and even despise—the "othered." In *Outbreak* and *Contagion*, for example, we can literally trace the disease and information vectors, watching them outlined on maps that display the path of the outbreak. In *24* (Fox, 2001–2010), *Covert One: The Hades Factor*, and *Toxic Skies*, it is clear with whom to ally and whom to despise, for whose death to cheer, whose crimes to condemn. And zombie narratives, whether they be as straightforward as *Resident Evil* (Anderson, 2002) and *Dawn of the Dead* (Snyder, 2004), or as nuanced as *The Walking Dead* or *iZombie*, revel in how permissive it is to smash, gouge, spear, or slice the zombied other.

Viruses remains a powerful and infectious metaphor, a way to demarcate "dangerous" people, a way to draw attention to the flaws and frailties of the bonds between people and between nations, and a way to spread and construct fear. As Peter N. Stearns writes, "we have come, as a nation, to fear excessively."[112] And one of the things we fear most is infection, both literal and metaphorical. The proliferation of digital media—our ability to digest all the information, all the time—makes this fear even more infectious. The power of panic—as well as the fear of infection—can now be multiplied the world over. *Going Viral* offers an attempt at working through these fears via an analysis of the outbreak narrative and everything it represents and feeds.

1

The Outbreak Narrative

Everyone, deep in their hearts, is waiting
for the end of the world to come.
—Haruki Murakami, *1Q84*

As defined by Amanda Ann Klein in her book *American Film Cycles: Reframing Genres, Screening Social Problems, and Defining Subcultures*, film cycles, like film genres, are "a series of films associated with each other through shared images, characters, settings, plots or themes." However, unlike genres, cycles "are financially viable for only five to ten years. After that point, a cycle must be updated or altered in order to continue to turn a profit."[1] This small period of financial viability is due to the fact that film cycles are specifically keyed to capitalize on specific historical and cultural events and/or the success of other films. This topicality and limited sustainability is a major characteristic of film cycles, as is the fact that they are often produced quickly in order to respond to these current events or trends.

Another characteristic of film cycles, keyed to their need to refresh and reinvent, is their play between dominant and subordinate traits. Leger Grindon explains that, at any given moment, there will be a dominant narrative convention—for instance, in terms of outbreak narratives, an emphasis on globalization as the key factor in the spread of disease. However, "repetition and predictability eventually become wearisome, so a subordinate trait . . . moves to the dominant position."[2] This can be seen with the terrorism outbreak narrative, for instance, where the subordinate trait of untrustworthy governments or corporations (otherwise known as "the establishment"), as seen in earlier films like *Outbreak* (Petersen, 1995), began to play a larger and larger part in later films and television shows.

A "cycle approach" is especially valuable in the context of media industry convergence. Current technological and industrial conditions have led Hollywood to rethink medium specificity, with producers speaking in terms of "content" rather than films, television shows, or video games. As John T. Caldwell explains in his article "Welcome to the Viral Future of Cinema (Television)," a set of wide-ranging forces—"the subcultures of production workers, conglomeration, branding, repurposing, convergence, and shifting economic and labor relations"—have not only blurred the lines between film and television scholarship but also caused film and television to become inseparable. Caldwell outlines just how inseparable the two have become, not to mention how "film now functions mostly as a subset of television and electronic media." This relationship can be seen in several ways: "First, in the current function film serves in the business practices of the new media conglomerates; second, because feature films are largely created by the very same production communities in Los Angeles that create prime-time television programs . . . ; third, because feature films since the 1980s have increasingly mimicked televisual form from an aesthetic and technical viewpoint; and fourth, the viewing conditions of film . . . now incorporate the reception conditions that have defined television for more than fifty years."[3]

When this article was published in 2005, it was DVDs that allowed the viewing conditions of film to incorporate the same reception conditions as television. Now however, with Hulu regularly streaming both box office hits as well as almost every broadcast television show, with Netflix expanding their production of original series content, and with Amazon allowing users to purchase both movies and individual television episodes or a "season pass" in addition to creating *their* own original series content, medium specificity feels like an anachronism. A cycle approach, therefore, can best position us to understand popular visual culture in the contemporary period, where films, television shows, and video games can not only feature the same or overlapping content but also are often produced, written, or directed by overlapping people. A cycle approach focuses on trends that traverse media, observing patterns and traits, capitalizing on specific aspects of the cultural and social zeitgeist.

Interestingly, the outbreak narrative, once suited for the big screen, seems to have evolved onto smaller and smaller screens, both televisions and smartphones, showing up as made-for-TV movies, television shows, and games where you either fight the virus (*The Great Flu* and *Killer Flu* are two examples) or where you are the virus trying to kill the world (such as *Plague, Inc.* or *Pandemic 2*, a browser-based game that was very popular during the swine flu scare of 2008). While big screen versions include *Outbreak, I Am Legend* (Lawrence, 2007), and *Contagion* (Soderbergh, 2011), a much more significant number are made-for-TV movies and miniseries. Outbreak narrative television shows are increasingly popular, including *The Strain* (FX, 2014–present), *The Walking Dead* (AMC, 2010–present), *The Last Ship* (TNT, 2014–present), and the recent reboot of *12 Monkeys* (Syfy, 2015–present), as well as specific episodes of shows such as *Person of Interest* (CBS, 2011–16), *Madam Secretary* (CBS, 2014–present), *Law & Order: Special Victims Unit* (NBC, 1999–present), and *Blindspot* (NBC, 2015–present). There is something appropriate about these narratives turning up on television, since television has such a unique relationship to news, information, entertainment, and catastrophe.

By virtue of their formula for success, cycles, even more persistently than genres, recycle and repurpose many of the same elements, creating a sense of familiar enjoyment that can be traced from the original throughout subsequent films.[4] The familiarity—or predictability—becomes part of the pleasure. One of the fascinating qualities of the outbreak narrative is that, while the cycle is routinely updated and altered to reflect changing cultural moments, there are still tropes that remain consistent. In particular, there are six key thematic tropes that have shaped visual depictions of infectious disease on-screen and off: one, the idea of the necessary accident; two, the othering, which creates the "them" in the first place, stigmatizing individuals, geographic areas, and/or lifestyles deemed threatening; three, establishing and policing security where these others pose a threat; four, contagious diseases bringing us together, unifying "us" versus "them"—the infected versus the uninfected; five, a constant emphasis on making the invisible visible, using maps, charts, or microscopes; and six, a fear of progress, with globalization as one form of progress. These tropes show up again and again in the outbreak narratives themselves (both the nonfiction and fiction versions)—until the apocalyptic outcome of an outbreak renders some of them irrelevant (there are no charts or microscopes or other forms of technology in *The Walking Dead*, for instance). The film *Outbreak* is a useful case study to demonstrate how the utilization of these tropes feeds a larger cultural narrative of fear and anxiety, a narrative that grew and evolved during subsequent decades.

Within these thematic tropes, there are several key visual characteristics that have now become common enough to represent viral outbreak at a glance, regardless of whether they appear in a newspaper or on a movie screen. These visual tropes are also used to feed the larger cultural narrative. Outbreak narratives, after all, are highly visual, and the visual signs compensate for what cannot be seen. Maps and charts, for example, become ways of visualizing the gravity of a threat. Maps render a faraway continent suddenly close and very real, as well as tracing the otherwise invisible path of disease vectors. Charts translate an otherwise unseeable threat into graphics and numbers. In *Outbreak*, for instance, the scientists diagram the chain of infection on a white board, each individual person connected both to whoever infected him or her, as well as to those he or she then infected. Rudy Alvarez (Daniel Chodos) infects Henry Seward (Leland Hayward III), at which point the new strain emerged. Seward, in turn, infects Corrine, his fiancée (Dana Andersen); Tracy H. (Jenna Byrne), who infects Jason H.; Mrs. Logan (Ina Romeo), who infects Baby Logan and Arthur; and someone named Neal. As each subsequent patient is identified, his or her personal interactions are added to the chart. Maps, charts, and networks, whether of commerce or information, emphasize and visualize connectivity, representing "a flattening or erasure of difference."[5]

Barriers are another repeated visual trope in the outbreak narrative. In the opening scene of *Outbreak*, for example, the Americans are wearing such opaque masks that, when they explore the village, we cannot even see their eyes, much less their faces. The next time we see Billy Ford (Morgan Freeman), he is wearing equally opaque sunglasses. During the introductory sequence at the CDC, the emphasis is on doors and windows, each laboratory a secure and confined space, some of the doors even looking like bank vaults. The barriers can be tangible, as in masks or protective gear or metal doors to block out dangerous microbes, or they can be political, as with quarantine regulations, travel restrictions, or border policies. Significantly, as Nicholas B. King emphasizes, while the intention of these barriers may be to act as prophylaxis, they—much like the networks, maps, and charts—serve to reflect vulnerability and fear about the frailty of both geographic and corporeal borders in the face of viral agents and vectors.[6] These visual tropes, much like thematic tropes, can be wielded and manipulated by Hollywood, journalists, and politicians to create and assuage panic in the face of disease.

The first key thematic trope is the necessary accident. In the three types of outbreak narrative (globalized, terrorized, and zombified), transgressions and accidents are essential. The necessary accident supplies dramatic tension, propelling the plot forward. Quarantines—or the equivalent—inevitably fail. Someone (a zombie, an infected victim, a terrorist) gets out or something (a zombie, a virus, a bomb) gets in. To illustrate, one of the central conflicts at the heart of the TV movie *Pandemic* (Hallmark, 2007) is the businessman who defies quarantine, slipping out of the carefully contained area where all the other infected people are being held, because he considers himself too busy and important. His ego results in numerous deaths as he spreads the virus in his wake throughout the city of Los Angeles. The same thing happens in the TV movie *Black Death* (CBS, 1992), this time with a congressman who tries to flee town, taking the infection with him. The disease always manages to spread, even to the scientists wearing protective apparel. Any attempt at quarantine on a large scale appears meaningless, and people are infected regardless of precautionary measures.

In his aptly titled essay "Contagion and the Necessary Accident," Bill Albertini explores the impossibility of containment in the outbreak narrative, despite the fact that containment is often the issue with which the cycle is most concerned. The issue of containment is, quite literally, at the center of *Containment* (CW, 2016), reflecting our continued interest in building higher walls and stronger borders. Initially, the "cordon sanitaire" is supposed to last only forty-eight hours, but it gets extended and extended through the first season. Shipping containers and armed enforcers are set up along the perimeter to prevent those on the inside from getting out and those on the outside from getting in.

In the outbreak narrative, security no longer means protection but *containment*, keeping the infected away from the uninfected. The infected are written off as worthless, and all that matters is keeping them inside and contained. We see this trope again and again. In outbreak narrative after outbreak narrative, the military or the National Guard shields the borders while the disease rages within, not only demonstrating the institutional unity of military with medical but also making visible the permeability of boundaries both on a body-level and on a political level. Biological security becomes political security. Bodily failure becomes failure of the body politic.

Security—and how to maintain it—is a pervasive theme in all outbreak narratives. The traditional understanding of contagion hinges on the dangers of close contact, underscoring a literal threat to bodily boundaries, but contagion can also be seen as a metaphoric threat for larger, national boundaries. The crux of the outbreak narrative, Albertini argues, is this "tension between the desire for containment and an opposing and powerful desire for accidental exposure and infection."[7] After all, without the accident, there would be no plot, no juicy conflict, no drama to play out on the screen. As viewers, we wait for it. There is even a predictable pleasure in watching the rupture occur. The accident is an essential but discomforting reminder that our bodies—much like our prophylactics—are unable to protect us. It is a metaphorical allusion to the inevitability of invasion, exposure, and infection—in a way that strategically removes responsibility or blame. Its occurrence also reinforces our fear of that inevitable mistake in our actual lives.

In *Outbreak*, there are multiple accidents, some fatal and some merely empty threats, to foreshadow the tragic accidents that will inevitably occur. The original viral spread is initially due to the faulty containment of the virus in 1967; monkeys carrying the virus scamper out of reach of the bomb blast that otherwise demolishes the infected village. One of these monkeys is later trapped and smuggled into the United States, thus bringing the virus from Africa to California. Ironically, the first shot of the ship sailing to California occurs seconds after General Ford (Morgan Freeman) says the virus is contained. A "fake" accident occurs when Major Salt (Cuba Gooding Jr.) vomits within his protective suit and pulls his mask off. Fortunately, at that point, the virus is not yet aerosolized, so nothing happens, but the threat reminds us of the ease of exposure. Another "fake" accident occurs when Casey (Kevin Spacey) finds a tear in Sam's suit (Dustin Hoffman). Luckily, he finds it before the two of them walk into the lab, and so Casey is able to repair the suit in time. However, this acts as foreshadowing, since Casey's suit will eventually tear, allowing the virus to infect him, and then, in turn, through yet another accident, he infects Robby Keough (Rene Russo). Another significant accident occurs in the laboratory at the Cedar Creek Hospital, where Henry (Leland

Hayward III), a distracted lab technician, accidentally shatters a test tube of blood, the infected substance spraying all over his face. This accident—and Henry's subsequent trip to the local movie theater—is what spreads the virus throughout the hospital and Cedar Creek. Without accidents, the virus would never have left the African continent, the CDC would have successfully contained the virus, and/or Casey and Robby would not have been infected. In fact, without the initial breach, the infected monkeys would never have survived the bomb blast.

"Othering" is the second key thematic trope of the outbreak narrative, both as a way to reflect on how a disease would (and could) spread and as a way of placing blame and indulging implicit racism and stigma. When Richard Preston was asked why Ebola continues to be so terrifying, he explained: "It's the nonhuman other that all human beings are contending with in many different ways."[8] This trope is not reserved only for entertainment purposes but also has historical and journalistic precedent. For example, Sheldon Ungar, in his analysis of American media coverage of the 1995 Ebola outbreak in Zaire, found that every source under consideration contained the view that Zairian "conditions are perfect for breeding a plague," repeatedly referencing the collapse of the public health system, the "staggeringly corrupt government," the soldiers "preying on a frightened populace," and describing the capital as "defined by decay."[9] Donna Haraway theorizes that, in response to the disease genocides that accompanied the European penetration of the globe, "the 'colored' body of the colonized was constructed as the dark source of infection, pollution, disorder, etc. that threatened to overwhelm white manhood (cities, civilization, the family, the white personal body)."[10]

Similarly, in an article for the *Washington Post* entitled "The Long and Ugly Tradition of Treating Africa as a Dirty, Diseased Place," Laura Seay and Kim Yi Dionne examine the tradition of describing not only the African continent in this way but also the African people as "savage animals." They examine the history of comparing African people to uncivilized primates and focus specifically on a *Newsweek* story that suggests "African immigrants are to be feared, and that apes—and African immigrants who eat them—could bring a deadly disease to the pristine shores of the United States of America."[11] The disease, in this case, is Ebola, and the article, predictably, warns that Ebola is on its way to American soil, "all but ignored by the popular press and public." The reason it is ignored is because the article's theory (that Ebola is within bushmeat smuggled into the United

States in luggage) is nonsense. As best as scientists can ascertain, Ebola is transmitted via bats, not meat. However, *Newsweek*, much like other media sources, continues to threaten that this is a valid risk, an insinuation that is not only misleading but irresponsible.[12] Also note the contrast between the ape-eating Africans and the "pristine" United States.

Unfortunately, this pattern is nothing new. Immigrants and foreigners have historically been seen as "contagious" and "diseased." Alan M. Kraut, in an essay entitled "Foreign Bodies: The Perennial Negotiation over Health and Culture in a Nation of Immigrants," describes how, at the beginning of the twentieth century, Chinese immigrants were seen as a threat to public health, specifically the bubonic plague, while the Irish were charged with bringing cholera to the United States in 1832. Italians were also stigmatized for polio, while tuberculosis was called the "Jewish disease."[13] During the 1990s, Haitians who tested positive for HIV were held at Camp Bulkeley in Guantanamo Bay and denied entry under a 1987 law barring immigration of HIV positive individuals into the United States.

Even now, in the twenty-first century, immigrants are seen as diseased and contagious. In July 2014, Representative Phil Gingrey accused immigrants from Central America of carrying deadly diseases such as swine flu, dengue fever, Ebola virus, and tuberculosis.[14] In July 2015, Donald Trump declared that "tremendous infectious disease is pouring across the border" in the bodies of immigrants.[15] Outbreak narratives allow for and encourage this kind of stigmatizing of individuals or locations deemed contagious or ripe for "plague breeding." This method of stigmatizing individuals or locations can be seen as a retaliation against the more homogeneous unity advocated by globalization, a way to redraw lines rendered meaningless by the process of globalization. Othering also becomes a way of creating reassurance that the virus is only meant for "at risk" people, enforcing a sense of difference and distance. Disease is consistently imagined as a foreign threat, traveling from the outside in, with—as Geddes Smith, author of *Plague on Us*, argues—quarantines as little more than attempts "to put a fence around an entire nation."[16]

In the outbreak narrative, the threat always comes from the outside in, spread via physical contact, breathing, technology, science, and/or conspiracy, but almost always originating in Asia or Africa, traveling from east to west. In *The Andromeda Strain* (Wise, 1971), the virus comes from outer space. In this case, it is literally aliens (a term also used to describe foreign inhabitants of the nation) who are to blame. The reference may be more abstract, but the process (othering) is the same. At that point in American history, Hollywood films were often centered around extraterrestrial threats. By the 1990s, however, it was common for the viral threat to come from an African country, even if it was repurposed by the American military as a bioweapon, as in the case of *Outbreak*. Not only does the virus come from an overtly primitive and dirty African village, but it is then transferred to "the pristine shores" of America via monkey, smuggled in by an Asian man, conveying layers of stigma and negative association. In *Contagion*, the virus comes from Asia—linked to the country's alleged lack of hygiene among food workers and the underclass—even if the spread westward is due to an American company and an American blonde. In *World War Z* (the book, written by Max Brooks and published by Three Rivers Press in 2007), the outbreak begins in China; however, in *World War Z* (the movie, directed by Marc Forster and released in 2013), the outbreak begins in South Korea. Thomas R. Feller posits that the reason for this change is the fiscally responsible reason that "China constitutes the world's second largest movie market after the US and the filmmakers did not wish to offend the Chinese authorities who could ban the film from being shown there."[17] In the miniseries *Covert One: The Hades Factor* (CBS, 2006), the virus was developed by Americans but spread by treacherous Muslims. The racial profiling may shift, but the other (whatever his or her skin tone) remains just as threatening, just as stigmatized.

In both real life and in the fictionalized outbreak narrative, it is not simply that diseases are blamed on an unfortunate group but that modernization is offered as the antidote to the diseased and dangerous "relics of 'primitive' other." *Outbreak*, for instance, opens in a tribal and disease-ridden African jungle space, which is in marked contrast to the next scene, set in the organized, protected, sterile, modern US Army Medical Research Institute of Infectious Diseases (USAMRIID)—the browns and greens of the jungle all the more chaotic when juxtaposed with the white sterility of the laboratory. The village is also full of tribal music, thatched roofs, dying people, and monkeys, while the "virology section" of USAMRIID is neatly compartmentalized into "biosafety levels," lists of levels and corresponding viruses distinguishing each section from the next. When the film returns to Africa, this time with the medical researchers, the Westerners walk into the village in their masks and yellow suits, their prophylactics emphasizing their boundaries—metaphorical, technological, and literal—protecting them from the disease and dirt, the dead and dying.

This kind of distancing from a threatening person or group of people continues to be just as relevant offscreen as on. The strident declarations by Donald Trump to ban all Muslims from entering the United States and to deport illegal immigrants are just another manifestation of an attempt to draw a line in the sand between "good people" and "hazardous people," when, really, those lines have become indistinguishable. In terms of 9/11, the obvious "other" was the Arab terrorist and the menacing Al Qaeda, but Elizabeth Goren argues that the first signs of distancing were the "actual erection of physical barriers around the disaster site itself," as if to contain the horror. This internal distancing was "mirrored by a strongly perceived invisible separation that developed between those outside and those within the zone of disaster." Those directly affected by the disaster were seen as "contaminated carriers of the catastrophe, who had to be almost quarantined" in order to protect others from the social contagion of what they had experienced.[18] The "contagion" of 9/11 was also evident in the way people fled the city after the event, either permanently or temporarily, tourists choosing other, "less tainted" destinations for their holidays. Ground Zero became, like patient zero, something to be shunned and avoided, an attribute further enhanced when the relief centers were moved off-site and uptown. The implication was that somehow the horror and trauma could be contained and localized.

A third key thematic trope is a focus on establishing and policing security in a world where "others" want to harm "us." Contagious diseases instill fears of sharing bodily fluids, bodily contact, or even just air space with potentially infectious creatures (animal or human, depending on the disease). If the horror, trauma, and microbes are geographically specific, then the aim is to get as far away from them as possible. This mentality persists, even when irrational. For example, after the Orlando shooting in June 2016, many Americans were shocked to discover that gay men cannot donate blood. The Food and Drug Administration banned gay and bisexual blood donation completely in 1983, revising the ban slightly in 2015 to allow gay men who have been celibate for a full year to donate. This qualification also applies to gay men in long-term relationships.

So one way to establish security is by literally drawing a line between "good bodies" and "bad bodies," "good blood" and "bad blood," and never the two shall mix. This can be done on a legal level, as in the FDA's ban, or it can be done with literal lines on the ground, through a quarantine, or by suggestion, through social distancing. In *Outbreak*, the entire town of Cedar Creek is quarantined, and then within that quarantine, the sick people are first isolated in the hospital and then fenced into a tented area after they become too contagious to share the hospital. *Contagion* (2011), rather than using traditional quarantine, depicts the use of social distancing, where individuals are told to remain three feet away from each other at all times. In *Containment*, social distancing expands to four to six feet. Staying home or wearing masks enhances the social distancing. Most people also stay indoors and wear masks.

Masks are also worn throughout *Containment*—both official medical masks and improvised masks, like a scarf wrapped around the head. Masks are a visual code for fatal infection. Scientists and medical personnel begin wearing masks even before the danger of the virus is determined, but things are serious when ordinary civilians start wearing masks as well, in addition to gloves and maintaining personal distance. In these narratives, there is layer upon layer of protection, layer upon layer of isolation, plastic and glass separating the characters from each other. Because they have run out of body bags in *Contagion*, when Erin dies, she is tightly covered with plastic and taped shut. Her body is sealed to contain potential contaminants, to reduce the risk of potential exposure. Even the air around her could be fatal. We also see Jory Emhoff (Anna Jacoby-Heron) kept apart from her boyfriend, only able to text him and to look at him through a window. While her father is being watched at the hospital, she communicates with him through a telephone and through a window.

Fear of infection makes one especially aware of the distance between bodies, making a suspected carrier feel uncomfortably close. Metaphorical lines are drawn between those who are not infected and those who are deemed infectious or more likely to be infectious. While it may be unattainable, distance from disease is an aspirational ideal. It is no coincidence, Jacqueline Foertsch writes, "that Sir Thomas More's *Utopia* is an island before it is anything else . . . The utopic desire for boundaries that hold ignites the rhetoric of the reactionary right throughout the cold war and AIDS eras, with destruction of these seen as equivalent to apocalypse."[19]

The utopic desire for boundaries that hold continues to ignite political rhetoric. Donald Trump, for instance, argued in an interview with CNN in 2015 that the United States has a "porous border" and that this is not acceptable: "To have a country you have to have a strong border, a really strong border."[20] He repeated this argument throughout much of his Presidential campaign messaging, including in a TV spot from January 2016. In that particular campaign ad, Trump demanded a temporary ban on Muslims entering the United States (keeping out "the questionable other"), as well as calling for a halt on illegal immigration via Mexico by building a wall (keeping out another type of "questionable other"). He concluded the ad by reiterating the argument that building higher and more effective walls "will make America great again."[21] Another example occurred during the November 2014 campaign season, when former senator Scott Brown, running for a senate seat out of New Hampshire, managed to pull all these metaphors together in one dizzying array, predicting that ISIS terrorists would sneak in via "porous" boundaries to spread Ebola, a prediction eerily similar to the plot of *Covert One: The Hades Factor.*[22]

Unfortunately for Trump, the outbreak narrative demonstrates that boundaries, walls, and safety apparel are never fully effective. For example, the prison is quarantined on *The X-Files* episode "F. Emasculata" (Fox, April 28, 1995), but the virus still spreads. The soldiers and the potentially infected are quarantined in *The Hades Factor*, but the virus still spreads. The hotel is quarantined in season 3 of *24* (Fox, 2001–2010), but the terrorists have more of the virus at their disposal. In *Global Effect* (Cunningham, 2002), Meredith Tripp (Carolyn Hennesy) attempts to quarantine South Africa, but the virus reaches the United States, anyway. The quarantine is violated in *Pandemic* and *Containment* by people defying orders and sneaking out of the containment zone.

The fourth key thematic trope is that, even though it separates us, contagious disease can also bring us together. The word "contagion," comes from the Latin *contagio*, meaning to touch together (*con*—"together with"—combined with the base of *tangere*—"to touch"). Integral to the word's origin is this bringing together, the formation of shared human bonds, and the connection and contagion therein. This is similar to the way that, on one hand, a traumatic event can isolate (no one else knows what you experienced; no one else can understand) but, on the other hand, a large-scale traumatic event can unify, creating a bond or community among those affected (because no one else knows what you all experienced). E. Ann Kaplan writes that, following 9/11 in New York, she felt a connection to strangers that she had never felt before: "On the subway, too, we looked at each other as if understanding what we were all facing. For at any moment, it seemed, another attack could take place . . . And we were in this together."[23] Similarly, in *Outbreak*, the mayor of Cedar Creek (Kurt Boesen) tells Robby Keough: "Cedar Creek is a small town. We're like a family. Everybody's scared." Everyone suffering through a virus is bonded together by the virtue of their shared suffering, much as those not yet infected can band together to avoid infection.

Contagious diseases create communities based on an "us against them" mentality, unifying groups of infected as well as groups of uninfected. In Robin Cook's 1997 novel, *Invasion*, one of the protagonists says of a deadly virus from outer space that arrives on Earth that "knowing it is happening and that all humans are at risk, I feel connected in a way I've never felt before," as if "humans are a big family."[24] Diseases also act as social equalizers, affecting both rich and poor (although *how* rich and poor are affected can vary widely). In *The Walking Dead*, *Dawn of the Dead* (Snyder, 2004), *Blindness* (Meirelles, 2008), and *Carriers* (Pastor and Pastor, 2009), we see how outbreaks create new kinds of families, survivors banding together in groups to form new types of social structure. Most overtly, the epidemic in *Outbreak* brings Robby and Sam Daniels (Dustin Hoffman) together, their romance rekindled by the act of saving the world.

The fifth key trope of the outbreak narrative is the emphasis on making the invisible visible. Part of this fixation stems from the fear of the seemingly healthy carrier. One of the most terrifying elements of contagious disease is that of the carrier who does not appear infected, innocently or maliciously spreading the virus in his or her wake, and against whom one must defend one's self. Typhoid Mary may have been one of the main instigators of this archetype—spreading tuberculosis to those around her while appearing to be in perfect health—but there have been many more since her, both in real life and on-screen. While there is no carrier in the first *Andromeda Strain* (since the infected people are already dead) and the carrier is conspicuously sick in *Black Death*, starting with *Outbreak* and intensifying with *Contagion*, the seemingly healthy carrier plays a significant role, underscoring the threatening implications of the latency period. The fear revolves around questions such as these: How can you protect yourself if you do not know from what (or from whom) you need protecting? How can you protect yourself if you do not know who is infected? The longer the virus takes to show symptoms, the more people will inevitably be infected. This is why viruses with high mortality rates do not spread as much; the carriers die before they can infect others.

Another part of this fixation stems from the fear that what you cannot see can kill you—and in terms of microbial threat, there is much that cannot be seen. Autopsies are one way of seeing the unseen, cutting open the body to reveal the otherwise hidden wreckage wrought by the virus. In *Black Death*, Sara (a.k.a. patient zero) is autopsied, thus revealing the enormity of her illness. "Dear God, this is one node!" shouts one of the doctors slicing Sarah open, before running to put on two additional pairs of gloves. In *Outbreak*, following Robby's autopsy of Jimbo (Patrick Dempsey), she tells Sam that "it looked like a bomb went off" inside him, that "all the organs were liquefied." After peeling the top of Beth's scalp in *Contagion*, the medical examiner (David Lively) says, "Oh my god." His assistant (Andrew White) asks if he should take a sample. The medical examiner replies, "I want you to move away from the table." "Should I call someone?" the assistant asks. "Call everyone" is the dramatic reply. In all three of these cases, we do not get to see what the doctors see, but we can surmise from their reactions that whatever lies inside these bodies is truly terrifying.

In response to the fear of the unseeable, outbreak narratives also fetishize the close-up, the magnification, the zooming-in to expose that which would otherwise remain unseen. For instance, the cover of *Time* magazine's September 12, 1994, issue featured magnified microbes and the title "Revenge of the Killer Microbes" (see figure 1). On May 20, 1995, the cover of the *Economist* featured a skull within a petri dish and the headline "Disease Fights Back" (see figure 2). Outbreak narratives frequently call attention to their high-powered microscopes, emphasizing the extreme close-ups of these invisible viruses. Sometimes they even feature animated sequences that depict the virus "at work," all with the aim of making the invisible contagions visible.

In this regard, outbreak narratives owe a significant stylistic debt to early public health films, which also struggled with how to visualize the invisible. A frequent trope of scientific documentaries and public health films is that microscopic view that allows us the pleasure of seeing what we cannot otherwise see. Kirsten Ostherr describes the "'aesthetic of astonishment,' in which pleasure revolve[s] around the fascination of seeing previously unimaginable views, including enlargements of bacteria and other revelations of the invisible, disease-carrying microbes that surround us."[25] Ostherr traces how directors of global conspiracy films in the 1970s, educational AIDS videos in the 1980s, and viral outbreak narratives in the 1990s

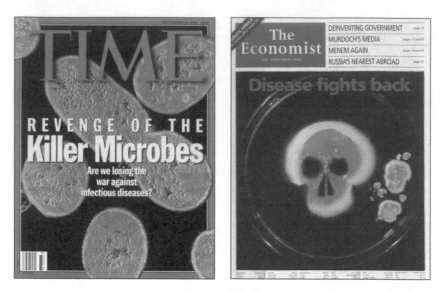

FIGURES 1 AND 2 Magazine covers for *Time* and the *Economist*, demonstrating our fascination with seeing the unseen.

all used digital-imaging technologies to make visual the invisible (to the naked eye) nature of contagion with increasingly realistic-looking animation as well as shot after shot of maps, charts, and lists tracking the virus's spread. Filmmakers, like doctors, are trying to visualize viruses in order to trace and follow the path of disease. Both need to see it in order to understand it and control it.

A pivotal scene in the original 1971 film *Andromeda Strain* features a dramatic zooming-in that results in the discovery of the elusive virus, depicting a mesh screen with a hole in it, the virus finally isolated and exposed in the tear. Screens are supposed to keep things out, but here is an example of a border that fails to protect, defenseless against the penetration and destruction performed by the virus. In a scene that might be painstakingly slow by today's standards, each click of the microscope is dramatically emphasized as we come closer and closer to the virus and the torn screen (see figures 3–6). There is a similar—albeit quicker—sequence in *Outbreak* and in the remake of *Andromeda*. The answer can be found if you know where and how to look and if you can look closely enough. When the scientists finally isolate the Motaba virus, Sam, Casey, and Major Salt gather around a set of monitors, looking at the impact of the virus on healthy kidney cells. First we see the impact after one hour, then after several hours,

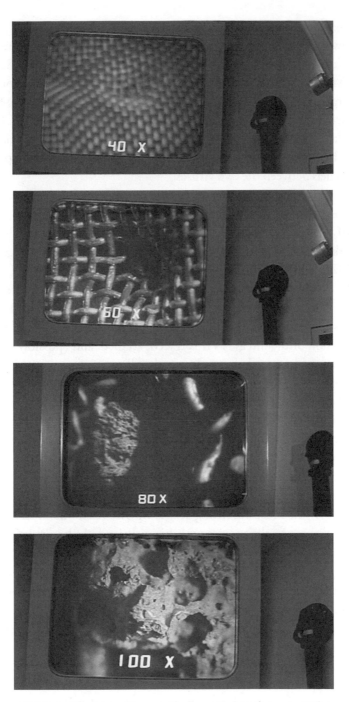

FIGURES 3-6 Increasing the magnification, searching for answers, *The Andromeda Strain* (1971).

and then after a couple more. For the grand finale, the microscope enlarges to allow us to see individual viral organisms, and then once more to see them closer, and then once again, and then one last time as Major Salt says, "Sirs, Mr. Motaba." The camera tracks even closer at this point onto the viral organism. "Mr. Motaba" shows up again, this time in a side-by-side comparison with the original virus from 1967, as General McClintock (Donald Sutherland) and General Ford (Morgan Freeman) discuss what should be done next, their lies about not recognizing the virus exposed in the parallels between the two viruses.

Public health films incorporate animated epidemiological maps to help visualize the spread of these invisible viruses. Hollywood films, too, use this kind of imagery—not only as a narrative tool or to make invisible global networks visible, delineating between "sanitary and unsanitary zones,"[26] but also to add yet another dose of chilling realism to the spread of their epidemics. The invisible made visible is seen repeatedly in outbreak narratives, as it is a way to cognitively map the unknowable world system. Viewers see not only the virus but also the paths the virus takes, the actual transmission of the disease as it is traced, studied, and (possibly) neutralized. These sequences help construct the illusion of a conspiracy narrative, heightening the suspense as we watch the disease pop up in countries around the world. In *Contagion* and *Outbreak*, we have shot after shot of charts visualizing the virus's spread, reminders that globalization has only exacerbated the speed with which disease—and panic—can travel. Most alarming, however, is that, despite this emphasis on making the invisible visible, technology has limits. Digital models may help identify the virus, but they cannot reveal the economic, political, and social forces behind it.

In one of the most unsettling scenes in *Outbreak*, one of the infected individuals goes to the movies with his girlfriend. As he sits in the theater, he coughs, and we can see, thanks to computer generated imagery, the minute particles that fly out of his mouth as he does so, emphasizing how deadly the unseen can be. The camera follows those particles—leaving everything else out of focus—as they spread throughout the theater, entering the mouths of the laughing crowd. It is a very self-reflexive moment, as when the film first came out, most people were watching it in a movie theater, also sharing contaminated and circulated air.

These types of visualizations also serve as reminders of the sixth and final key trope: fear of progress combined with the development of an integrated "risk society." These narratives are conservative in the sense that they always recommend caution, slow change, a halt to development. Progress is the issue, with globalization as one form of the progress. Globalization has eroded borders that might otherwise protect us, and when combined with technology and transportation, globalization also exacerbates the speed with which disease—and panic—can penetrate what borders are left. "In contrast, in *Black Death*, the virus merely travels from California to New York." Three years later, in *Outbreak*, after the virus travels from Africa to Cedar Creek, California, globalization is barely mentioned. The only implication that the virus might have global consequences (after it wipes out the United States) occurs when General McClintock (Donald Sutherland) instructs those in the White House briefing to "be compassionate but think globally" as he tries to sell them on his plan to bomb Cedar Creek. Beyond that, there is no mention of the fact that the rest of the world exists. In fact, there are only two maps in *Outbreak*: one in the CDC epidemic control center and one in the White House briefing room. Tellingly, both show just the United States. Similarly, in 2007, in *Pandemic*, the virus hitches a ride on a flight from Australia to Los Angeles, those on board vulnerable to the virus lurking inside one of the passengers. The distance may be great, but there remains a clear course of travel, from point A to point B.

However, with each passing year, as travel and viral spread increase, the course of travel complicates. In 2011, it was a drastically different scenario in *Contagion*. The opening of *Contagion*, for instance, cuts from city to city, country to county, our only indication that we are in a new location the text on the bottom of the screen. The virus passes effortlessly from one geographical point to the next, from one ethnicity to the next, from one body to the next. A clear travel trajectory has been replaced with an infinitely interlocked network. Even Beth, the one who originally spreads the virus from Asia to Europe and the United States, works as a global marketing operations manager for the American corporation Alderson International Mining and Manufacturing (AIMM)—a symptom and result of increased globalization, much like the cause and spread of the disease itself.

A constant in the outbreak narrative is the issue of blame, although who (or what) is to blame can and does shift. While the Muslim, African, or Asian "other" is often to blame for instigating the outbreak in the Western world, the extent and speed of the spread is attributed to human development; "progress" is often critiqued for causing, if not the outbreak itself, its spread. Frank Furedi observes the frequency of perceiving "human activity through a narrative that emphasizes its selfish, destructive, and toxic behavior" and argues that this is what "underpins our culture of fear."[27] The sense of culpability in our own destruction is a major theme in both our culture of fear and the outbreak narrative. For example, in *The Hot Zone*, Richard Preston writes that AIDS, Ebola, and any other emerging diseases are "a natural consequence of the ruin of the tropical biosphere," an immune system response against humanity by earth herself.[28]

This idea of environmental retribution is most often manifested with the message that, by moving things that should not be moved, destroying habitats that should be preserved, we unleash the virus, and then have no one to blame but our greed. Or, like the medicine man says in *Outbreak*, "This is what happens when men go chopping down trees where no man should be. The gods got angry. This is punishment." As demonstrated in the *Andromeda* remake and in *Contagion*, recklessly destroying ecosystems can have detrimental consequences. *The Andromeda Strain* specifically warns about the hazards of abusing the environment, exhausting natural resources that the world will one day need. In the film, the president is about to begin underwater mining in order to tap into resources beneath the ocean. Activists are protesting but to no avail. However, the antidote for the Andromeda virus lies precisely in these same underwater mines. The warning received from the future is that exhausting this resource will leave the world unable to combat viruses like Andromeda. As Dr. Jeremy Stone (Benjamin Bratt) puts it, "It's a slime from the bottom of the ocean that could save us, something we were prepared to obliterate." The cautionary message behind Dr. Stone's statement is that mankind must heed restraint and not the ego. The virus is contained only because the antidote still exists in untouched mines.

In his explanatory sequence at the end of *Contagion*, Steven Soderbergh demonstrates how globalization and modern living have stripped away traditional food sources from people and animals, forcing both to eat what they would not normally eat as their traditional habitats are destroyed in the interest of capitalistic advancement. We see in *Contagion* the same breached boundaries Allison Fraiberg wrote about twenty years prior "boundaries 'breached,' or at least 'leaky,'" including "those between human and animal, between animal-human and machine, and between the physical and the non-physical."[29] Or, as Eugene Thacker and Alexander R. Galloway write, "These emerging infectious diseases are composed of assemblages of living forms: microbe-flea-monkey-human, microbe-chicken-human, microbe-cow-human, or human-microbe-human,"[30] unnatural combinations that should not happen and would not have happened had it not been for glob-alization. Fruit bats, as used in *Contagion*, are significant to the film's critique of capitalism and environmental destruction because, as Laurie Garrett observes, they "are so stressed by the combination of apparent rising tempera-tures in the upper canopy of the rain forest and human encroachment that they are increasingly going into human areas in search of food . . . and pass-ing ancient viruses, via either their saliva [when they feed] or their urine."[31] Environmental trespass breeds disease, and then globalization spreads that disease.

In a *Newsweek* article from 2003 entitled "How Progress Makes Us Sick," Geoffrey Cowley describes that what specifically turned AIDS into a "holocaust" was not just the virus itself but also the "proliferation of roads, cities, and airports" that allowed the virus to spread.[32] The implication is that the price we pay for development is an increased susceptibility to emerging diseases and an increased risk of self-destruction. Torin Mona-han argues that the Fox television show *24* functions as a "metaphor for modernity" by depicting the new social order and impacts of globalization. While the show portrays the necessary global flows of people and goods essential to a healthy economy, it also depicts how these same flows exacer-bate vulnerabilities such as terrorism, military intervention, and economic instability.[33] Both the fictional and the nonfictional tap into the same set of vulnerabilities and capabilities.

In 1995, Geoffrey Cowley wrote in an article for *Newsweek* entitled "Outbreak of Fear" that "most experts [had] thought of new viral diseases as accidents of genetic mutation." But they had become "less fearful of random genetic change and more terrified of the effects of human social change." Cowley provides several specific examples. For instance, the emer-gence of HIV in sub-Saharan Africa can be linked to trucking and tour-ism, as well as war and commerce. Experts assume the virus had existed for decades before it emerged in the 1970s but simply would not have escaped the isolated rural villages without the trucking and tourism industries that brought the world to Africa or the war and commerce that brought the villagers out into the world. Sex work, in particular, thrived both along the truck routes and in the rapidly growing cities. Throughout the world, rapidly growing cities have put unprecedented numbers of people closer together—many of whom are in the developing world, where access to sanitation, clean water, and health care is limited—as well as causing more people to move into once rural areas. Encephalitis, for instance, has become an issue in rural areas of Wisconsin not only because more and more people are moving into those areas but also as a result of ecological disruptions in those locations, creating more places for the mosquitoes to breed.[34] All these examples indicate the impact of human action, Morse's causality of local to global coming into play.

Heather Schell, however, sees the issue of responsibility a little differently. She interprets the drive to posit humans as the ultimate cause of epidemics as a way to maintain a fiction of general human control. This fiction is a rebuttal or response to concerns about the lack of human control. Schell argues that recent science fiction is less assured of human control, as evidenced by the failure of medicine and technology to "repel the onslaught of disease organisms."[35] We see this in films like *I Am Legend*, where the cancer vaccine turns people into zombies, or television shows like *The Walking Dead*, where the CDC is unable to do anything to help and does not even know how the infection started. Science fails when it creates a deadly virus (*Covert One: The Hades Factor*, *I Am Legend*, *28 Days Later*, *Resident Evil* [Anderson, 2002]), technology fails when it creates a machine that tries to kill and cause destruction (*The Andromeda Strain*, *Resident Evil*, *The Walking Dead*). In order to compensate for a lack of control in real life, these narratives are created to shift blame and make sense of the world around us.

These narratives that shift blame often incorporate the language of conspiracy. Conspiracies, as observed by Frederic Jameson, can act as attempts to map the structure of an otherwise unknowable global system. In his analysis of conspiracy films in *The Geopolitical Aesthetic*, Jameson writes that conspiracy theories are an "unconscious, collective effort at trying to figure out where we are and what landscapes and forces confront us in a late twentieth century whose abominations are heightened by their concealment and their bureaucratic impersonality."[36] Conspiracy theories, after all, create a sense of agency and purpose for that which cannot otherwise be understood. They reflect the assumption that, for better or for worse, "everything is connected," that everything has a purpose, that there is a master plan.[37] This effort to make sense of "where we are" via conspiracy theory is a sign of how much people need to believe in a hidden agenda to make sense of the chaos of contemporary life. In *Outbreak*, the fault of the virus may not initially have been with the government, which tried to destroy the virus when it was first discovered in 1967, but it is a government conspiracy that allows the virus to spread. It is a government conspiracy that prevents Sam Daniels from doing his job and delays the resolution of the epidemic.

Outbreak narratives frequently integrate conspiracy with the issue of responsibility: government conspiracy, as in *Outbreak* or *Covert One: The Hades Factor*, or corporate and government conspiracy for economic gain, as in *Toxic Skies* or in the *X-Files* episode "F. Emasculata." *The X-Files,* despite its campy tone, managed to tap into many of the same anxieties and conspiracy fears that would permeate future outbreak narratives. In the episode "Deep Throat" (Fox, Sept. 17, 1993), for example, Agent Dana Scully (Gillian Anderson) asks, "Doesn't the government have a right and a responsibility to protect its secrets?" Agent Fox Mulder (David Duchovny) replies, "Yes, but at what cost? When does the human cost become too high for the building of a better machine?" Scully, ever the voice of reason and compliance, retorts, "These are questions we have no business asking." One of the central themes of the show is Mulder's attempts to ask the questions he has no business asking, while Scully tries to reason with him to toe the line and accept the easy answers. The two act as foils to illuminate not only the depths and complexities of government and corporate conspiracies but also the lies we tell ourselves and the questions we do not ask so that we can sleep at night. In the episode "Squeeze" (Fox, Sept. 24, 1993) Mulder observes, while looking at one of their captured targets, "All these people putting bars on their windows, spending good money on high-tech security systems, trying to feel safe? I look at this guy, and I think, 'it ain't enough.'"

The impossibility of truly effective safety pervades all outbreak narratives, reinforcing the theme that all boundaries are porous and indefensible. In *The Hades Factor*, for instance, an American government–engineered virus spreads on domestic soil, having fallen into terrorist hands. In *Toxic Skies*, it is, perversely, a pharmaceutical company that deliberately weakens American's immune systems so as to make higher profits. That which should keep us safe actually makes us sick. In *The Walking Dead*, there is always a threat of attack, either from zombies or other humans. There is no safety, even in the fortified town of Alexandria. Similarly, in every season of *24*, Jack Bauer must fight to keep America safe from yet another threat. Ruth Mayer argues that fictional texts are better able to reflect and respond to real-life events than political and journalistic nonfiction texts because the markedly fantastic dimension of fiction gives it more freedom to reflect on current fears and fascinations.[38] With its markedly fantastic elements—squirting pustules, rotting zombies, frothy seizures, and blood-filled eyes—the outbreak narrative has no shortage of elements with which to tap into the unconscious.

In 2016, the CW network hopped onto the outbreak narrative bandwagon with *Containment*, its version of the Belgian television show *Cordon* (vtm, 2014). *Containment*, which would not be renewed for a second season, premiered on the CW network on May 7, 2016. The show looks at what happens when a deadly virus breaks out in Atlanta and authorities are forced to quarantine the area of the city immediately surrounding the local hospital's infectious disease center. Before the initial premiere, the network launched a trailer that encapsulates some of the show's highlights while also providing insight into why the show failed.

The trailer opens with a man in a white medical coat speaking to a woman behind a window. A surveillance camera monitors her, indicating that she is somehow a threat, worthy of monitoring. "You understand the precautions we need to take, Dr. Sanders?" the man asks, his back to us. She nods, and we can see blood caked around the bottom of her nose, which, according to Hollywood code, is an instant red flag. "Tell me one more time," he says. Now we see his face, his clean and orderly appearance in clear contrast to hers. This triggers a flashback to Dr. Sanders (Elyse Levesque) administering her rounds earlier that day. At this point, she looks the height of professionalism. Her first patient of the day, she tells us via voice-over, "presented with flu-like symptoms." Immediately, there are two more red flags: one, the "flu-like symptoms" that, according to Hollywood code, signify imminent outbreak; and two, the man hovering behind the sick patient is wearing a taqiya, which is also Hollywood code, this time for "danger." To make matters more suspicious, the patient himself is Syrian, Hollywood code for "terrorist." The female doctor recounts, "There was no exposure to fluid, no high-risk contact," but we know this is irrelevant. When the virus wants to spread, it always finds a way—because Hollywood has shown us that people always make mistakes. Instantly, as if on cue, the female doctor remembers lending the sick patient her pen. She now holds it in front of herself gingerly, as if it is still contagious—which it probably is. This is how the virus was transmitted. *Containment* does not need to tell us. We can read the signs, interpret the code. We have seen it all before.

At this point, the trailer cuts to another location, this time an Atlanta train station, where the MARTA train is just pulling in. Those on the platform step forward to board the train, but the train leaves without stopping. This is another red flag. Social order is beginning to fray at the seams.

Trains are not abiding protocol. Our suspicions are further reinforced by the police officers shepherding everyone out of the station. As veteran viewers of television and movies, we are experienced at collecting and assimilating all the clichéd red flags Hollywood serves up. We know this cannot be good for the citizens of Atlanta.

Cut to another scene, this time a briefing for police and CDC officials. There are whispers among those in the room as to the cause for the briefing. It is quickly revealed that the initial patient with the "flu-like symptoms" is patient zero and that the virus is not presenting as anything that can be identified. This is another frequent device in the outbreak narrative, since anything that could be identified *could* be solved, or at least managed. But when it is an unknown or mutated strain, that is when narratives can get away with their unrealistic and accelerated death tolls, and that is exactly what happens in *Containment*.

At this point, the cuts get faster, giving us quick glimpses of the police interviewing the Syrian family harboring patient zero, children at the hospital waiting for a doctor who does not appear, the hospital being locked down, police with riot gear, blood on the walls, masks on faces, doctors declaring the virus fatal and highly contagious, and shots of Dr. Sanders getting sicker and sicker before dying. The hospital and the surrounding area are cordoned off under threat of national security. Interspersed with all these shots are title cards: "We can't see it," "We can't contain it," "We can't control it," and "Ordinary people will defy the odds." The fundamental tension of the series becomes the mayhem that ensues within the quarantine zone—the familiar struggle to contain and control both the virus and the infected—and the chaos shown at the end of the trailer hints toward this.

So if the outbreak narrative is as relevant as I argue that it is, if it taps so acutely into contemporary American fears, why would a show like *Containment* be canceled after only one season? Why would a show that hits so many of the outbreak narrative tropes not be a resounding success? While there are other explanations, to be sure, including the fact that *Containment* diverged dramatically from the CW's standard teenage fare, one key reason for the show's failure lies in the concept of the film cycle.

In a chart constructed by Richard Nowell for his book *Blood Money: A History of the First Teen Slasher Film Cycle*, Nowell outlines what he sees as the evolution of the film cycle arc, using the first teen slasher film cycle as his example. The cycle begins with the "Pioneer Production," which he lists as *Black Christmas* (Clark, 1974). A Pioneer Production is a film that tests the waters or breaks the ice of whatever new cycle is about to be formed. The "Speculator Productions," which he lists as *Halloween* (Carpenter, 1978) and *Silent Scream* (Harris, 1979), are stage two. Out of these, the successful one becomes the "Trailblazer Hit." This is the film that rakes in the box office cash and establishes that particular cycle as successful and worthy of imitation. In this case, it is *Halloween*. Stage three is for those films attempting to capitalize on the success of the Trailblazer Hit. These "Prospector Cash-ins," as Nowell describes them, are *Friday the 13th* (Cunningham, 1980), *Prom Night* (Lynch, 1980), and *Terror Train* (Spottiswoode, 1980). These films mimic the Trailblazer Hit in order to capitalize on its success but are usually more cheaply made. Out of these, the successful ones are the "Reinforcing Hits." The success of those leads to stage four, the "Carpetbagger Cash-ins"—films trying to capitalize on the success of the Reinforcing Hits, often even more cheaply made. In this category, Nowell lists eleven films, all from 1981, including *Friday the 13th Part 2* (Miner), *Final Exam* (Huston), *Happy Birthday to Me* (Thompson), and *My Bloody Valentine* (Mihalka).[39]

The outbreak narrative fits the same pattern as Nowell's teen slasher cycle. It, too, has a Pioneer Production, Speculator Productions, Trailblazer Hits, Prospector Cash-ins, Reinforcing Hits, and Carpetbagger Cash-ins (see table 1). Interestingly, however, the outbreak narrative cycle can be fleshed out using three distinct "waves." The first wave, originating in the mid-1990s, focuses on the impact of globalization and progress, while the second wave, beginning at the start of the twenty-first century, focuses on increased fears of terrorism. The third wave, which reflects the current moment's fascination with what the world would look like after a viral outbreak, begins with the cult classic *Braindead* (Jackson, 1992) and the success of Capcom's original *Resident Evil* video game in 1996. Its peak popularity, however, occurred during the first two decades of the twenty-first century. Its success was so great that this wave warrants an additional category: Stage 5, "Parody and Other," includes not only zombie parodies, such as *Shaun of the Dead* (Wright, 2004), *Pride and Prejudice and Zombies* (Steers, 2016), and *The Walking Deceased* (Dow, 2015), but also the web series *Bite Me* (Machinima, 2010–2012), about three die-hard gamers who find themselves in the middle of the zombie apocalypse, and the web-based "reality" show *Fight of the Living Dead: Experiment 88* (YouTube Red, 2016), in which a group of YouTube stars try to survive a simulated zombie apocalypse. I also include the FX television series *The Strain*

(2014–present) in this category because of the way it fuses zombie and vampire tropes with infection. These lists are by no means complete. They are merely intended to provide a sense of not only the scope of the outbreak narrative but also how its three distinct waves evolved.

In the case of the original wave of the outbreak narrative, the "Pioneer Production" is arguably the television movie *Black Death* (also called *Quiet Killer*), which aired on CBS on March 24, 1992—just a few months before Richard Preston's infamous article "Crisis in the Hot Zone" was published in the *New Yorker*. *Black Death* began the shift from disease-of-the-week movies to pandemic narratives. Disease-of-the-week movies—a slightly snarky title for a particular breed of made-for-TV movie focused on people struggling with an illness or disability (frequently blindness or cancer)—became popular during the 1970s and 1980s. These TV movies were often melodramatic and cheaply made, lending them a distinctive and easily duplicated style.

In *Black Death*, based on the 1977 novel of the same name by Gwyneth Cravens and John S. Marr, an infected girl flies home to New York after a camping trip in California—tapping into fears of disease spread via air travel—and threatens to infect the city (and then the world) with the Black Plague, which she most likely caught from a squirrel via flea bites—tapping into fears of zoonotic diseases. Zoonotic diseases (those spread from animals to humans, like rabies and Ebola) would surface again and again in later outbreak films, such as *Outbreak* and *Contagion* (2011). Realizing that Sara has died of the plague, a pandemic that spread throughout Europe during the fourteenth century killing an estimated two hundred million people, Dr. Nora Hart (Kate Jackson) tries to warn the authorities, but the mayor refuses to do anything, more worried about causing a panic than stopping a plague. This is another plot device that appears frequently in future outbreak narratives: those in power are usually reluctant to take action due to the economic and social repercussions of panic. Already, in 1992, the various tropes of the outbreak narrative can be seen in their infancy, foreshadowing their future impact.

Per Nowell's chart, the Pioneer Production is followed by the Speculator Productions, out of which one (or more) becomes the Trailblazer Hit. In this case, the Speculator Productions can be seen to be early versions of the outbreak narrative, such as the made-for-TV movie *The Stand* (based on the book by Stephen King), which aired on ABC in May 1994, about what happens after a virus kills off most of humanity; the made-for-TV movie

Table 1

The outbreak narrative film cycle.

Stage One	Stage Two		Stage Three		Stage Four	Stage Five
Pioneer Production →	Speculator Productions →	Trailblazer Hit →	Prospector Cash-ins →	Reinforcing Hits →	Carpetbagger Cash-ins →	Parody and Other
Globalization						
Black Death a.k.a. Quiet Killer (1992)	The Stand (1994)	Outbreak	Pandora's Clock (1996)	Contagion	Containment (2016)	
"Crisis in the Hot Zone" article (1992)	Outbreak (1995)		Pandemic (2007)	The Andromeda Strain		
	Virus a.k.a. Formula for Death (1995)		The Andromeda Strain (2008) Contagion (2011)			
Terrorism/Conspiracy						
Contaminated Man (2000)	Global Effect (2002)	24	Covert One (2006)	The Crazies	The Blacklist "The Front" (2014)	
Venomous (2001)	Contagion (2002)		Toxic Skies (2008)		12 Monkeys (2015)	
	24 (2003)		The Crazies (2010)		Blindspot "Bone May Rot" (2015)	
					Person of Interest "Reassortment" (2016)	
					Inferno (2016)	
					Madam Secretary "Desperate Remedies" (2016)	

Postapocalypse/Zombies

Resident Evil video game (1996)	Resident Evil	Resident Evil (2002)	Resident Evil: Apocalypse (2004)	Resident Evil: Apocalypse	Fear the Walking Dead (2015)	Shaun of the Dead (2004)
Braindead a.k.a. Dead Alive (1992)	28 Days Later	28 Days Later (2002)	Dawn of the Dead (2004)	Dawn of the Dead	The Last Man on Earth (2015)	Bite Me (2010)
The Walking Dead comic book (2003)		S.A.R.S Wars (2004)	28 Weeks Later (2007)	28 Weeks Later		The Strain (2014)
			Resident Evil: Extinction (2007)	Resident Evil: Extinction		iZombie (2015)
			I Am Legend (2007)	I Am Legend		The Walking Deceased (2015)
			I Am Omega (2007)	Zombieland		Fight of the Living Dead (2016)
			Grindhouse: Planet Terror (2007)	The Walking Dead		Pride and Prejudice and Zombies (2016)
			Zombieland (2009)	World War Z		
			Carriers (2009)	The Last Ship		
			The Crazies (2010)			
			The Walking Dead (2010)			
			World War Z (2013)			
			The Last Ship (2014)			

Virus (also known as *Formula for Death*), which aired on ABC in May 1995, in which a virus breaks out in Los Angeles; and, of course, *Outbreak*, released by Warner Bros. in March 1995. *Outbreak*, with its box office draw of almost $190 million, would become the clear Trailblazer Hit.

In the years to come, the Prospector Cash-ins would appear. Most of these would be TV movies or straight-to-video releases—like *Pandora's Clock* (NBC, Nov. 10, 1996), about a deadly virus on a flight from Germany to New York City (reinforcing the threat of air travel, or as Dr. Roni Sanders [Daphne Zuniga] warns in *Pandora's Clock*, "The world's airline system is a potential instrument for viral holocaust"), or *Venomous* (Ray, 2001), about genetically modified rattlesnakes released from a secret government lab and that spread a deadly virus (reinforcing threats of government conspiracy, biowarfare, and zoonotic diseases), or *Pandemic* (Hallmark, 2007), about the bird flu spreading through Los Angeles, transmitted from Australia via an airline passenger (reinforcing again the threat of air travel as well as faulty quarantines). These were campy low-budget affairs, but they still helped keep viral outbreaks on the television screen and in the cultural consciousness until *Contagion* (Soderbergh, 2011).

Contagion—with its worldwide box office of $135 million—would be the last big-budget big-screen viral outbreak blockbuster, helping to wrap up the first incarnation of the outbreak narrative. As the only one of the Prospector Cash-ins to truly succeed, it would be part of the Reinforcing Hits category, indicating to Hollywood that the cycle still had some juice left, and giving the CW network enough confidence to produce *Containment*. *Containment* would then be a Carpetbagger Cash-in, an attempt to recycle the same formula as the Trailblazer for at least some of that film's profits. The box office success of *Contagion*, on the other hand, can be partially explained by the fact that it updated the original outbreak narrative template by making the spread of the virus more global. While using all the key tropes, it also aimed to update the formula. Having director Steven Soderbergh at the helm and acclaimed screenwriter Scott Z. Burns as the writer also helped *Contagion* rebrand the outbreak template and grant it legitimacy and artistic integrity. However, *Containment* did almost nothing to reinvent the template, and by 2016, the original format of the outbreak narrative template had been stretched too thin. Without significant alterations, the show was doomed to fail.

While terrorism and conspiracy are not new to Hollywood, the twenty-first century embraced their integration into the outbreak narrative cycle.

This second wave of the outbreak narrative had the low-budget *Contaminated Man* (Hickox, 2000) as a Pioneer Production, an early integration of biowarfare and terrorism into the theme of viral outbreak. After 9/11, this incarnation picked up steam. The *Global Effect* (Cunningham, 2002) and *Contagion* (Murlowski, 2002) may not have hit in the box office, but *24* became a massive success, and season 3 (Fox, 2003–2004) revolved entirely around the threat of a bioterrorism. The idea of viruses as terrorist weapons has now become commonplace, manifesting in the television remake of *12 Monkeys*, episodes of *The Blacklist* (NBC, "The Front," Oct. 20, 2014), *Blindspot* (NBC, "Bone May Rot," Oct. 12, 2015), and *Person of Interest* (CBS, "Reassortment," May 24, 2016), and back to the big screen with *Inferno* (Howard, 2016).

This same kind of film cycle structure can be found with the third outbreak narrative wave, the postapocalypse or postoutbreak incarnation. This wave launched with the *Resident Evil* videogame (Capcom, 1996) and *The Walking Dead* comic (2003) and proved its potential with the first *Resident Evil* movie (Anderson, 2002) and the release of *28 Days Later* (Boyle, 2002). In the subsequent years, Reinforcing Hits like *Resident Evil: Apocalypse* (Witt, 2004), the *Dawn of the Dead* remake (Snyder, 2004), *Resident Evil: Extinction* (Mulcahy, 2007), and *28 Weeks Later* (Fresnadillo, 2007) proved that zombies were far from dead. By the time *The Crazies* (Eisner) and *The Walking Dead* (AMC) television show premiered, both in 2010, this incarnation was in full stride. The incarnation was in such full stride, and the tropes so familiar, that this wave even began to spawn parodies, such as *Shaun of the Dead* (Wright, 2004) and *Pride and Prejudice and Zombies* (Steers, 2016), as well as Carpetbagger Cash-ins such as *Planet Terror* (Rodriguez, 2007), *iZombie* (CW, 2015–present), and even a YouTube Red "zombie reality show," *Fight of the Living Dead: Experiment 88* (2016).

While the outbreak narrative does not fall as neatly into Nowell's film cycle categories as the horror genre, plotting the films out using his categories can help explain how one feeds into the next. For instance, the film *Carriers* may have just cost $10 million to make, but it only grossed $5.8 million worldwide, making it a clear commercial disappointment. However, its depiction of a world devastated by a viral outbreak, with most of the population dead and the few survivors forced to figure out a strategy for this new world, resonated enough with audiences, writers, and producers to be returned to again and again. This incarnation of the outbreak narrative set a template that would prove profitable and was likely inspired by *The Walking Dead* comic, which was first published in 2003. The success of the *Resident Evil* franchise, *I Am Legend* (Lawrence, 2007), *Zombieland* (Fleischer, 2009), *The Walking Dead*, *World War Z*, and *The Last Ship* further solidified this new wave of the cycle.

Because plots within each wave of the outbreak narrative mirror each other so transparently, there is less medium specificity than might exist within the tighter constraints of some film genres, where a television show must be evaluated completely different than a movie. The outbreak narrative is remarkably consistent regardless of whether it is in a television show or a movie, a miniseries or a book. The message is the content, and the medium itself becomes irrelevant; the same story is repurposed regardless of screen size or delivery mechanism. The outbreak narrative traverses between the big screen and the little screen with little variation, launching with a made-for-TV movie, hitting its stride with big-screen spectacle, and reinforcing itself with television shows and miniseries and journalistic depictions of real-life outbreaks. In other words, the outbreak narrative is not only a rhetorical pattern between individual films but also a pattern that persists across media forms and platforms—television, movies, and even the written word. The outbreak narrative continues its transmedia appeal, pulling from books (*The Andromeda Strain, Black Death, The Stand, Formula for Death, Pandora's Clock, I Am Legend, World War Z, 28 Days Later, Covert One: The Hades Factor, The Last Ship, The Day of the Triffids*), video games (*Resident Evil*), and comic books (*The Walking Dead*), and even manifesting in board games (*Pandemic*) and phone apps (*Plague, Inc.*). As briefly outlined in the introduction, the outbreak narrative gained initial attention with a combination of media texts, including those early articles like "Crisis in the Hot Zone," books like *The Coming Plague* and *The Hot Zone*, as well as television movies like *Black Death*, news items on AIDS and Ebola, and the cinematic success of *Outbreak*. The message crossed all platforms: A virus was coming to get us.

The outbreak narrative, through its fantastical and metaphorical representations of real-life anxieties—on many types of screens, dispersed through many types of networks—provides portrayals of scenarios ripped from our nightmares and our headlines. We may fear these scenarios—we may even relish them within the safety of the screen—but what remains unwavering is that while the cycle may update, the outbreak narrative remains keyed in to the pulse of the zeitgeist.

If one is searching for manifestations of America's fear of viral contagion, its fears that deadly diseases or deadly carriers will migrate from primitive unknowns to America's neatly groomed suburbs, causing panic and social breakdown, then the place to turn is the outbreak narrative. Displaying not only a preoccupation with the body's vulnerability to disease, the outbreak narrative seems equally—if not more so—concerned with what the repercussions of an epidemic, of an American infrastructure beset by fear and infection, would look like. The consequences of contagion—immunological, political, social, ideological—are at the heart of the outbreak narrative.

2

The Globalization Outbreak

> How the world is framed may be as
> important as what is contained within
> that frame.
> —Anne Friedberg, *The Virtual Window*

While the impossibility of truly effective safety pervades all outbreak narratives, this fear would grow more pronounced as the impact of globalization grew more visible. In particular, the combination of eroding barriers and rapid global communication would change both the world and the outbreak narrative. Viral outbreaks would make us afraid of globalization—of the encroachment of germs, bacteria, and their carriers—and outbreak narratives would feed into this fear. After all, globalization *does* exacerbate the threat of infection, and so film and television narratives can easily emphasize the insecurity of boundaries, regardless of whether the infection is literal—spread via zombies or viruses—or metaphorical. In turn, in a viral fashion, these Hollywood narratives encourage an increase in pandemic reporting, putting us on the lookout for more juicy stories, more dramatic retellings, primed for the real-life outbreak we have been told to expect. And so the cycle of fear spreads.

The Cold War, despite the panic and anxiety it caused, had also established a certain bipolar, black-and-white stability under which individuals, organizations, and governments could be unambiguous about their stations and locations in life. When it ended, geo-politics became far more nuanced and confusing, opening the door for new superpowers like China, Brazil, and India to emerge. By the end of the twentieth century, the worlds of finance and commerce had almost completely globalized. This was due to a rapid-fire succession of historical events and political alignments: the end of the Cold War in 1989; the collapse of the Soviet Union in 1991; the creation of the European Union in 1993 and the launch of the euro in 1999; the signing of the North American Free Trade Agreement in 1994; a steady erosion of trade barriers throughout the eighties and nineties; faster, cheaper transportation by car and by plane; and the proliferation of electronic communications, such as cell phones and the Internet.

Traditional understandings of the nation-state grew increasingly outdated as globalization grew in power and relevance, as illustrated by transnational labor, the global outsourcing of production, the growing distribution of products worldwide (cultural and otherwise), and the reliance of military and law enforcement personnel on networked machines. Political, economic, and social activities became worldwide in scope. Roland Robertson, sociologist and theorist of globalization, attributes to this era a "compression of the world and the intensification of the consciousness of the world as a whole."[1]

As individual governments and nations saw their power erode, multinational corporations saw their power increase. This led to the further proliferation of networks into everyday life and everyday function. Alexander R. Galloway and Eugene Thacker write that the "networks of FedEx or AT&T can be seen as more important than that of the United States in terms of global economies, communication, and consumerism."[2] Corporations of this magnitude can now play a large role in "determining the economic, political, and social welfare of many nations," allowing them to control "much of the world's investment capital, technology, and access to global markets."[3] The growth of these corporations and their networks further encouraged the shift from the vertical and hierarchical to the horizontal and networked. In fact, Galloway declares these decentralized networks to be "the most common diagram of the modern era."[4]

These shifts had another, more personal impact. As national identities evolved or evaporated, so, too, did traditional understandings of individual identity. When the World Wide Web was first invented in 1991, it "formed the basis of a new type of networked communication" that was mainly a variety of generic services that you could join or utilize, but the service itself would not automatically connect you to others. However, with the advent of Web 2.0, shortly after the turn of the millennium, "online services shifted from offering channels for networked communication to becoming interactive, two-way vehicles for networked society."[5] Technological networks became even more integrated into everyday lives, into how we presented and shaped our identities, both online and off, bringing individuals together—while still physically separated—through a complex web of connections. Perversely, while people were more networked than ever, they were also more isolated.

All these shifts—financial, commercial, technological—changed the way life would be experienced and understood. In 1996, Spanish sociologist Manuel Castells described the contemporary world as based on networks and paths of flow(s).[6] His perspective reflects the movement of an increasingly globalized world, as newer, more flexible and capillary models were replacing older hierarchical structures, exemplified most familiarly by the innovations of Microsoft, Google, and others.[7] Much like globalization, these shifts also enhanced the sense of being "a citizen of the world" and the increasing irrelevance of national borders. Sites like Blogger (1999), MySpace (2003), Facebook (2004), and YouTube (2005) created online connections and communities, networks that had little to do with nation-state boundaries or geographic location. Nation-state boundaries and geographic locations could be (and would be) superseded by rapid global communication.

In turn, global communication and global networks changed the way we understood time and space, eradicating temporal and spatial limitations in order to bring the farthest reaches of the globe into homes and onto screens. Ideas and information could now circle the world in seconds. This had an impact that transcended mere economics. These technological innovations, as well as the steady expansion of networks—both local and international—combined to create a moment arguably defined by rapid global communication. The proliferation of digital technologies and networks of electronic connectivity mirrored chains of infection, permitting users to send information worldwide in the blink of an eye. Thanks to the ubiquity of media in our lives, information—and its accompanying media platforms—has become all the more pervasive, all the more *viral*.

Over the last twenty years, network discourse has proliferated with an epidemic intensity. Galloway and Thacker argue that "Peer-to-peer file-sharing networks, wireless community networks, terrorist networks, contagion networks of biowarfare agents, political swarming and mass demonstration, economic and finance networks, online role-playing games, personal area networks, mobile phones, 'generation Txt,' and on and on" have become integral to every aspect of our lives.[8] It has become increasingly difficult to find people or locations that are "off the grid."

In turn, viral epidemics have been collapsing time and space since the mid-nineteenth century, "rendering seemingly stable geopolitical and biological distinctions tenuous, if not moot."[9] This kind of collapse has become even more pronounced in the twenty-first century, as technology and networks shrink the world and change our relationship to it. For instance, in *Casino Royale* (Campbell, 2006), M (Judi Dench) has a subdermal microchip inserted in James Bond's (Daniel Craig) arm so that she can track him. "So you can keep an eye on me?" he asks her. "Yes," she replies. "Don't worry about keeping in touch. We'll know where you are." Technology renders physical location irrelevant.

Further enhancing this notion of always being "in touch," a couple hours after the November 2015 terrorist attack in Paris, Facebook activated "safety check," a safety feature triggered by geolocation to allow users in Paris to mark themselves safe, thus reassuring other users who may have been unable to get through with other methods of communication. First introduced in October 2014, this feature is activated during natural disasters or crises, such as Tropical Storm Dianmu in Vietnam during August 2016 or the bomb explosions in Thailand that same month. Significantly, a Facebook spokesperson told *Politico* that "the feature is not used during longer-term crises, like wars or epidemics, because such emergencies have no clear start or end, making it difficult to determine when an individual is 'safe.'"[10] It is precisely this quality—the inability to distinguish when the threat is over—that makes epidemics so terrifying.

If geographical factors are no longer relevant, they are also no longer protective, leaving ordinary citizens vulnerable. Global (rather than local) health and security have become pivotal issues (in real life and in Hollywood), partially due to the seemingly constant threat of worldwide infection spread via juicy stories and dramatic retellings. Human networks have become "conduits of viral destruction," with air travel, in particular, making "especially apparent the intricate networks of human existence and human interdependence."[11] Or, as Thierry Umutoni (Fana Mokoena) says in *World War Z* (Forster, 2013), "The airlines were the perfect delivery system." This wave of the outbreak narrative—the globalization outbreak—plays off the fear that global boundaries are now fully porous. *Contagion* (Soderbergh, 2011), for example, expands the traditional outbreak narrative seen in *Outbreak* (Petersen, 1995). Rather than focus on one town, Soderbergh portrays the struggle of the Centers for Disease Control and Prevention (CDC) and the World Health Organization (WHO) to keep up with a terrifying epidemic that hits Hong Kong, London, Chicago, Minneapolis, and Tokyo almost simultaneously. *Contagion*, a Prospector Cash-in that became a Reinforcing Hit in the outbreak narrative film cycle, is a useful text for demonstrating the differences between modern and postmodern outbreak narratives because it emulates some of the original Trailblazer Hit (*Outbreak*) while reinventing the cycle enough to stay relevant. Significant differences are that *Contagion* reflects the postmodern era of globalization, including its emphasis on global communication, networks, and the transnational body. Much as *Contagion* is not about a hero saving the world, it is also not about disease, per se, at least not in the conventional sense. We do not see bodies oozing with pus or torn open. When people get sick, they tend to die fairly quickly and/or quietly. The specific terms of the disease seem to be fairly inconsequential. The emphasis, instead, is on a general threat to the world, a world that is both increasingly borderless and interconnected.

Contagion also depicts an increased awareness of the ways that globalization and technology have exacerbated the speed with which disease—and panic—can travel, fueling terror over the potential of both to harm and destroy. These fears feed into the desire for a return to walls and barriers, as demonstrated by the popularity of politicians like Donald Trump and Scott Brown, who advocate for an end to immigration and the creation of reinforced borders, as well as by referendums like Brexit in 2016, in which the United Kingdom withdrew from the European Union—all actions that call for a retreat from contemporary globalized standards.

It is not merely the nation that has become less relevant as a result of globalization, but the individual has become less relevant as well. The shift of scale and scope does not only apply to the physical sprawl of the virus or to the locations featured in the film or television show. The shift of scale also applies to the protagonist. When scope is huge, conflict is no longer man-to-man or even country-to-country. It is network-to-network. The individual action movie hero has been replaced with teams—teams of scientists, military personnel, and politicians—often located in different cities, if not different countries. There is no one person for whom you really cheer, no one person with whom you identify. Networks are favored over singularity. Rather than pitting good versus bad, the postmodern globalization outbreak narrative looks instead at the ways different organizations work together, how the global infrastructure operates, and how people themselves interact with each other. In a globalized and interconnected world, major networks and infrastructures are our only recourse toward solving a large-scale epidemic. When a disease hits on such a massive scale, it is no longer just about the virus or a particular hero but about the networks and the organization of such networks and their effectiveness (or lack thereof).

In comparison, in earlier (modern, colonial) eras of globalization, villains and heroes were clear, geographical locations defined, and the narrative worked toward a happy resolution (closure). This is evident in *Outbreak*, for instance, where the hero is clearly Colonel Sam Daniels (Dustin Hoffman), who defies authority to save his ex-wife and then the world. Who to blame is equally clear: corrupt military men are responsible for the conspiracy while primitive Africa is to blame for the virus. However, in later (postmodern) eras of globalization, heroes are elusive, othering does not fully take, geographical locations are fluid, and the resolution is only partially satisfying because we see how easily these sorts of things can happen (and happen again!). For example, in lieu of a hero, the *Andromeda Strain* remake (A&E, 2008) features a network of scientists—employed by the government (another network)—and a rogue journalist who work together to save the world and expose government conspiracy. The villains are other government employees (forming a different network) trying to keep the conspiracy under wraps. Both villains and heroes are networks and the geographical area threatened by the virus is worldwide (as opposed to the tiny town of Piedmont decimated in the original *Andromeda* [Wise, 1971]). The resolution is uneasy, as the government tucks its Andromeda sample away for later use. In *Contagion*, the network of scientists—working with or for government networks, most conspicuously represented by the CDC and the WHO—try to understand how the outbreak happened and struggle to stop it. The villain is the virus, the geographic scope worldwide.

Both films emphasize the impact of a globalized, networked world in which individuality has been forsaken for the network.

Based on variations within the outbreak narrative, there seem to be two possible responses to the increasingly rhizomatic modes of contemporary life. The first response, as seen in *Outbreak*, favors one iconic character who has the fate of the world on his or her shoulders. This structure continues to resonate through films like *I Am Legend* (Lawrence, 2007) and *World War Z*, both of which revert to heroic tales of salvation in a nostalgic and familiar fashion. The continued appeal of the classical hero in these narratives can be seen as a response to the shift from hierarchical social ordering to the horizontal and networked sprawl common to the twenty-first century, much like the acceptance of the hypersovereignty that would emerge after 9/11. For instance, the hero in *I Am Legend* is Robert Neville (Will Smith), a successful scientist who somehow survives a man-made plague that turns everyone around him into diseased vampire-zombies. His precise status as a hero is debatable, depending on which ending you prefer (more about that in chapter 4), but it is clear, however questionable his methods, that the fate of the world *does* rest on Neville's shoulders. Similarly, in *World War Z*, the fate of the world rests on the shoulders of Gerry Lane (Brad Pitt), who must save it from being taken over by zombies.

These single heroes reflect the characteristics of the thriller genre, "whose emphasis has always been on heroic individualism and personal, rather than collective, agency."[12] Ironically, *World War Z* (the book upon which the film was based) avoids giving us a single perspective, emphasizing the lack of one preeminent individual protagonist. There is no privileged narrator, much as there is no privileged geographic location. Each chapter switches to a different character's voice. In contrast, in *World War Z* (the movie), there is a clear and deliberate attempt to reduce the networks to a single hero (Gerry Lane).

The second response includes those that refuse to simplify in this way, such as Steven Soderbergh's *Contagion*, or *The Andromeda Strain* remake. Instead of echoing more traditional action films, which offer the single action hero with whom to ally, in these outbreak narratives, the single hero is often missing, replaced by the prevalence of networks or by a woman. The role of the hero is revamped to reflect not only a new kind of hero but a new kind of national identity. As Stacy Takacs outlines, the definition of "hero" becomes less about gender difference than difference between patriot and "other." With a "global context defined by the dissolution of the geographic boundaries that once stabilized an 'inside' through contrast to 'outside,' the very concept of patriotism had to be redefined," Takacs writes. Post-9/11 spy thrillers, for example, "with their mixture of male and female, black, white, yellow, and brown agents," demonstrate just how much multiculturalism has become a defining feature of post-9/11 American identity, "how expansive the conception of patriotism became."[13] For these narratives, gender and race matter less than citizenship, allowing the role of the hero to expand to include not only women but teams of people—of mixed race and mixed gender—working together.

There are several potential reasons for this shift. One, as stated above, is that gender matters less than citizenship, allowing the role of the hero to be redefined. Two, coding networked agency feminine or making the hero a woman acknowledges the limitations of the traditional melodramatic hero in a risk society. The female scientist (unlike, for example, the male CDC scientist in season 1 of *The Walking Dead* [AMC, 2010–present]) often has the winning combination of rational thought *and* empathy that allows her to save the day—a nurturing yet brilliant persona who can care for her patients without any of the male machismo driving the frequently antagonistic male military characters.

A variation of this can be seen in the original *Andromeda Strain*. In the book upon which the film was based, Dr. Leavitt is a man. In the film, Dr. Leavitt is the only female working in the lab. In *The Andromeda Strain: Making the Film* (Bouzereau, 2001), director Robert Wise describes his reaction to screenwriter Nelson Gidding's suggestion to make Leavitt a woman. Nervously envisioning "Raquel Welch in a submarine again," Wise called "two or three scientists" who assured him that having a woman as a scientist would be fine, that there are "many fine women scientists" and adding one "would not violate the film at all."[14]

During the film, Leavitt receives much the same treatment as her male colleagues. Bonnie Noonan, author of *Gender in Science Fiction Films, 1964–1979*, observes that, other than having a separate dressing room, all the team members go through the same grueling decontamination procedures and complete equally challenging work. The significant difference is that, in creating Leavitt as a woman, Gidding endowed her with particular characteristics that can be read as analogous to the circumstances of the woman scientist. She operates differently than her colleagues in a "particularly gender coded way." For example, Noonan writes that, unlike her research partner, Dr. Jeremy Stone—who is methodical and reliant on

tradition—Leavitt is intuitive. He pressures her to be thorough and to follow established procedures, leading her to experience self-doubt. When she
observes the organism mutate, arguably the most important development
in the film, she initially believes she has imagined it. This intuitive nature
can be seen as a female characteristic. Leavitt is also the only member of
the team with two obvious handicaps: her glasses—a mark against someone whose profession requires microscopic observation—and epilepsy—a
condition she keeps secret, knowing that "no top lab would have her if they
knew," explains Stone, in defense of Leavitt's secrecy.[15] There is no such
sympathetic explanation for Peter Leavitt's epilepsy in the original novel.
When *The Andromeda Strain* was remade in 2008, it featured *two* female
scientists, both of them attractive, one played by Christa Miller and the
other Viola Davis.

A third potential reason for the repeated use of female lead characters
is that it allows the outbreak narrative to appeal to a female audience. This
strategy can be seen as an embodiment of a "distinctive Hollywood storytelling mode" that David Holloway describes as "allegory lite": a commercial aesthetic "packed with different hooks pitched at different audience
groups," providing multiple audiences multiple ways into the story and
"alienating as few customers as possible."[16] If the outbreak narrative has
replaced the disease-of-the-week TV movie, perhaps the character of the
female scientist is a nod to the traditionally female audience that watched
many of those original movies, especially when they appeared on networks
like Hallmark.

The connection of the outbreak narrative to the science fiction genre
provides a fourth reason for its reliance on female scientists. Science fiction
frequently depicts women as scientists, assistants to scientists, or students
of science, displacing their expected roles as housewife and contented
mother.[17] And so the outbreak narrative—as a fusion of soap opera with
science fiction, of the B movie with melodrama and/or horror—provides a
natural home for the larger-than-normal role of the female scientist.

And this role *is* larger than normal. In 2013, the *New York Times* published an article by Eileen Pollack entitled "Why Are There Still So Few
Women in Science?" The article references a recent study by Yale researchers that found physicists, chemists, and biologists (both male and female)
are more likely to view a young male scientist favorably than his female
equivalent. In fact, only 14 percent of physics professors in the United
States are women. Pollack quotes astrophysicist Meg Urry, who investigated

why there are so few women in the sciences. Her results support the argument that female scientists are underappreciated, made to feel uncomfortable, and encounter roadblocks along the path to success. Specifically, Urry also argues, "American men can't seem to appreciate a woman as a woman and as a scientist; it's one or the other."[18]

Real life notwithstanding, in outbreak narrative after outbreak narrative, whether television show or film or made-for-TV movie, the character of the female scientist is integral to the discovery of the virus's cure and, in turn, to saving the world. Observing gender roles, noticing who has information and who does not, who finds the cure and who does not, who controls the story and how, provides a more nuanced understanding of the film and television texts and the ideology behind them.[19] In an analysis of the key texts analyzed in this book (see table 2), all but three have female scientists or female doctors (or both): *28 Days Later* (Boyle, 2002), *World War Z*, and *The Walking Dead*. All the women, with the exception of Dr. Ruth Leavitt (Kate Reid) in the much earlier *Andromeda Strain* (1971) are also traditionally feminine and attractive women.

The least classically feminine one from the current texts is the first incarnation of Dana Scully (Gillian Anderson) on *The X-Files* (Fox, 1993–2002, 2016–present), whose no-nonsense persona was meant to contrast with Fox Mulder (David Duchovny), her partner. Initially, her subordinate status was emphasized by the fact that the studio required Anderson to stand a few feet behind her male partner on camera. "I can only imagine that at the beginning, they wanted me to be the sidekick," Anderson says. "Or that, somehow, maybe it was enough of a change just to see a woman having this kind of intellectual repartee with a man on camera, and surely the audience couldn't deal with actually seeing them walk side by side!"[20] However, as the show progressed, Scully was able to walk alongside Mulder and grew more classically feminine.

Beyond this, the outbreak narrative features a long list of gorgeous and physically fit female scientists, played by actresses like Nicolette Sheridan, Rene Russo, Madchen Amick, Tiffani Thiessen, Kate Winslet, Marion Cotillard, and Mia Maestro, all of whom save the day by stopping the virus. Many of them are main characters, and if they are supporting characters, it is as part of an ensemble cast in which they figure prominently. Two of them (Robby Keough in *Outbreak* and Kayla Martin in *Pandemic* [Hallmark, 2007]) are supervisors. None, with the exception of poor Ruth are "nerdy" or antisocial. And all, again with the exception of Ruth, appear to be in their thirties, if not younger. Two are married: Robby (*Outbreak*), but the marriage is on the rocks; and Charlene (*The Andromeda Strain*, 2008), but the husband and children are far away from the top secret lab where she is stationed. The one who is dating (Sophie Amsden in *Covert One: The Hades Factor* [CBS, 2006]) dies before the relationship can progress or conclude. Olivia Moore (Rose McIver in *iZombie* [CW, 2015–present]) dates unsuccessfully. The rest are single. But in general, these female scientists do their jobs without romance and without a need for male approval. In fact, they often do their job *in spite* of male disapproval, like in *Toxic Skies* (Erin, 2008), where Tess Martin (Anne Heche) perseveres despite the efforts of the mayor of Spokane (Kevin McNulty), the CEO of Kellor (Barclay Hope), and Major Stein (Tobias Slezak) to quash her investigation.

Interestingly, it is the journalist who often provides the voice of male authority. In certain outbreak narratives—*The Andromeda Strain* remake, *Containment* (CW, 2016), or *Contagion* (2011), for instance—the journalist plays an actual role within the plot, acting as a character within the general narrative rather than merely as a commentator upon it. In fact, during the climax of *Outbreak*, Sam Daniels becomes a guerilla journalist in order to find the cure for the virus. Despite being ordered to respect a media blackout, he barges his way into a TV station so that he can broadcast news of the virus to the country and plead for the location of the missing monkey. Both hero *and* journalist, he becomes the ultimate voice of authority.

In most outbreak narratives, however, the journalist is outside the actual narrative, rarely speaking with any of the central characters unless it is via interview questions or press conferences. In this case, the journalist's primary purpose is to relate the immediacy of the events. He or she is either on the scene or reporting from a news desk, acting as the audience's go-between. In the television miniseries *Pandora's Clock* (NBC, 1996), ICN news is the link between the passengers trapped on the plane and the outside world, a mediating voice that links the viewers in the diegetic world of the film to the quarantined passengers and the film's audience. Similarly, in *Pandemic* (Hallmark, 2007), we often see the news footage directed at us, as if we are watching the news ourselves, before cutting to the footage itself within a screen, as we see a character watching the news, before cutting to shots of the journalist or the press conference happening in front of us, without the buffer of the TV cameraman's eye. All these cuts emphasize the shared space of the reporter and the viewer, both diegetic and nondiegetic.

Another result of having a journalist mediate the events is that their lack of knowledge—emphasized as we cut to a military or political briefing room where the full story is known—emphasizes how controlled and limited our access to the truth often is. Sometimes, characters like Alan Krumwiede (Jude Law), the news blogger in *Contagion* remind us that journalists may even intentionally mislead us to further their own agendas. Krumwiede, specifically, tells his readers that the homeopathic treatment Forsythia is a cure from the virus—even though there is no proof of this—so that he can get a share of Forsythia's profits when sales skyrocket. Other films make the point, as well, that politicians, much like everyday people, may also find out their information via the broadcast news, occasionally knowing no more than we do about horrific and catastrophic events. In *Pandemic*, for example, we cut from location to location, seeing the televised news first in the governor's office, then hearing the news on the radio in the mayor's car, then on the television in the home of an ordinary citizen, emphasizing not only the viral spread of media information but also that this is the way most people experience catastrophe—through the frame of a screen, through the vector of an information network.

In addition to complicating the role of the hero, outbreak narratives often complicate the role of the villain. Categories are fuzzier as blame becomes harder to place. In *The Andromeda Strain* remake, for example, just as in *Containment*, the government is guilty of cover-up and conspiracy, but the actual spread of the virus happens accidentally, with no one group or organization to blame. In *Containment*, CDC Dr. Sabine Lommers (Claudia Black) is the one who institutes the cordon sanitaire, but, as is discovered later in the season, she also conceals the identity of the true patient zero and the illegal gain-of-function studies that led to the current virus mutation sweeping through Atlanta. Dr. Lommers's culpability is her involvement in setting up Dr. Burns (David McKahan) with a lab to recreate the deadly virus, thus creating the potential for the inevitable outbreak. However, as the show and Lommers repeatedly make clear, her intentions are never malicious but, rather, to strengthen America's bioterrorism capabilities. In this case, the "villain" is a patriot who puts the needs of a country ahead of the needs of a group of quarantined individuals, which makes it harder to vilify her.

In *Contagion*, right from the start, Soderbergh makes it clear that Beth Emhoff (Gwyneth Paltrow) is the one responsible for spreading the virus worldwide, infecting people who then spread the virus themselves. However, the exact origin of the virus—and the "necessary accident" that brought it to Beth—is unclear until the very end of the film, at which point, the notion of "blame" becomes even more complex. This can be seen in contrast to previous incarnations of the outbreak narrative, where the othering was more clear and seemingly more "successful" (i.e., where blame stuck). Now the othering does not fully "take" because anyone can travel in a global world; it is the global context that is the causal agent, not some easily identifiable other.

The final sequence of *Contagion* interrupts the otherwise linear progression of the film to flash back to the very beginning, gradually revealing the virus's origin. The last moments of the film are a critique of global corporate capitalism and environmental destruction, with some additional racial and gender inflections. First, a bulldozer for AIMM, the company Beth Emhoff worked for, razes a tree for an unexplained demolition project, sending displaced bats flying over a pig farm, where a bat drops a piece of fruit (necessary accident #1). This fruit is then eaten by a pig that is shipped to a restaurant to be cooked (necessary accident #2), where a Chinese chef with poor hygiene habits spreads it to Beth Emhoff by shaking her hand (necessary accident #3).

Even if she is not solely responsible for the outbreak, Soderbergh is still very clear about blaming Beth for her actions. When Dr. Leonora Orantes (Marion Cotillard) traces Beth's final steps through recordings delivered to her by the casino, we do not see what Leonora sees. While Orantes watches the "clinical version" (see figure 7), the version the audience sees is a more emotional version (see figures 8–11), a version shot on a handheld camera, a version that bobs and weaves, as if filmed by a person in the crowded casino rather than by a security camera fixed to a wall. The version we see is warm and joyous, full of light and noise, the frame saturated with golds and yellows, in marked contrast to the clinical surveillance footage, neutrally colored and filmed at an objective and automated distance from the action. This contrast is played up every time Leonora watches the footage.

The "surveillance footage" that we watch is not surveillance footage at all. Instead, it reflects the innocent and lighthearted joie de vivre that existed in a previral world, in a world before Beth spread a virus from China to Minnesota, before millions of people died, before the air we breathed and the surfaces we touched killed us. If our perspective had been as removed and neutral as Leonora's footage, our opinion of Beth might

FIGURE 7 Dr. Leonora Orantes's (Marion Cotillard) laptop footage, *Contagion* (2011).

have been just as neutral, and then the disease vector, much like the narrative itself, would be less pointed. However, the "fake footage" provides a stark contrast with the rest of the film—where contact is minimal and barriers frequent—and is instrumental for communicating Beth's carefree former life, with her overindulgence in gambling, sex, drinking, and food. The "fake footage" both exposes her character and creates a perspective from which it is easy to condemn her.

A reference to the fear of progress evident in most outbreak narratives, this trope of the "misbehaving female leaving lives in her wake" feels as old as the link between the spread of disease and transgressing boundaries. Kirsten Ostherr, in her book *Cinematic Prophylaxis: Globalization and Contagion in the Discourse of World Health*, describes *How Disease Is Spread*, an educational health film from 1924. The crux of the film is that a diseased traveler goes about her day, shopping and eating out, spreading germs carelessly in her wake. We are shown, in graphic detail, how easily the disease is spread, and the very real impact of inappropriate and reckless consumption and socializing. None of this would be happening if the woman had just stayed home. Furthermore, the film links the disease-spreading process "to particular scenarios that only occur in modern, urbanized consumer culture. The commodification of activities such as transportation, communication, and food service creates a circuit of exchange that enables diseases to spread through networks of production and consumption."[21]

FIGURES 8-11 Beth Emhoff (Gwyneth Paltrow) in the casino, *Contagion* (2011).

This is only one of several parallels between this particular film and *Contagion*, which would not be released for another ninety years. Not only does *How Disease Is Spread* attempt "to train viewers to imagine germs that they cannot actually see,"[22] but most significantly, it casts a middle-class white woman as the villain whose inappropriate behavior gets this whole thing started. As Ostherr writes, "In this vision of modernity, the middle-class white woman is representative of the domestic sphere and serves as an antidote to the evils of the public sphere—but only if she stays at home," thus casting the "misbehaving middle-class white woman" as one of the "problematic subjects of modernity."[23] This is unsurprising since outbreak narratives are frequently conservative in the sense that they always recommend caution, slow change, a halt to development. Beth, as our disease vector, is seen as one of the problematic subjects of modernity, with her appetite for adventure, whether via food, sex, corporate success, or travel. It is not merely that she is a carrier but that she is a voracious and jet-setting one. Interestingly, this fits in with Soderbergh's body of work. As Joshua Clover argues, these epidemiological vectors can be seen as a progression from the "entangled libidinal liaisons of *Sex, Lies, and Videotape* [released in 1989 and Soderbergh's first feature film], and the lines of commerce and political debt of *Traffic* [released in 2000]."[24] First there was sex, then there was commerce, and then there was sex, commerce, and disease.

Unlike *Outbreak*, which establishes a clear binary between primitive Africa and "the pristine shores" of America, *Contagion* contains some aspects of that kind of othering (stigmatizing individuals, geographic areas, and/or lifestyles deemed threatening), but it also complicates this othering. For instance, while the disease may originate in a "dirty" country, it is a blonde (how pristine can you get, in terms of Hollywood's visual code?) with immoral behavior who brings it back to America, not an ethnic minority guilty of illegal animal smuggling. Similarly complicated, while the "root" cause of the virus can be traced to the action of an American company, it is the Asian chef who does not wash his hands or wear gloves who spreads the virus to Beth. Rather than setting up a more traditional hero–villain binary, *Contagion* makes visible the constant and impossible-to-control flow of bodies, goods, and information in our twenty-first-century life.

Brent Bellamy argues that *Contagion* does not just depict the struggle to contain the virus "but also figures the representability and manageability of the *globe* as a problem," as well as "the way disease, rumour, speculation, and capital spread around the world."[25] This more complex take on disease is a reflection of the more complex interconnectedness of contemporary globalization. After all, we cannot just blame "natives" for being superstitious and unhygienic. We cannot always simplify right versus wrong, just as we cannot always contain a virus. The globe is now the issue. The antagonist, if there is one, is the virus. The hero is an amalgamation of the various organizations, doctors, and scientists determined to stop the virus.

Another complication to the expected hero–villain binary in *Contagion* is the positioning of government officials as the "good guys" who clean up the mess, finding a cure and a vaccine so the world can be put back together. This may seem surprising in a post-9/11 world, when conspiracy theories are as common as tales of bureaucratic ineptitude, but the impact of this decision is significant. Within Soderbergh's films, he generally seems less concerned with simple good versus bad; in his film *Traffic*, he portrays the illegal drug trade from different perspectives: dealers, abusers, and law enforcement officials. In *Contagion*, it is not only that he is not interested in simple good versus bad but also that he is concerned with a depiction of globalization's complexities, exploring the logistics and policy questions that bring us together and separate us. International infrastructures, for instance, often struggle with the tensions between increased globalization and government regulation, between the local and the national as well as between the national and the global. Another conflict depicted in *Contagion* is between the CDC (as a federal institution) and state health departments. As *Contagion* screenwriter Scott Z. Burns explains, "Even though the CDC is the government's best defense, it doesn't have primacy over state health departments, and for them to get involved, any state's department of health has to invite them in . . . When an outbreak doesn't respect state lines, you start having issues with different policies on either side of [the] state line and that can get very complicated."[26]

This shift toward understanding the world as intricately interconnected, both global and tiny at the same time, manifests in an emphasis on two kinds of simultaneity: a simultaneity in *viral* spread—in that a virus from China is a virus in London is a virus in New York, all seemingly overnight—as well as a simultaneity in *information* spread, in that an outbreak in China can feel like an outbreak in London, because information is everywhere at once.

Contagion emphasizes both kinds of simultaneity: the world is ostensibly a level playing field, everything visible at the same time, geographic distance notwithstanding. The movie flashes from country to country, city to city, continent to continent, with speed and ease, as if everything were just around the corner, as if we, like the virus, were everywhere. When scientists finally isolate the virus, we get a montage of the same information projected in conference rooms around the world at the same time, emphasizing the simultaneity in information spread, vectors of data operating much like vectors of diseases.

In contrast, nothing spreads in the original *Andromeda Strain*, a historical relic from an era when borders still existed. Borders, bodies, and information are all contained. Even the outbreak is contained, and since the victim's blood turns into powder, there is not even blood to drip. There is no sense of trajectory or travel. The only trajectory in that film is downward, as demonstrated by the lengthy "decontamination sequence." The characters make their way through a five-level decontamination, each level deeper underground, each level automated, each level increasingly isolated, as a disembodied computer voice directs the characters. Almost everything in the lab is automated, including robots for handling the microbial cultures, as well as the central computer and the nuclear device set to destroy the lab in the event of contamination. The six scientists and the two survivors from Piedmont are the only elements not automated. All the drama takes place in the lab, under the microscope, with as much as possible computerized and isolated. The spreading is still minimal and geographically contained twenty-four years later in *Outbreak*. Despite its trajectory from Africa to Cedar Creek, with a minor appearance in Boston, the virus's exposure is limited and quarantine is maintained.

Released in 1996, a year after *Outbreak*, the television miniseries *Pandora's Clock*, based on the novel by John J. Nance, is all about geographical trajectory but between rigid borders. A deadly virus is thought to be on a plane traveling between Germany and New York. When the potentially infected passenger has a heart attack, London will not let the plane land for medical care, determined not to let the virus out within its borders. The pilot tries for Frankfurt and is also denied permission to land. The same thing happens with Dutch air traffic control. Even Canada, Greenland, and Iceland deny the plane permission to land. Eventually, the American air force is summoned to escort the unwanted plane down covertly onto an American base in England. However, England finds out about it, and the plane is forced to move yet again, this time to Africa. The primary issue in this miniseries becomes who owns the land and who owns the air above it. National boundaries are inflexible, and even the air space above each respective country is claimed and nonnegotiable, marked by boundaries that cannot be crossed.

In 2007, the Hallmark channel aired its own outbreak narrative miniseries, *Pandemic*. *Pandemic* still features geographical specificity in that the virus clearly travels (via plane) from Australia to Los Angeles International Airport. A quickly made quarantine proves ineffective, and one arrogant businessman gets out, the virus spreading in his wake. As he makes his way across Los Angeles, everyone with whom he has contact becomes infected. We are told that outbreaks of the virus are also happening in other cities around the world, even though they do not appear in the miniseries; this narrative is firmly centered on the Los Angeles outbreak. So while there is no geographical specificity in terms of the outbreak, there is geographical specificity in terms of what we see. The focus is on Los Angeles. The situation worsens when another passenger, a convicted drug lord in the custody of the FBI, also manages to escape quarantine. Despite two escapees, the spread of the virus is still restricted to a handful of easily distinguished people. *Pandemic* can be seen as an intermediary between the more geographically limited films and television shows before it, when borders were resolute, and the outbreak narratives that came after, when borders were anything but.

For example, the remake of *The Andromeda Strain*, which aired in 2008, only one year after *Pandemic*, depicts a very different world. Quarantine zone after quarantine zone are violated. The virus gets out, killing civilians and military personnel as it spreads further and further from Piedmont. Birds pick up the virus, and then it gets in the water, rushing into neighboring states, threatening to reach Las Vegas and an international airport. As Dr. Charlene Barton (Viola Davis) warns, "One international flight and Andromeda is worldwide."

Starting with *Pandemic* and the *Andromeda Strain* remake, before hitting its critical and commercial peak with *Contagion*, the outbreak narrative began focusing more intensely on the failure of global boundaries rather than city boundaries, depicting and feeding into anxieties surrounding the revelation that these constructed barriers are not as real as we wish them to be. Unlike *Outbreak*, where the virus is primarily confined to Cedar Creek, in *Pandemic*, the virus travels from Australia to Los Angeles, California, before threatening the world. In *The Andromeda Strain*, the virus first destroys Piedmont, Utah, before threatening neighboring states and the world. In *Contagion*, there is not even an initial local outbreak. In *Contagion*, everything spreads; every boundary is crossed. The virus seems to emerge in Hong Kong, London, Chicago, and Minneapolis simultaneously. After all, the plot focuses on the impact of a virus that has gone global within the first few minutes of the film, portraying an outbreak and the corresponding efforts by scientists and public health officials worldwide to contain it. The film also depicts the ensuing panic as thousands of people die before scientists discover the vaccine. National boundaries leak as the virus hops from Kowloon, Hong Kong (population 2.1 million) to London, England (population 8.6 million), to Minneapolis, Minnesota (population 3.3 million), to Tokyo, Japan (36.6 million)—all within the first four minutes of the movie. The world is now one big network of cities and population numbers. Similarly, the global spread of zombies is the central narrative of *World War Z*, a significant shift from most other zombie narratives, which are much more geographically limited. In *World War Z*, Gerry Lane (Brad Pitt) must save the world *before* he can save his family.

Another way to trace the evolving depictions of the world through outbreak narratives is by looking at the proposed solutions. For instance, in both of the *Andromeda Strain* movies and in *Outbreak*, as well as in *Pandora's Clock*, *Global Effect* (Cunningham, 2002), and John Murlowski's *Contagion* (2002), the government's response to the respective epidemics is to threaten to blast away the infected area with a nuclear bomb. When the virus is localized, a nuclear bomb is considered a viable option. In these narratives, a nuclear bomb is no longer the ultimate threat but the lesser of two evils. It is a tool of sterilization, or, in the words of *Resident Evil: Apocalypse* (Witt, 2004), "sanitation." In this film, the all-controlling Umbrella Corporation actually does this, annihilating Raccoon City. In *Global Effect*, the strategy for containing the virus is to blow up South Africa. There is even a moment when one of the military advisors draws a big "X" through South Africa on the map, advocating the necessity of cutting off the foot to save the body. Even if it is the wrong move—which all the films emphasize that it is, largely because of the innocent civilians caught in the blast—a nuclear bomb goes from being the unthinkable to being a reasonable plan B, at least until the virus spreads too far. When the virus is contained, as it is in *Outbreak* and *Andromeda*, a nuclear bomb seems to be the best solution. However, in *Contagion* (2011), as in *World War Z*, the disease has gone too far, infected too many people. A single nuclear bomb would no longer solve anything; it would have to blow up the world. Interestingly, a nuclear bomb is used at the end of season 3 of *The Strain* (FX, 2014–present); however, it is the villains who set it off. The bomb is part of a coordinated plan to conquer Manhattan and black out the sun. First, the Master (Robin Atkin Downes) spreads the contagion to build his army, and then he annihilates whatever is left with the bomb.

In *Outbreak*, *Pandora's Clock*, and the original *Andromeda Strain*, there is a fixed sense of geographic distance and narrative resolution. These older films paint a localized understanding of the world that now feels dated (but safer) by comparison. There is a sense of trajectory, a need to get from point A to point B, from one border to the next. The pressure comes as a result of time and distance. How are we going to get to the girl? How are we going to find the monkey? How much gas is left? In contrast, the newer outbreak narratives, more global in scope, become less a tale of a few sick people and a need to get from point A to point B. They are studies in global circulation. Geographical specificity is not an issue. We are seemingly everywhere at once. Pandemics have no end point or temporal dimension. Soderbergh further emphasizes the irrelevance of national, state, or local boundaries in *Contagion* by abandoning captions that distinguish our geographical location after the first time each city is identified. We never even see Beth Emhoff on a plane. She just arrives at each new destination. Disease has evolved from a constrained and tidy threat to a terrifying international phenomenon that can spread in the blink of an eye, capable of killing millions while government infrastructures struggle—and often fail—to keep up.

Regardless of plot specifics, many outbreak narratives emphasize how faulty existing regulation or infrastructure can be when it comes to dealing with any large-scale threat (a threat that feels larger the more recent the outbreak narrative), depicting how quickly social order can collapse. The scenes of panic and mayhem in *Contagion* feel especially realistic because they echo similar scenes aired on the news. Images of riots—such as the ones in Ferguson, Missouri, in 2014 following the fatal shooting of Michael Brown by a white police officer or in Venezuela in 2016, where armed guards transported the nation's food and stood watch over grocery stores as street gangs and civilians fought for supplies—could have seamlessly been edited into *Contagion*. These types of scenarios are not merely ones Americans have been warned about. These types of scenarios happen now, even if without the viral component, and the makers of *Contagion* aimed to portray these scenarios, as well as the various details surrounding the science of the outbreak, as accurately as possible. As *Contagion* screenwriter Scott Z. Burns says, "I was certainly aware there were other pandemic movies, but I wanted to do one that really felt like what could happen."[27]

Science fiction films and television shows intentionally create an atmosphere of credibility in order to enhance the unsettling impact of their narratives, but Soderbergh and Burns went above and beyond, even enlisting several key experts to work on *Contagion* as consultants, including Laurie Garrett, author of the nonfiction bestseller *The Coming Plague*, who worked closely with Burns on the script. W. Ian Lipkin, director of the Center for Infection and Immunology at Columbia University's Mailman School of Public Health, also served as a consultant on the film, helping to design the virus itself and constructing production models, as well as teaching the actors how to perform certain tasks. His lab served as inspiration for one of the labs built for the film, and the director of that cinematic lab was named "Ian" after the original doctor.[28] The production designer based the war room on the CDC's actual war room. Even the virus itself, Burns recalls, was actually based on the Nipah virus, which affects bats in Southeast Asia, and the genetic sequence used in the film is accurate.[29] Unlike *World War Z* and *The Strain*, which paint spectacularly melodramatic portraits of apocalyptic futures full of zombies, vampires, and destruction, films like *Contagion* and *Andromeda* are more minimalist and realistic. And that is precisely why they are so chilling. The more realistic the film or the television show, the more it plays into and feeds off our fears.

However sensational many aspects of the show could be, accuracy was also important for *Containment*. The CDC was "involved from pretty early on, even in the pilot stage," explains Melinda Burns, research assistant for the show. Burns says the show kept her "busy with various research projects for even the smallest of elements." Producers and writers for the show interviewed CDC specialists in epidemiology and virology "to get a general understanding of how viruses work and what the CDC protocol is during an emergency outbreak situation." The show even hired a CDC consultant to read all the scripts as they came out to flag things that warranted further discussion, as well as to offer more general advice.[30] Not only does this emphasis on accuracy allow a film or television show to be more chilling, but it also elevates it from campy schlock to a more serious piece of craftsmanship.

As hyperbolic as the premise of *Containment* may sound, it is still credible. The threat of biological warfare escaping containment, intentionally or unintentionally, *is* a real one, much like the threat of governments using found viruses for biowarfare. In fact, between 1949 and 1969, the US Army intentionally conducted 239 secret germ warfare tests by releasing "bugs" throughout the United States, including at Washington's Greyhound bus terminal and a national airport, and in the New York City subway system and San Francisco. Leonard A. Cole, the director of the Terror Medicine and Security program at Rutgers New Jersey Medical School, quoted from "Special Report No. 142: Biological Warfare Trials at San Francisco, California, 20–27 September 1950" in his book *Clouds of Secrecy: The Army's Germ Warfare Tests over Populated Areas*: "Nearly all of San Francisco received 500 particle minutes per liter. In other words, nearly every one of the 800,000 people in San Francisco exposed to the cloud at normal breathing rate (10 liters per minute) inhaled 5,000 or more fluorescent particles . . . per minute during the several hours they remained airborne."[31] In addition to those experiments, the army also sprayed simulated germs into the air at a number of bases, including Fort Detrick, Maryland; Fort Belvoir, Virginia; and the marine training school at Quantico, Virginia. The army insisted that the bacteria used in the tests was harmless, but it caused at least eleven cases of pneumonia and at least one death, and more than five hundred workers connected with biological warfare activities suffered infections, according to the army's count.[32]

Ian Sample, writing for the *Guardian*, explains that, more recently, public health experts warn that "controversial experiments on mutant viruses could put human lives in danger by unleashing an accidental pandemic."[33] (This is actually what happens in some zombie outbreak narratives, where controversial experiments on mutant viruses result in an accidental pandemic of zombies—but more about that in chapter 4.) The repercussions of disrespecting the power of both science and technology are specifically emphasized in the *Andromeda* remake. At the close of the miniseries, for example, Dr. Jeremy Stone (Benjamin Bratt) talks to a reporter. Stone acknowledges that while technology and science may have saved the world this time, "it was our arrogant misuse of both that got us into this trouble in the first place. Just because we have acquired a technological or scientific capability doesn't mean we should rush out to use it."

Modern society is based on the fact that rules are to be obeyed and protocol to be followed. Outbreak narratives, however, aim to provide a credible vision of what happens when those rules are not obeyed, when an arrogant misuse of science or technology backfires. They depict what happens when the infrastructure stops working in ways that, while hyperbolic, also aim to be plausible enough to terrify—or at least unsettle. Policemen are supposed to catch bad guys, and 9-1-1 is supposed to be there to help you. However, in an outbreak, the police, along with the military and the National Guard, are not interested in protecting you. They are interested in *containing* you. Infrastructures intended to keep society together suddenly vanish, the illusion of a functional society disappearing in a blink of an eye—or twenty-eight days later, as the movie with that name implies. The crux of narratives like *Containment, Contagion, World War Z*, and *I Am Legend* is how a city (or the world) falls apart once there is an outbreak, how quickly it runs out of food and military personnel, and how isolating it can be to be trapped in the middle of it when no one can help. In *Containment*, it is not only that cell phones are turned off. Calling 9-1-1 does not work because there is no one to answer.

This feeling of isolation is a complex one, but it lies at the heart of many outbreak narratives either literally or metaphorically—or both. In his book *The Culture of Fear Revisited*, sociologist Frank Furedi examines "the relative weakness of institutions which link the individual to other people in society" and the way that contributes to an intensification of isolation. In contemporary society, many "are literally on their own," he writes, and "many of society's characteristic obsessions—with health, safety, and security—are the products of this experience of social isolation."[34] In other words, isolation always exists in contemporary society—compounded by technological networks that enhance communication while facilitating physical isolation—but outbreaks enhance this existing isolation with fears of contagion and death.

This kind of enhanced isolation was felt following the attacks of September 11, 2001. In his book, *American Fear: The Causes and Consequences of High Anxiety*, Peter N. Stearns compares the difference in emotional response to the attack on Pearl Harbor and 9/11. Arguing that American responses to the two events were significantly different, Stearns writes that, following 9/11, "Americans were over three times as likely to be afraid, and the level of their fear, when expressed, ran much deeper as well." Americans were also much less likely to express "statements of confidence in American government." This was despite the fact that shock was great following both attacks and the death rate and symbolic components were similar (in that the two events were symbolic attacks of key expressions of American power). One of the fundamental differences was that American culture had changed between 1941 and 2001: "The 2001 data and collected stories reveal a marked increase in attention to self and family. . . . Despite some comfort in postdisaster displays of unity, it was easier to believe that threats had to be faced as individuals and as families, not in terms of society as large."[35]

Director Steven Soderbergh emphasizes this sense of isolation in *Contagion* through composition, color, editing, and lighting. In contrast, in the earlier *Outbreak*, there is no such emphasis on isolation, and families are often seen together. In fact, one of the most disturbing scenes in the film is at the Cedar Creek movie theater, where local residents share the same air, clustered together, allowing the virus to spread. Even Jimbo (Patrick Dempsey) gets a warm embrace from his girlfriend, when he is conspicuously sick, thus spreading the virus to her. Fear of contagion, much less fear of intimacy and social contact, appears nonexistent. The twenty-first century, however, as depicted by Soderbergh, encourages a greater emphasis on the self, on isolation, and on the realization that distance—in other words, action you take rather than action that doctors or government officials take on your behalf—may be the only thing that can prevent infection.

A frequent technique Soderbergh uses to separate his characters from each other and from us is to put obstructions between them and the camera, as well as between individual characters. For example, during the scene when Beth has her seizure, our view is obscured by the kitchen counter, as we seem to be following her son's point of view. In this shot (see figure 12), we see most clearly the cabinet doors and only a fraction of Beth's

FIGURE 12 Beth (Gwyneth Paltrow) has her seizure, *Contagion* (2011).

body as she convulses on the floor. Our vantage point is also low, much like that of her young son. In this case, Soderbergh seems to provide us with someone's point of view, which partially justifies the obscured view.

However, when Mitch (Matt Damon) finds out that his wife is dead (see figures 13 and 14), we get a different kind of indirect shot. In this case, we are not following anyone's point of view, but instead go back and forth between peering awkwardly over Mitch's shoulder and then the doctor's, obscured from a proper close-up of either one's face, or even a direct shot of either one. Soderbergh makes us feel as if we are outside the conversation,

FIGURES 13 AND 14 Mitch (Matt Damon) finds out his wife is dead, *Contagion* (2011).

eavesdropping, an unseen fourth party, which makes the scene more awkward than it already is. Mitch is unable to accept the fact that his wife is dead, and the doctor is unable to explain what happened to her. Even the body language is telling. Soderbergh films the two men in such a way as to emphasize the distance between them and the lack of physical contact. Not only is there is no physical contact—no gesture of condolence—but the doctor stands with his arms folded while the woman behind him holds her own neck, as if retreating into herself. This body language, as well as the distance between the characters (the black of the woman's sweater separating her definitively from the white of the doctor's jacket), emphasizes their isolation from each other. Physical contact, after all, can be deadly.

We continue to get obscured shots throughout the film to emphasize this sense of isolation. For example, when Mitch takes a cab home from the hospital, the camera is placed between the two front seats, looking up at him, the out-of-focus chairs separating us from him on either side, two big blobs of black reinforcing a sense of imprisonment already implied by the diagonal lines to either side of him. Mitch, it is clear, is trapped and alone. Similarly, when Dr. Erin Mears (Kate Winslet) catches the virus, she, too, is imprisoned by her surroundings (see figure 15). Soderbergh shoots her blocked in by barricade upon barricade, devoting a third of the frame to the dark door of her hotel room—and only a thin sliver to Erin's reflection. She is "imprisoned" by the walls of the bathroom as they reflect in the

FIGURE 15 Dr. Erin Mears (Kate Winslet) in the bathroom, *Contagion* (2011).

mirror. Our view of her is layered, indirect, and narrow, and it is not even actually her. It is just a reflection, a representation of a being.

Another type of barrier that Soderbergh uses throughout the film is glass. We repeatedly look at people through windows, windshields, and glass walls. Many of the buildings and airports within which Soderbergh shoots have glass walls, creating a terrarium-like effect for the people "trapped" within these buildings, as well as allowing Soderbergh to shoot through the glass walls, further emphasizing the terrarium effect. For example, when Cheever (Laurence Fishburne) and Mears have their first meeting (see figure 16), Soderbergh films them through glass windows, "imprisoned" not only by the glass but also by the beams holding the glass in place. Glass, after all, is a frequent separation device because it allows you to see without contact, and it is unsurprising that Soderbergh would use so much of it in this film since, it is, after all, arguably more isolating to see something that you cannot touch. A similar kind of beam-like window structure is seen in the hospital, when Jory Emhoff (Anna Jacoby-Heron) arrives to see her father. We see her first through a glass door, and we watch her lay eyes on her father from within the window frame, as if she were the one in the terrarium (see figure 17). It becomes clear, however, that Mitch is the one in the actual terrarium, quarantined by the hospital personnel until they can determine if he is still contagious.

FIGURE 16 Cheever (Laurence Fishburne) and Mears (Kate Winslet) have their first meeting, Contagion (2011).

In Soderbergh's world, all buildings seem to share the same glass walls, emphasizing protection and confinement and alienation. This stylistic pattern is repeated over and over. As Mears meets with her team to plan their strategy against the virus, the initial shot places them in layers of rectangles, isolated together from the world around them, the Minnesota Department of Health conference room seemingly designed by the same architect who designed the CDC offices in Atlanta and the AIMM offices in Minnesota.

Another recurring motif of isolation in *Contagion* is telephones—and the physical contact that they replace. Reflective of our increasing loss of physicality and alienation from each other, as well as the compression of space the film emphasizes, people frequently talk to each other through the telephone. In fact, the film *opens* with a telephone conversation. Beth, alone at an airport bar, talks on the phone with her lover—her lover whom she left without saying good-bye. Their good-bye, which, thanks to the virus becomes their final good-bye, takes place over the phone. It is implied that they have just had sex. Supposedly, they just had an intimate moment. But all we see is one woman, alone at a bar, on her phone. We hear his voice, but we do not see him. We just see her, holding a small rectangular black box to her face. That has become our substitute for intimacy. Similarly, Mitch finds out about his son's death through another small black rectangular box. While under quarantine, Mitch and his daughter communicate by telephone, separated by glass, unable to have any actual

FIGURE 17 Jory Emhoff (Anna Jacoby-Heron) at the hospital, *Contagion* (2011).

contact (see figure 17). Intimate relations are now frequently mediated via digital communications through black rectangular boxes (phones or computers or tablets). Ironically, by today's standards, a phone call is unusually intimate when compared to the default of texting.

Images of separation and isolation are so much more frequent in outbreak narratives that the rare image of intimacy, real interpersonal intimacy, feels awkwardly out of place. We see this intimacy when Cheever gives his wife the vaccine. We still get a sense of voyeurism, peering at our characters from an awkward vantage point behind the armchair, but this time, the warm light and yellow, gold, and red tones, in addition to the framing of the two figures, creates a sense of intimacy and security rather than hostility, danger, or isolation. If the scene had been shot with the blue tones Soderbergh uses frequently throughout the film to signify the location of Minnesota, or the hot yellows and reds he uses to represent Hong Kong, or even the greenish yellows of Tokyo, the scene would read differently, creating an uneasy and ominous atmosphere. However, because of the warm tones, we get a rare moment of intimacy between Cheever and his wife as he gives her the ultimate gift: an early dose of the vaccine.

Near the end of *Contagion*, Soderbergh uses similarly constrictive framing to shoot Cheever giving his personal fast-tracked vaccine to the son of Roger (John Hawkes), a janitor at the CDC. In this case, the framing also creates a sense of intimacy reinforced by the provocative impact of two men shaking hands, which, as we have been shown throughout the film, is a gesture that can be deadly. As Cheever explains to the janitor's son, shaking hands is a sign of trust, demonstrating that neither man is carrying a weapon. At the height of a global epidemic, shaking hands *is* tantamount to using a weapon, and so for the two men to shake hands demonstrates both trust and a renewed sense of intimacy in a world that is starting to heal. The light, providing us with the silhouette of the two men, provides even more focus on the men and their handshake, neatly centered in the frame, drawing our eyes in and directly to it.

This kind of self-sacrifice occurs a couple other times in the film—for instance, when Dr. Hextall (Jennifer Ehle) tests the vaccine on herself in order to avoid losing time to official testing protocol, or when Dr. Orantes (Marion Cotillard) discovers that a fake vaccine is being used to discourage terrorists. Earlier in the film, she is kidnapped by Sun Feng (Chin Han) and taken to his village. His strategy is to use her as leverage to make sure the people in his village get the vaccine as soon as possible. Since it takes months for the vaccine to be developed and then produced, Orantes bonds with the villagers as they wait together for freedom and safety. When the vaccine is finally delivered to Feng in exchange for Orantes, everyone is happy—at first. But then Orantes discovers that the vaccine is a fake that was engineered merely for her release. She has grown so connected to the villagers, her former friends and neighbors, that she races back to the village to warn them, startling her boss, who expected Orantes to be more self-serving, to exemplify the me-centric attitude more common within the outbreak narrative cycle, when self-preservation trumps self-sacrifice. As an example of this attitude, Colonel Ferrus (Louis Ferreira) tells General Mancheck (Andre Braugher) near the end of the *Andromeda Strain* remake, "Your kind of honor is a bit outdated, sir. I'm not going to fall on my sword for you or anybody else." Orantes, however, willing to risk her life to save others, is clearly an anachronism, much like Cheever and Hextall.

One of the final scenes of *Contagion* features two teenagers dancing within their domestic quarantine, reasserting singularity in the couple formation. This is a rare moment of romantic intimacy. Mitch's daughter and her boyfriend are having an improvised prom in Mitch's living room, the two of them providing an unconventional twist to a tradition which otherwise makes everyone the same. Prom is often portrayed in film (and in related real-life marketing) as a required ritual for high school seniors, where everyone shops for their prescribed formal wear and corsages and boutonnieres, before filing into limousines or shared cars to head to either their high school gym or a rented ballroom to celebrate the completion of their adolescence. However, the fact that the two teenagers in *Contagion* are performing a ritual alone that customarily takes place with groups is conspicuous, as is the fact that they are confined in the home. In its celebration of the couple, the scene also emphasizes that Mitch has been stripped of his partner, forced merely to look at pixelated versions of her on a digital camera. Prom, usually the event in which everyone from a school year comes together, now seems riddled with solitude. But there is still a refreshing quality to an activity that depicts shared intimacy between two people, real physical bodies, monogamous and loyal, a marked contrast to Beth's violation of monogamy and loyalty at the beginning of the film. Prom has taken on a new meaning, been given a new construct. It is no longer about conforming to the masses but about the triumph of the individual to remake ritual and tradition. The film, which opens with a castigation of a wayward and globe-trotting woman, concludes with a reassertion of the importance of the hetero-normative and a condemnation of global expansion and consumption.

There is only one moment of intimacy in the *Andromeda* remake, where everyone appears to be isolated, either quarantined in the lab or within the video chat window. This moment occurs between Dr. Jeremy Stone (Benjamin Bratt) and Dr. Angela Noyce (Christa Miller) in the lab's exercise room. However, this moment of intimacy is limited, much like the prom scene with Mitch's daughter and her boyfriend, since both partners are fully dressed In fact, in *Andromeda*, both characters are wearing long-sleeved workout clothes. They manage one kiss before Jeremy is summoned to the conference room. That short scene is the only moment of romance or intimacy in the film. Other than that, the scientists in the lab keep their distance from each other.

Containment also ends with several hetero-normative couples unified by the outbreak, one with a baby and an engagement ring, the underlying message being that even in this kind of abject crisis, singularity can be asserted in the (hetero) couple formation. One of the flaws in *Containment* is actually this overinvestment in romance, something that is normally forsaken—or at least minimized—in the outbreak narrative. Perhaps to appeal to the CW audience, *Containment* writers forced several separate romance plots into the season's arc, which had the effect of slowing down the main story and creating an air of contrived and unnatural intimacy. There is a reason personal intimacy and romance is usually left out of the outbreak narrative: it does not belong.

In the *Andromeda Strain* remake, video chatting and conferencing are popular means of communication. Video screens make anyone anywhere present and visible even if not physically present. Video conferencing also makes it easier to forget that the scientists are quarantined in a lab far below the surface of the earth, allowing distance to feel irrelevant as long as a screen is nearby. However, the scientists are reminded just how tenuous this connection is when General Mancheck cuts off all communication between the lab and the outside world. Their only recourse is a guard's cell phone and the information they use to blackmail Mancheck into restoring communication.

Writing in 1990, Mary Ann Doane argues that "television's ubiquity, its extensiveness, allows for a global experience of catastrophe."[36] However, there is a key difference between "global experience," as Doane describes it, and globality defined by Daniel Yergin as the end-state of the globalization process.[37] While it is true that television and technology can create a global audience, which the Internet and the spread of viral media only intensifies, this global audience does not necessarily translate into global unity. With broadcast television (which Doane was referencing), there is a shared experience of simultaneous consumption. With the Internet, however, there is fragmentation, political siloing, and me-casting (tailored experiences that do not necessarily overlap, exacerbated by invisible barriers that separate departments, divisions, or just groups of people). Audiences may be watching the same thing, but they are rarely watching it at the same time and certainly not in the same place. To put it simply, despite the greater technological connectivity, there is still increased isolation.

As we interface via screens more and more, real-life interactions seem to be an afterthought. In place of intimacy, in both *Contagion* and the *Andromeda Strain* remake, we see screens all the time—in the background, in the foreground, in people's hands. We see telephone screens and cash register screens, computer screens and television screens, a screen in almost every scene. We watch as a man on his phone films another man die and the video goes viral. We watch through television monitors as a press conference is filmed, and then see the footage played on an airport television screen. We watch video conferencing happen on television screens and within computer screens. The CDC briefing room in *Contagion*, much like the briefing room in the *Andromeda* remake, is lined with screens—computer screens on people's desks and monitors on the walls (see figure 18). Officials brief each other simultaneously on their (lack of) progress with the virus, each screen showing a representative of a different country or maps of affected areas or screens within screens. Laptops and cellphones are everywhere, and they are always on, flickering and glowing. Even the mystery of the outbreak's origins in *Contagion* is literally discovered via screens, as Dr. Orantes scrolls back through both time and surveillance footage to trace Beth's steps. The truth is on the screen. The invisible is visible on the screen. The people are on the screen. Screens are interfaces for information and communication. Even though globalization is usually used to describe economic integration, this integration is intrinsically linked to—and often a direct result of—technological innovation.

In contrast, back in 1995, technology—and the accompanying screens—was less prevalent. Interestingly, the few times we see computers in *Outbreak*, they are turned off and in the background, representative of an

FIGURE 18 The CDC briefing room, *Contagion* (2011).

earlier age when screens were less ubiquitous and less necessary. The original version of *The Andromeda Strain* also features screens that are frequently turned off and in the background, almost like objects of décor (see figures 19 and 20). Some monitors are never turned on during the entire film. It is as if, in an earlier era, it was enough to showcase the monitor in order to create the appearance of technological prowess. The monitor could remain blank as long as it was just there. In *Outbreak*, the only working screens are the ones connected to the microscopes in the lab and two television screens near the end of the film. Now, however, a blank monitor, a black monitor, is a sign of failure, disconnection, and breakdown.

Appropriately, in *World War Z*, there are barely any screens because technology, much like civilization, has been destroyed. In a postapocalyptic dystopia overrun by zombies, screens are conspicuously and appropriately absent. (There are also no screens in *The Walking Dead*.) Instead, there are lots and lots of (rotting) bodies. However, where they do show up, monitors provide an organized structure of viewing and an illusion of control. The most spectacular appearance of screens is on the ship that has become the unofficial central command post for the military while the rest of the world is overrun with zombies. This scene echoes cultural theorist Paul Virilio's writing about Desert Storm, the combat phase of the Persian Gulf War that occurred between 1990 and 1991, and the way military logistics and perception have changed: "War henceforth takes place in a stadium, the squared horizon of the screen, presented to

FIGURES 19 AND 20   Turned-off monitors, *The Andromeda Strain* (1971).

spectators in the bleachers."[38] We see this literally in *World War Z*, as the command center safely watches the chaos happening in the world through a bank of monitors.

These days, information can come via any kind of electronic screen. Identical footage, for example, is played on a phone as well as on TV screens in the *Andromeda Strain* remake. As all our different screens—phones, televisions, computers, electronic signage—converge, "their comparative differences seem increasingly trivial,"[39] media scholar Vivian Sobchack writes. What matters most is their ubiquitous presences in our lives: "We live today primarily in and through screens rather than merely on or with them. No longer a small, if significant, part of our lifeworld, screens now are our lifeworld."[40] Screens are everywhere, which means information is everywhere, more viral than ever.

As a result of the increasing pervasion into daily life of digital communication, fear and speculation can spread like wildfire, echoing the spread of an actual virus. This conceit has fueled many an outbreak narrative's promotional campaign. For example, the tag line for *Pandemic* was "The fear is real. The panic is spreading." While "nothing spreads like fear" was the tag line for *Contagion*, it was also used as the URL for the promotional website (www.nothingspreadslikefear.com). An editorial for *USA Today* from October 14, 2014, was entitled "Fear Spreads Faster than Ebola: Our View."[41] Similarly, an article for the American Psychological Association from 2015 was entitled "An Epidemic of Fear," and its opening sentence presented the concept of "fearbola."[42]

Therefore, a common occurrence in the outbreak narrative is for those in power to restrict information because they know that panic is going to be the real problem. This makes those in charge wary of imposing quarantines or publicizing details of the epidemic before real dangers are confirmed, arguing that the hysteria is often worse than the disease itself. When Dr. Cheever confronts Alan Krumwiede, the blogger who intentionally lies in order to further his own agenda and fuel hysteria, Cheever tells the television journalist conducting the interview that "in order to get sick, you have to come in contact with a sick person or something that they touched. In order to get scared, all you have to do is come in contact with a rumor, or the television, or the Internet. I think what Mr. Krumwiede is spreading is far more dangerous than the disease." At another point in the film, Cheever even says, "The virus is the least of our worries." In *Pandemic*, a representative of the CDC, speaking at a press conference, tells the journalists that they are overreacting, making the story bigger than it really is: "Responsible news coverage should make it clear that there is absolutely no need for public panic." Panic is the real problem. But in the twenty-first century, how does one contain the spread of information?

In *Outbreak*, the government literally places a media blackout on the town of Cedar Creek to limit the dissemination of information about the virus, and this strategy works. A journalist, speaking to the cameras, declares that the residents of Cedar Creek have been silenced: "All phone communication has been cut off, and those we can hear, those with the information, will not speak." However, with today's viral media and global communication networks, panic can happen immediately and everywhere, and information can come via any kind of electronic screen. It is impossible to contain. In *Contagion*, it is impossible to have a media blackout; the government cannot even stop Krumwiede's manipulative blog, and it is the readers of his blog who bail him out after he is arrested, demonstrating that even the government cannot keep him imprisoned. In *Containment*, where the main area impacted by the virus is relatively small, the cell towers are turned off, but radio broadcasts can still be transmitted over the barricades.

Globalization means many things. It involves many factors that create many issues. It impacts politics, economics, science, media, and technology, as well as the transmission of bodies, goods, and information across eroding local, national, and international boundaries with increasing speed. Even when information is not particularly noteworthy, it is still, as Mary Ann Doane observes, "always *there*, a constant and steady presence, keeping you *in touch*,"[43] just like M and Bond. The eradication of temporal and spatial limitations through the spread of networks and information has destabilized the localized, organic body, even the very idea of "local" in favor of the transnational body.

Networks are now crisscrossed, interlocked, and seemingly infinite. Viral outbreaks in particular bring together various networks—biological, transportational, institutional, communicational—and cross species, national, and economic boundaries, drawing together "viruses, organisms, computers, databases."[44] Ironically, as these networks—both centralized and decentralized, technological and otherwise—become more integrated into our lives, they also become harder for us to see. The more comprehensive their role, the more "embedded, hidden, off-shored and merely forgotten about."[45] Galloway and Thacker argue that "computers, databases, networks, and other digital technologies are seen to be foundational to contemporary notions of everything from cultural identity to war. Digital media seems to be everywhere, not only in the esoteric realms of computer animation, but in the *everydayness* of the digital (e-mail, mobile phones, the Internet)."[46] And yet, despite this everywhere-ness, networks are easily forgotten about until the threat of a viral outbreak reminds us of them.

These new networks, while at first seemingly liberating for their excise of dated categories like "local" and "national," have also created a whole new set of problems. While epidemics have existed for centuries, our progressively interconnected world has facilitated the spread of large-scale epidemics. The story outbreak narratives love to tell is how bodies—intimacy with them and the blood within them—have become threatening, deadly, and impossible to avoid, while boundaries, in our increasingly networked society, have become ineffectual at protecting both us and our countries.

The virus—and, in turn, the outbreak narrative—demonstrates how unstable boundaries are between inner and outer, between human and world, between infected and uninfected. These unstable boundaries reflect the similar collapse of nation-state boundaries, a blurring facilitated both by the impact of globalization, as well as by the integration of technology into seemingly every aspect of modern life.

In all outbreak narratives, quarantine and containment are emphasized—but also fundamentally ineffectual. All the outbreak narratives mentioned in this chapter accentuate that, in order to understand the transmission of viruses, the world needs to be recognized as a complex and interlocked system where barriers are just as unable to keep viruses *out* as they are to keeping viruses *in*. Globalization and technology have created a thoroughly interconnected and interdependent world. In the twenty-first century, the threat of contagion is no longer held over a singular body or a singular location but over a *transnational* body. These newer narratives increase fear and anxiety over porous and ineffective boundaries, over the speed with which viruses can leap over continents, over the deadly ramifications of an increasingly networked world. Global health and security have become intertwined issues, fed by the seemingly constant risk of worldwide infection—a sense of risk fed, in turn, by these narratives.

3

The Terrorism Outbreak

In a globalized world order, the boundary between "outside" and "inside" has become precarious, and the forces and devices of good and evil have become remarkably similar.
—Ruth Mayer, "Virus Discourse"

On the morning of Tuesday, September 11, 2001, nineteen Al Qaeda terrorists simultaneously hijacked four passenger planes. Two of the planes were flown into the World Trade Center in New York City, one into the North Tower and the other into the South Tower. Shortly thereafter, hijackers flew the third plane into the Pentagon in Arlington County, Virginia. When passengers attempted to seize back control of the fourth plane, the hijackers intentionally crashed that plane into a field in Pennsylvania. Everyone on all four planes died, as well as more than 100 military and civilian personnel in the Pentagon, and most staggeringly, 2,753 at the World Trade Center. In total, almost 3,000 people were killed. The financial, emotional, and social costs were immense, including property and infrastructure damages of ten to thirteen billion dollars and ancillary costs to the city of New York (due to lost jobs, lost taxes, damage to infrastructure, etc.)

of ninety-five billion dollars.[1] In many ways, for Americans, the trauma of 9/11 would define the end of the twentieth century and the beginning of the twenty-first.

The events of 9/11 were seen as acts of war, and at first, President George W. Bush was seen as America's great defender. Public approval for Bush skyrocketed by as much as forty percentage points, reaching a remarkable 90 percent in late September 2001 and lingering around the high eighties in the months that followed. Sweeping measures against terrorism initially seemed justified in order to restore a sense of safety and security. For example, a week after the attack, Congress passed the Authorization for Use of Military Force Against Terrorists (AUMF), which allowed the President "to use all necessary and appropriate force against those nations, organizations, or persons *he* determines planned, authorized, committed, or aided the terrorist attacks that occurred on September 11, 2001."[2] On October 26, 2001, President Bush signed the USA PATRIOT Act into law (the name is an acronym that spells out "Uniting and Strengthening America by Providing Appropriate Tools Required to Intercept and Obstruct Terrorism"). The PATRIOT Act was meant to strengthen the government's ability to combat terrorism by allowing, among other things, the indefinite detentions of immigrants; searches of private property without the owner's or the occupant's consent or knowledge; and the Federal Bureau of Investigation (FBI) to search telephone, e-mail, and financial records without a court order.

In his book *Discipline and Punish: The Birth of the Prison*, Michel Foucault observes that, in earlier centuries, it was illness that was met with control, containment, and heightened regulation. With responses that foreshadowed the United States following 9/11, viral outbreaks, and specifically plague, provided opportunity for "the penetration of regulation into even the smallest details of everyday life." Rulers dreamed of an outbreak so that they could experience absolute power. During an outbreak, for instance, inspection could function ceaselessly, information about each individual's life and death passing through representatives of power. "Omnipresent and omniscient power" allowed "ultimate determination of the individual." More specifically, various forms of disease necessitated different types of regulation and jurisdiction. The leper, for instance, "gave rise to rituals of exclusion," whereas the plague "gave rise to disciplinary diagrams."[3] The infectious other was removed or excised, while those still healthy were regulated and contained. The physical self was compartmentalized and controlled—much as the biological self was classified and segregated—based on health, illness, susceptibility for illness, and proximity to infection.

Protocol for regulating and controlling the body was then repurposed for regulating and controlling cities. For example, towns were divided into districts, districts into quarters, quarters by roads and houses, and so on.[4] These were methods of imposing quarantine and delineating zones of infection and safety. Each individual was meant to stay fixed in his assigned place. If he moved, it was at the risk "of his life, contagion, or punishment."[5] The justification that outbreaks required this kind of "spatial partitioning and subdivision" was taken to its extreme point in order to restrict "dangerous communications, disorderly communities, and forbidden contacts."[6] All these regulations were ways of trying to restore a sense of control in an otherwise uncontrollable environment and were justified as being for the greater good. This premise is also used to justify the inevitable quarantine in, among others, *Outbreak* (Petersen, 1995), *Global Effect* (Cunningham, 2002), *Contagion* (both versions: Murlowski, 2002 and Soderbergh, 2011), season 3 of *24* (Fox, 2003–2004), *Pandemic* (Hallmark, 2007), *Toxic Skies* (Erin, 2008), *The Crazies* (Eisner, 2010), and *Containment* (CW, 2016).

Similarly, threats like 9/11 can also prompt institutions (government, medical, and military) to impose acts of containment and regulation in the name of security while encouraging citizens to submit willingly to this kind of regulation. There is even a comfort to defining who is "us" and who is "them," who belongs and who does not, whom to fear (and contain) and whom to support. The reassurance of a national identity, fused with a sense of safety and belonging, presents an easy choice to make, especially during a threatening time. Some pariahs are excised and profiled, while others are curfewed and quarantined. Xenophobic impulses to limit outside threats—whether Ebola victims or Syrian immigrants—can be seen as retaliation to the heightened awareness of "leaky borders" exacerbated by an increasingly networked society.

Much as the PATRIOT Act is an example of the government increasing its ability to regulate and control without legislative or judicial oversight, the National Security Agency (NSA) also enters naturally into this cultural moment, justifying surveillance of our networks, e-mails, phone conversations, and even our global footprint via our cell phones. Alexander R. Galloway and Eugene Thacker write that legislation supporting increased electronic surveillance "further reinforce[s] the deep penetration of networked technologies and networked thinking" into our lives.[7] Like the state of plague Foucault describes, the "War on Terror" following 9/11 became the excuse for this kind of inspection, omniscient power, and expanding networks, encouraging American leaders to grasp for absolute power while urging terrified American citizens to allow and support it.

Peter N. Stearns, in his book *American Fear: The Causes and Consequences of High Anxiety*, discusses the seemingly infinite "capacity of many Americans, including many leaders, quickly to reinvent threats and hyperbole, as if the emotional rhetorical habits of long years of hot and cold wars could not be cast aside." Stearns is quick to emphasize the role that the "complicit media" play in this reinvention of threats and hyperbole: they are "eager to sell crises and blessed with new technology that facilitate[s] instantaneous images from almost any hot spot." With these tools at America's disposal, is it any wonder that "an Iraqi dictator—an undeniable nuisance who arguably needed some attention" would become a latter-day Hitler or Stalin?[8] Stearns stresses that this kind of hyperbole is not exclusively tied to the events of 9/11. In fact, Stearns traces fears of terrorist attacks to well before September 11, 2001: these fears were also fueled by "the 1993 World Trade Center bombing, plus assaults on American embassies and military equipment, along with the more general emotional volatility born of a long diet of crises." In fact, a poll "taken six weeks before September 11, 2001, revealed that about 90 percent of all Americans were actively afraid of international terrorism and weapons of mass destruction."[9] The events of 9/11 just confirmed that all these fears were warranted.

Starting in 2002, fears of bioterrorism and genetically engineered viruses began showing up more and more in films and television shows, whether the virus was released accidentally (*28 Days Later* [Boyle] in 2002; *The Andromeda Strain* [A&E] in 2008; *The Crazies* in 2010) or intentionally (*Global Effect* in 2002; *Contagion* in 2002; season 3 of *24* [Fox] in 2003–2004; *Covert One: The Hades Factor* [CBS] in 2006; *Toxic Skies* in 2008; *The Blacklist* [NBC] in 2014; *Blindspot* [NBC] in 2015; *12 Monkeys* [Syfy] in 2015, *Madam Secretary* [CBS] in 2016, *Person of Interest* [CBS] in 2016; *Inferno* [Howard] in 2016). These narratives reflect the renewed patriotism that followed the 9/11 attacks, as well as the popularity of rogue heroes—seemingly America's only weapon against radical terrorist groups. While the typical outbreak narrative may function as a metaphor for modernity, the terrorism outbreak narrative literalizes the martial metaphors often used to describe disease, as well as the disease metaphors used to describe terrorism. This second wave of the outbreak narrative cycle reflects the fears dominating American consciousness at the start of the twenty-first century, much as celluloid portrayals of terrorists reflect fears of infected bodies as weapons.

This combination of viruses and terrorism seems inevitable. As Alison Bashford writes, "Chemical and biological warfare is perhaps the site at which panic and disease have come together most intensely."[10] After all, pandemics, like terrorist attacks, trigger a specific kind of fear and anxiety created by events with no end point or temporal dimension. For instance, on an MSNBC broadcast following the terrorist attacks in Paris on November 13, 2015, American television journalist Harry Smith opened a segment on the psychological effects of terror by emphasizing that a key tactic of terrorism is "to instill the fear that it could happen to you, to your family, no matter who you are and where you are."[11] That kind of vague and unrelenting mental anguish adds another larger layer to the actual physical destruction of the terrorist attack. Therefore, in the aftermath of events like the Paris attacks or 9/11, it is common to have a sense of terror that extends well beyond the blast radius itself, much as fears of contagion spread well beyond the radius of the outbreak. Both terrorism and contagion emphasize that nowhere (and no one) is safe. If pandemics reshape trauma by being open, messy, and timeless, terrorism, too, disrupts traditional understandings of trauma by being open, messy, and timeless. Anyone, anywhere may be vulnerable, however implausible those fears may actually be.

Jonathan Metzl, director of the Center for Medicine, Health, and Society at Vanderbilt University, emphasizes the strength of the "psychological mechanism that happens well beyond the blast radius and the aftermath of seemingly senseless acts of violence like terrorism or mass shootings." Metzl describes this mechanism as a "catastrophic loss of innocence" resulting not just from the direct effects of terrorism but also from the heightened sense that places that normally provide safety and security—like churches, concert halls, places of business—suddenly shift to being "places of peril." This sense of anxiety, he argues, is "heightened by the sense that the usual rules or safety markers that we use to unconsciously reassure ourselves—things like a sense that the government is in control or that we are all playing by the same rules of society—that these factors are not at play."[12] Terrorism—like a viral outbreak—happens when the normal rules of society and space are disregarded, when boundaries of protocol and geography are ignored. This creates a sense of anxiety and fear that transcends the point of actual physical impact.

It is not just that terrorism, like a virus, can take place anywhere but that it can take place at any *time*. Kevin J. Wetmore describes the color-coded terrorism threat scale that has been used by the Department of Homeland Security since March 2002. Green represents low risk, blue represents general risk, yellow means elevated or significant risk, orange represents high risk, and red is severe risk. Wetmore emphasizes that, significantly, there is no color for no risk.[13] Similarly, the first panel of Art Spiegelman's post-9/11 graphic novel *In the Shadow of No Towers* captures the relentlessness of the anxiety under the heading "the new normal" (see figure 21). First, in the image dated "Sept. 10" via a calendar in the corner, there is a family (two parents, their daughter, and their cat) drowsing in front of the TV. Then, in the image dated "Sept. 11," the same people are watching the television with their hair standing straight up, cat included. In the final graphic, where the calendar has been replaced with an American flag, the parents are drowsing in front of the TV with their hair standing up, while the daughter and the cat keep a watchful eye on the television. The last panel depicts the relentlessness of the anxiety in America following 9/11.[14] There is no reprieve because nowhere feels immune. Terrorism can hit anywhere, anytime. Or, as attorney Marion Springer (Jayne Atkinson) warns on the *Law & Order: Special Victims Unit* episode "Savant" (NBC, Oct. 16, 2007), putting many people's fears into words, "There is a terrorist around every corner . . . you just don't know about it."

Fusing terrorism with viral fears doubles the terror of both, literalizing a metaphorical relationship that goes back centuries. Military metaphors have been used to describe disease since at least the 1600s, when John Donne wrote that we work arduously to maintain our health—"a long and a regular work"—but, in a minute, "a cannon batters all, overthrows all, demolishes all."[15] Military metaphors for describing illness became even more specific following Louis Pasteur's discoveries in the late nineteenth century, when it was no longer the illness that was the invader but the *microbe*. Since then, this kind of martial terminology has continued to "infuse all aspect of the description of the medical situation," notes Susan Sontag in her book *Illness as Metaphor and AIDS and Its Metaphors*.[16] Phrases like "the invader is tiny," or "[the body] begins to mobilize an array of cells," or "the AIDS virus . . . evades the rapidly advancing defenders" in

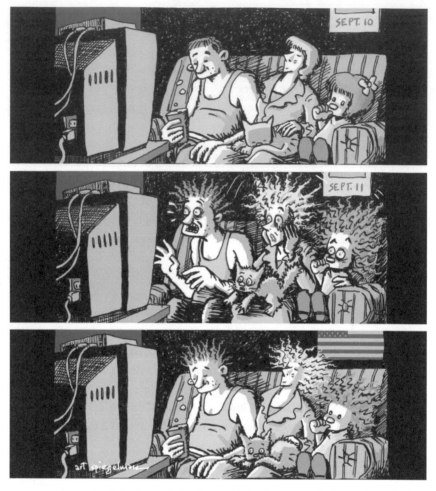

FIGURE 21 From Art Spiegelman, *In the Shadow of No Towers* (New York: Pantheon Books, 2004), 1.

order to hone in "on the master coordinator of the immune system" reflect not only military metaphor but also, Sontag writes, "the language of political paranoia, with its characteristic distrust of a pluralistic world."[17]

Joanna Burke describes the image of the AIDS virus on the cover of the January 1987 issue of *Scientific American* as "looking like a grenade, primed for detonation"[18] (see figure 22). Emily Martin expounds at length about this kind of description in her book *Flexible Bodies: The Role of Immunity in American Culture from the Days of Polio to the Age of AIDS*. Beyond using military terminology to describe disease, it is used to describe the body's process of self-defense. Martin writes, "The portrait of the body conveyed

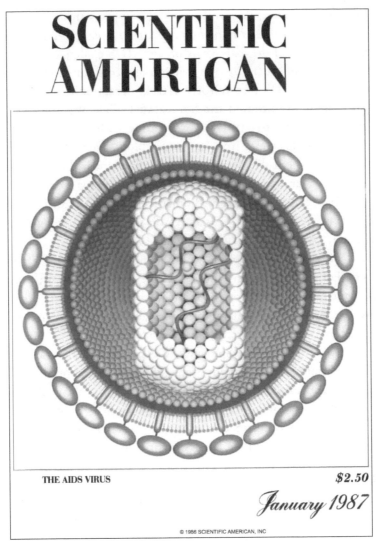

FIGURE 22 *Scientific American*, January 1987.

most often and most vividly in the mass media shows it as a defended nation-state, organized around a hierarchy of gender, race, and class," with the immune system as a defense system maintaining the boundary between self and nonself, with the nonself world visualized as "foreign and hostile."[19] Similarly, in an article in *Time* magazine entitled "Returning Fire against AIDS" from June 1991, the virus is portrayed as possessing "hidden parts that do not show up on the immune system's radar screen."[20]

This kind of militaristic terminology also appears throughout Randy Shilts's book *And the Band Played On: Politics, People, and the AIDS Epidemic*, a chronicle of the early years of the AIDS epidemic with a focus on the political and social apathy that initially confronted the outbreak. Shilts compares AIDS to a terrorist attack, observing that "thinkers in the gay community believed the homosexual plight was less like being in a war than living with terrorism. At any time, without any coherent reason, the virus could emerge from its victims' blood and violently seize their lives. Gay men who had lived with terrorism in countries like Israel argued that AIDS was an even more insidious enemy."[21] Paula Treichler, in her article "AIDS, Homophobia and Biomedical Discourse: An Epidemic of Signification," even gives the virus an Arabic identity, describing the AIDS virus as a "terrorist's terrorist, an Abu Nidal of Viruses."[22]

Conversely, disease metaphors are frequently used to describe invading enemies. For instance, during the Cold War, Communism was seen as a "malignant parasite"; the Soviet Union infected by "germs of a creeping disease."[23] Communist guerilla movements during the Vietnam War were described as "a disease of transition to modernization . . . rooted in the pathology of economic development."[24] Colleen Bell, in an article entitled "Hybrid Warfare and Its Metaphors," details how "metaphors of infectious disease and its treatment" can also be used to "express the goal of immunizing local populations against becoming insurgents."[25] Insurgency is portrayed as being purely destructive, with guerillas relying on terror in order to further their mission. Like viruses, their primary task is "to debilitate and destroy."[26] David Kilcullen, former special advisor to the US secretary of state from 2007 to 2009 and senior advisor to General David Petraeus in Iraq in 2007, outlines the process of the accidental guerilla using a disease model: infection, contagion, intervention, and rejection. The infection occurs when the guerilla establishes a presence, the contagion step demarcates the period when the guerilla's influence spreads throughout the country at large, external authorities begin to take action during the intervention step, and rejection mirrors "an immune response in which the body rejects the intrusion of a foreign object."[27]

Terrorism, specifically, is imagined as a foreign disease that can infiltrate boundaries, a virus that can permeate anywhere or anyone. To illustrate, on October 15, 2001, Richard N. Haas, then acting as a representative of the US Department of State, gave a speech in which he compared international terrorism to a terrible lethal virus:

Sometimes dormant, sometimes virulent, it is always present in some form. Like a virus, international terrorism respects no boundaries—moving from country to country, exploiting globalized commerce and communication to spread. It can be particularly malevolent when it can find a supportive host. We therefore need to take appropriate prophylactic measures at home and abroad to prevent terrorism from multiplying and check it from infecting our societies and damaging our lives . . . We also need to make sure that the virus does not mutate into something even more deadly through the acquisition of nuclear, biological, or chemical weapons of mass destruction.[28]

Similarly, as Nicholas B. King argues, "Dangerous states and ideologies have given way to dangerous fragments, circulating globally and freely transgressing the boundaries of the modern world."[29] It is not merely that there has been a shift from vertical to horizontal, from states represented by armies to individuals acting with their own sovereignty but that the bio-terrorist operates "at the junction between commercial, informational, and scientific economies," representing the darkest potential of globalization, transforming "global networks into conduits of infection," and symbolizing "American fears of racial, ethnic, and national contamination."[30]

Just one week after 9/11, an anthrax attack in the United States threw these metaphorical connections into stark relief; it condensed these fears into a neat real world bundle. Beginning on September 18, 2001, letters containing anthrax spores were mailed to five news media offices and two Democratic senators. Five people died and seventeen were infected. The FBI eventually identified the culprit in 2008 as Bruce Ivins, a scientist in the army's biodefense lab at Fort Detrick, in Maryland, although many still feel their investigation was inconclusive.[31] In fact, a congressional inquiry even identified major gaps in the case.[32] The length of the investigation, as well as its inconclusive results, combined with the death of Bruce Ivins, a victim of an apparent suicide, further compounded fears of future incidents of biowarfare. If the American government was unable to prevent anthrax and 9/11, or even to apprehend those responsible, why should they be any less inept at preventing future attacks? At the time, the fact that the anthrax used in the attacks was traced back to Fort Detrick also intensified questions of whether the greatest danger was already within our borders, possibly in the hands of our own government.

A repeated plot point in many terrorism outbreak narratives is that a virus the American government has created is then used against the very

Americans it is supposed to protect, echoing the premise set forth by Romero in the original film *The Crazies* (1973). This is also exactly what happens in *Covert One: The Hades Factor*. In *The Hades Factor*, Hassan (Conrad Dunn), the terrorist leader, declares to his fellow terrorists, "No one will know they are infected until it's too late. All the targets have been chosen to inflict the most infection. We will turn America against itself. Let them feel the sting of their own creation." He infects his men with an American-engineered virus that he then attempts to spread throughout America. In the campy film *Venomous* (Ray, 2001), a group of Jihadi terrorists break into an American government lab and release genetically modified rattlesnakes the American government had bred as weapons. The snakes breed and multiply underground, eventually coming to the surface after an earthquake. Anyone they bite can, in turn, transmit the virus. Much like in *Outbreak*, the military, desperate to conceal evidence of their biological warfare development, is more invested in blowing up the town to cover up all evidence than it is in helping the inhabitants. While a biological weapon is also used in *The Crazies* (both versions), a significant difference is that the release of that virus is accidental. A military aircraft containing the Trixie virus crashes into a local river, infecting the water supply. What is not accidental is the military's response: to shoot all the civilians, even those not infected, and to blow up the town.

Although anthrax is not a contagious disease, the anthrax attacks demonstrated the seemingly facile ways in which terrorists could spread disease and the current power of ordinary social networks to harm us. Both natural viral outbreaks and terrorist-orchestrated outbreaks call attention to the significance and power of networks in contemporary life. Whereas bombs and gunfire are location-specific, a viral outbreak can—and often does—travel the world via networks—both visible and invisible—and can be impossible to contain. A viral outbreak is literally contagious information spreading throughout globalized vectors of disease, and a terrorist-planned outbreak merely makes the spread of that contagion deliberate. While a natural viral outbreak and a terrorist-fueled outbreak may have similar results, a terrorist-fueled outbreak is chilling for the intentionality of the destruction.

As these narratives remind us, contemporary life makes us all interconnected, leaving us especially vulnerable to bioterrorism. Who thinks twice before opening mail addressed to them? Before drinking water? Walking down a city street? These actions, based on this crop of outbreak narratives—as well as recent news headlines—could kill you. You do not even need to board a plane. The plane may crash into you. The occasional real-life terrorist attack, however infrequent, establishes a precedent of plausibility that is reinforced every time a similar scenario plays out on television or in the movies. After all, viruses do not only spread organically. Unlike Typhoid Mary, who was a passive carrier of germs within her body, the bioterrorist is an active agent, "blending science and nature into political weapons."[33]

A core part of America's identity following 9/11 became its oppositional role against Al Qaeda. Fear was a foundation for national unity. The shared sense of purpose also provided a unifying focus, as well as a way to cope with the trauma caused by 9/11. Simultaneously, patriotism could literally be seen (not just felt) in the proliferation of raised flags displayed throughout cities, on buildings, and over homes. The unknown Arab had become the deadly contagious "other" threatening to infiltrate America's borders, only able to be kept at bay by this relentless patriotism. The Bush administration declared to the American public, "You are either with us or against us."[34] If you were not unequivocally supporting Bush's agenda in the Middle East, if you were not behind the "War on Terror," you were in bed with the enemy. This simplistic binary hearkened back to the black-and-white clarity of the Cold War; a Muslim man with a beard had merely replaced the Communist villain. These rhetorical strategies were employed by politicians, journalists, and Hollywood to impose a narrative on an otherwise confusing situation.

However, unlike the black-and-white clarity of the Cold War, this new kind of warfare remains confusing and complex, despite rhetorical efforts to simplify the situation. Much of this had to do with the fact that, rather than a classic "hierarchical terror organization," Al Qaeda is one "devoid of organizational boundaries," penetrating many levels of Islamic society around the world. Al Qaeda, much like many terrorist organizations, is a network; "highly decentralized and dispersed," it has "diffuse structure, indirect connections, and nontraditional modes of communication."[35] American historian and political commentator Walter Laqueur, in his 1996 essay on "postmodern terrorism," writes that, in the past, "terrorism was almost always the province of groups of militants that had the backing of political forces like the Irish and Russian social revolutionary movements of 1900," which made it much easier to understand allegiances and agendas. Now, however, terrorists are individuals or like-minded people working in very small groups, often with varying allegiances and agendas.[36] This approach was seen with terrorists such as Ted Kaczynski, also known as the Unabomber, who mailed or hand-delivered a series of bombs, or Timothy McVeigh and Terry Nichols, the perpetrators of the 1995 bombing of the Alfred P. Murrah Federal Building in downtown Oklahoma City. Dzhokhar Tsarnaev and Tamerlan Tsarnaev, the two brothers responsible for the Boston marathon bombing on April 14, 2013, claimed to have been inspired by extremist Islamist beliefs, but they were still self-radicalized and self-taught, unaffiliated with any specific terrorist group. Laqueur also describes the "bewildering multiplicity of terrorist and potentially terrorist groups and sects . . . espousing varieties of nationalism, religious fundamentalism, fascism, and apocalyptic millenarianism" who defy geographic, as well as ideological, containment.[37] This is a new kind of war for a new kind of world.

The idea of power working without a sovereign center echoes French philosopher Gilles Deleuze's argument that we are moving toward control societies, where, rather than the closed and orderly environments of disciplinary societies, we will have corporations made up of multiple bodies. One key difference between older and newer outbreak narratives is arguably this shift from discipline to control, from hierarchical social ordering to horizontal and rhizomatic modes of self and peer-to-peer policing.[38] The acceptance of the hypersovereignty that emerged after 9/11, attempting both to cover every space and control every contingency, can be seen as a compensatory representation designed to alleviate anxieties inspired by these fears. If we cannot determine whom to trust, much less whom to fear, we rely on our leaders to determine it for us. We will also do whatever we can to feel safe, regardless of whether that safety is an illusion or not.

In many ways, the 9/11 attacks could be described as a blow by cellular, networked, modular, nimble terrorists against a centralized tower, an icon, a pillar, demonstrating the global shift from centralized hierarchical powers to distributed, horizontal networks.[39] This evolution mirrors that of many brick-and-mortar institutions, sovereign power structures, and central bureaucracies, all of which have been increasingly eroded or even replaced with the flatness of interconnected networks. However, it is not merely that the terrorist organizations are networks but that terrorist organizations *use* networks. King, in his 2002 article "Dangerous Fragments," writes that contemporary terrorist attacks are facilitated by the "ability to navigate and manipulate networks." Global networks of transportation, trade, and information, as well as the acceleration of international trade and commerce, allow the terrorist to secretly acquire or construct, and rapidly and efficiently disseminate, weapons of mass destruction to American cities.[40]

The importance of these networks also makes them prime targets for terrorists. In season 1 of *The Strain* (FX, 2014–15), for example, Eldritch Palmer (Jonathan Hyde) hires computer hacker Dutch Velders (Ruta Gedmintas) to disrupt the city's entire Internet and telecommunications systems, thus weakening the infrastructure of New York City. In season 1, episode 2 of Syfy's *12 Monkeys* ("Mentally Divergent," January 23, 2015), Katarina Jones (Barbara Sukowa) studies the pattern of the viral outbreak and concludes that it followed an intentional design aimed at making the virus hit with maximum impact. "They made sure to infiltrate centers of power, police, government, health," she tells Cole (Aaron Stanford), because these are the targets not only for spreading disease but also for crippling social order.

Before the "War on Terror" began, America had been trapped in a liminal state of helplessness and vulnerability exacerbated by the confusion of this new kind of warfare, where enemies were unclear and geographical boundaries irrelevant. However, once war began in Afghanistan, the unknown Arab could be painted as, according to Lynn Spigel, "the antithesis of Western humanity and progress,"[41] and an adversary worth conquering. The American desire for vengeance would surface in an increase of narratives featuring "heroic saviors and violent redemption," as well as "fantasies of national and subjective coherence," such as *The Agency* (CBS, 2001–2003), *The Grid* (TNT, 2004), and *Threat Matrix* (ABC, 2003–2004).[42] These thrillers, very much fueled by Bush's "War on Terror," aimed to make sense of the political situation, imposing a clarifying binary and patriotic simplicity to the situation. Evil often germinated in the Middle East, the threat was most likely Jihadi radicals, and the American government had tools and tricks that would allow them to remain one step ahead. They also depicted "the covert, small-scale, 'low-intensity' combat" that would become increasingly common after 9/11.[43] This kind of small-scale combat appears in all the texts I discuss in this chapter: battle is between single individuals—often American agents versus terrorist infidels—involving hand-to-hand combat, computer screens, and microscopes rather than battlefields. After all, as Lacquer had already written in 1996, "terrorism is becoming the substitute for the great wars of the 1800s and early 1900s."[44]

In order to compensate for the confusion that followed 9/11 about who America's enemy was and why America had been attacked, these new film and television narratives revolved around uncomplicated narratives of American "good" versus foreign "evil."[45] These stories made it quite clear that the threat came from without rather than within. Even if the threat was on American soil—which it almost always was—it came from a terrorist who had slipped over the border. This fits with the criteria associated with patriotism according to Silvio Waisbord: "Patriotism establishes that only external forces pose threats to the nation. It excludes the possibility of internal actors interested in disrupting a seemingly unified community."[46] Even if the threat looked American, it never actually was.

For instance, in the episode "The Plague Year" (Mar. 7, 2002) from the CBS's television show *The Agency*, Tom Gage (Beau Bridges) exclaims that Omar (Grayson McCouch), the terrorist, "doesn't look Middle Eastern." Jackson Haisley (Will Patton) confirms that Omar was born in Algeria, and Quinn (Daniel Benzali) explains that Omar "surgically altered his appearance: bleached his skin, lightened his hair, cosmetic contacts surgically implanted." All this, of course, so Omar could move about the United States without causing suspicion after literally cutting his way through the fence on the Arizona–Mexico border. Omar's agenda? To spread smallpox to his girlfriend, who would, in turn, spread it to a United States senator with whom she was having an affair. Once infected, the senator would then spread smallpox throughout Capitol Hill. Appropriately, Wolfgang Petersen, director of *Outbreak*, was executive producer of *The Agency*.

Featuring unprecedented filming at the headquarters of the Central Intelligence Agency (CIA) in Virginia, the show was developed in collaboration with CIA liaison Chase Brandon and "was supposed to make the case for the continued necessity of the CIA in a post–Cold War world of geopolitical complexity."[47] Making this case was even more of a challenge after the intelligence failures that led to 9/11. Each episode became a public relations device of sorts, showing all the implausible gimmicks that this fictional version of the CIA had at their disposal, tools enabling them to bring home the bad guys every time in narratives loosely (and sometimes not-so-loosely) inspired by real-life events. For example, the original pilot hit so close to home—with its depiction of a plot by Al Qaeda to blow up a London department store and repeated mentions of Osama bin Laden—that the episode was delayed from September 27, 2001, to November 1, 2001. CBS pulled completely an episode dealing with an anthrax attack on New York City.[48]

CBS did, however, air the episode "A Slight Case of Anthrax" (Nov. 8, 2001)—about a terrorist planning to release anthrax in Washington, DC—fewer than two months after the real-life anthrax attack. The episode capitalized on existing fears by emphasizing just how dangerous anthrax could be—but not to worry, the CIA was *on it*. FBI special agent Shelton (Leslie Silva) describes an incident when less than a teaspoon was accidentally released in a lab and sixty-four people died. In response, Carl Reese (Rocky Carroll) warns that "someone with a Dixie cup and a plan could kill thousands." To complicate the episode's plot further, it is discovered that the anthrax in question had originally been engineered in a government lab in Virginia, much like with the real-life anthrax attacks of 2001. From the lab, the American government sold the anthrax to the Iraqis—when the United States was supporting them in their war against Iran—who then engineered a new strain to resist antibiotics, making its fatality rate 100 percent. Now that the Iraqis were no longer friendly with Americans, the anthrax posed a serious threat. Ironically, seconds after the episode's conclusion, the Oregon CBS affiliate broadcasting *The Agency* promoted its upcoming nightly news with a clip about a mysterious rash closing local schools. "We'll have the latest," the voice-over declares.

Conceived before 9/11, *The Agency*, much like *Alias* (ABC, 2001–2006) and *24* (Fox, 2001–2010), "[was] designed to respond to anxieties about global interconnection and boundary dissolution with fantasies of national and subjective coherence."[49] These anxieties would intensify after the attacks of 9/11, making these shows even more relevant. While *The Agency* reflected the efforts of American agents to protect the United States from terrorist attack, *The Grid*—a 2004 miniseries coproduced by the BBC, Fox TV, and Carnival Films that aired on TNT in the United States and the BBC in the UK—tackled more global efforts to stop terrorism, reflecting not only efforts by the NSA, the Pentagon, the CIA, and the FBI, but also those of British agencies MI5 (the United Kingdom's domestic counterintelligence security agency) and MI6 (the United Kingdom's foreign intelligence agency). Responding to the complexities of intelligence work in a globalized world, representatives of these various antiterrorist agencies are forced to work together as an international counterterrorism team.

In the first episode of *The Grid*, "Hour One/Hour Two" (July 19, 2004), sarin gas is accidentally released by a group of incompetent terrorists—a network including a former Al Qaeda commander—without authorization from any terrorist council. This reflects the new kind of warfare common to the twenty-first century, with its decentralized and nontraditional terrorist organizations. Even though the accidental release occurred in London, an informant tells FBI agent Max Canary (Dylan McDermott) that other extremists are bringing sarin gas across the Mexican border to Los Angeles. Again, the Mexican border becomes a repeated plot point due to its supposedly porous nature. Interestingly, the show engages directly with the deep-seated fear many Americans still feel about Muslims, using CIA agent and Middle East analyst Raza Michaels (Piter Marek) both to demonstrate the racism that many Muslims experience as well as to give them a voice. When NSA agent Maren Jackson (Julianna Margulies) declares, "To me, Islam is one thing: fear," Raza tells her that Islam is the religion of almost a billion people. "Are you saying that all one billion are criminal? I find it inexcusable that a woman with your standing could judge an entire religion by the actions of a fundamentalist faction. How would you feel if I judged all Christians by the actions of the KKK? . . . Because of some narrow thinking by governments like ours and people like you, we are judged by our worst example."

Even when they state that fear of all Muslims is not the answer, shows like these do reinforce the suspicion that much of America's threat comes from the Middle East. These narratives also reinforce the strength and appeal of clearly defined heroes working together—as a network and/ or a team—fighting against just-as-clearly-defined enemies. In the words of James William Gibson, author of *The Perfect War: Technowar in Vietnam*, these stories advocate for "the primacy of heroic male warriors, magic weapons, and horrific enemies as fundamental cultural categories."[50] Virtually nonexistent on TV since the 1960s, this type of story surged in popularity on small and large screens after 9/11, achieving "a new raison d'être in the wake of the attacks."[51]

The explicitly patriotic overtones found in these narratives are not accidental. Shortly after 9/11, Karl Rove, senior advisor and deputy chief of staff in the George W. Bush administration, met with film producers, directors, screenwriters, and media executives in Hollywood in order to strategize how best to make patriotic films that portrayed the government in a positive light. However, as Justin Lewis, Richard Maxwell, and Toby

Miller conclude, the meeting was really "an intelligence briefing designed to bring the Hollywood power elite up to date on the White House's war aims."[52] To further the government's public relations initiative, many television programs also "received assistance, both before and after 9/11, from U.S. security agencies, the Department of Defense, and/or the State Department."[53]

However, despite these efforts by Hollywood and Washington, public support began to turn away from the government in the years that followed. In 2005, Italian philosopher Giorgio Agamben wrote that President Bush's constant references to himself as "commander in chief" after September 11, 2001, should be seen as a "presidential claim to sovereign powers," a claim further reinforced by Bush's attempts "to produce a situation in which the emergency becomes the rule."[54] In January 2006, in an article for the *New York Times*, American author and Harvard law professor Noah Feldman describes this increasingly unchecked presidential power:

> The administration of George W. Bush, emboldened by the Sept. 11 attacks and the backing of a Republican Congress, has sought to further extend presidential power over national security. Most of the expansion has taken place in secret, making Congressional or judicial supervision particularly difficult. Administration lawyers have gone so far as to claim that the president as commander in chief is not bound by laws that ban torture because he is empowered by the Constitution to fight the nation's wars however he sees fit . . . The administration has also suggested, in other memos, that the president may violate international treaties if necessary to fight the war on terror. When added to the newly declared presidential right to arrest American citizens wherever they might be and detain them without trial as enemy combatants, these claims add up to what is easily the most aggressive formulation of presidential power in our history.[55]

By March 2006, at 33 percent, Bush's overall approval ratings were the lowest of his presidency, and only 42 percent approved of his handling of terrorist threats, a decline of 20 percent since January 2005. The word "incompetent" became the word most frequently used to describe the president.[56] In June 2006, the Supreme Court struck a significant blow against the Bush administration with its ruling for *Hamdan v. Rumsfeld*, declaring that the president "did not have the right to hold military commissions to try terror suspects held at Guantánamo Bay." This decision also "slapped down his assertion that, as a wartime commander in chief, he had the authority to exclude Congress from decisions concerning national security."[57] Public sentiment had officially shifted.

Despite the significant increase after 9/11, trust not only in Bush, but in the government as a whole, began declining in the years that followed, a tumble that only fell faster during debates over the war in Iraq, White House and congressional scandals, the gross mishandling of rescue efforts following Hurricane Katrina, and a worsening economy. A CBS–*New York Times* poll conducted in October 2008 found that only 17 percent of those surveyed "trusted the federal government to do what is right."[58]

This change of heart was reflected by Hollywood. While pro-American patriotic messages had filled the airwaves immediately following 9/11, in the years after, film and television narratives began to emphasize that the voice of freedom inevitably stems from the rogue hero fighting *against* the military machine or the corporate establishment. These narratives were still patriotic in that American ideals of freedom and justice always prevailed, but the difference was that sometimes these ideals would be met *in spite of* government or corporate efforts to the contrary. Once again there was the individual hero working outside the system. Jennifer Gillan describes these heroes as "Cowboy Knights"—"unorthodox, yet honest; unrefined, yet honorable; ordinary, yet extraordinary."[59]

Examples of these rogue heroes abound. In *Toxic Skies*, for example, Tess Martin (Anne Heche) stands up to the military and pharmaceutical establishments. In *The X-Files* (Fox, 1993–2002; 2016–present), Fox Mulder (David Duchovny) routinely questions government protocol and behavior. In the miniseries *Covert One: The Hades Factor*, it is army microbiologist Colonel Jon Smith (Stephen Dorff), who defies government orders and flees a secured military base. In *The Crazies* remake, it is David (Timothy Olyphant), the Ogden Marsh sheriff, who discovers the initial conspiracy, shuts off the town water against the direct order of the mayor, escapes quarantine, and shoots military personnel, first as an attempt to save the town, but then, after that fails, himself and his wife. Jack Bauer (Kiefer Sutherland), the lead protagonist on Fox's *24*, is repeatedly described not only as a patriot by *24* creator Joel Surnow but also as the only man who can save America. "There are not a lot of measures short of extreme measures that will get it done. America wants the war on terror fought by Jack Bauer," Surnow explains.[60] Howard Gordon, one of *24*'s executive producers, describes *24*'s success as a reflection of American audiences' desire for heroes "who will do whatever is necessary to save society from harm."[61] While protagonists might *prefer* to think things through and follow the rules, the circumstances that put modern societies at risk do not allow for it. Rogue heroes who operate outside the system "are the only ones that can act sufficiently."[62]

The television show *24* is an example of a television show that integrates all these core elements: rogue heroes, patriotism, surveillance, networks, technology, binaries of good and evil. The main plotline of season 3 was bioterrorism. Originally launching on November 6, 2001, *24* immediately became distinctive for its format as well as for its timeliness. The show runs in "real time," with a minute of the show equaling a minute of real life. In order to emphasize this narrative device, the show regularly features a digital clock displaying the time it is within the world of the show, as well as split screens depicting multiple scenes happening simultaneously. The screen splitting echoes a style frequently used on broadcast news programs and in surveillance footage. This documentary aesthetic is reinforced by the camera work, which is often gritty and jittery, almost always moving as it follows Jack Bauer through his various exploits. The format of *24*—its real-time elements, serial structure, camerawork, and split screens—reinforces the show's illusion of live-ness and realism despite the amplified and melodramatic plotlines, providing a contagious sense of patriotism and a depiction of the unrelenting complexity of contemporary life.

The various screens—and the emphasis on the information conveyed within them—not only communicate the globalization of the crisis, as also seen in *Contagion* (2011) but also force the viewer to engage with multiple events happening simultaneously. This simultaneity echoes shifts occurring in day-to-day life, where multiple-frame images are increasingly common. As Anne Friedberg describes, over the last twenty years, "the introduction of computer-generated images and digital display technologies has radically transformed the space of the screen . . . Multiple-frame images are a readable new visual syntax, a key feature in the contemporary remaking of a visual vernacular."[63] Viewers now frequently watch and interact with not only multiple frames simultaneously but multiple separate screens.

However, it is not merely the split screens that, in the words of Matthew B. Hill, "present the show as a high-tech or computerized experience."[64] The show itself places heavy emphasis on the use of technology and the transfer and acquisition of data in order to resolve whatever particular crisis is at hand. Whenever the show presents us with a scene shot within

CTU (the Counter Terrorism Unit) headquarters, it is always filled with glowing monitors; some rooms are even lined with them from floor to ceiling. Hill writes that, in *24*, the "War on Terror" is presented "as a high-tech information war . . . a computer war, managed, defined, and at times won by data and those who possess it and process it, technowar transformed into icons and IP addresses."[65] This provides an apt reflection of just how foundational computers and networks—along with the data transmitted by both—have become.

As I mention in the introduction, flows of information are integral components in all types of networks, including computer, political, social, and biological. These flows of information (contagious or otherwise) create and sustain networks. Bauer, as the central figure in *24*, both produces and consumes "the data processed and stored by CTU. He is a node . . . on the network of computers, databases, analysts, and communications systems."[66] In fact, his ability to connect with others—and their ability to connect with him—is such a pivotal part of the show that whenever Bauer goes off grid, intentionally or unintentionally, things fall apart. Bo Kampmann Walther observes that Jack's number one weapon is his cell phone and that whenever it begins to malfunction "we know for sure that something bad has happened and is about to occur."[67]

One of the tag lines for season 3 of *24* is: "To stop a weapon that has no cure . . . You need a man who knows no limits." The "weapon that has no cure," is a virus, of course, and in this case it is the Cordilla virus, engineered by rogue Ukrainian scientists who want to sell it to the highest bidder. Similar to the hantavirus, Cordilla causes nosebleeds, hemorrhaging, skin abscesses, and death. The villain here is crystal clear. It is Stephen Saunders (Paul Blackthorne), a vengeful former MI6 agent, who targets nine American cities, including Los Angeles, New York, San Francisco, Seattle, and Las Vegas. Saunders uses the threat of a nationwide (and then worldwide) epidemic to try to force President Palmer (Dennis Haysbert) to comply with a list of demands, including giving up a list of American undercover agents abroad. This aim is to take down the American intelligence/military apparatus as revenge for how it abandoned him when he was on a mission with Delta Force, the United States' primary counterterrorism unit.

"The man who knows no limits" is classic rogue hero, Jack Bauer. In *24*, Jack Bauer is often seen as the only true patriot, and it is "the government and the military . . . that ha[ve] strayed from the ideals of American nationhood."[68] Hill describes Bauer as a "nearly savage mythic hero who possesses the 'dark understanding' of the Others (the terrorists) . . . He thinks like them and fights like them."[69] When Hill writes that Bauer "fights like them," part of his meaning is that Bauer does not play by the rules. Time and time again, Bauer must circumvent rules, regulations, and incompetent superiors in order to save the day. "The majority of those appointed or elected to preserve the life, liberty, and happiness of normal Americans are depicted as incompetent . . . Heroes like Bauer must work outside of the system to 'save' it from itself."[70] In this sense, Bauer's extremism reflects America's extremism, justifying the torture and the violence that went hand in hand with the "War on Terror." Rogue heroes must operate outside the system because the system itself is frequently part of the problem. Those heroes willing to break a few rules "for the greater good" are the only ones who can act sufficiently. They are the true patriots. Much like in earlier colonial-esque outbreak narratives, these metaphors create a good versus evil binary, where motives are absolute, eradicating any uncertainty and ambiguity that exists.

Similar themes manifest in the TV miniseries *Covert One: The Hades Factor*. The national security apparatus is also portrayed as ineffectual and corrupt, and again, the rogue hero is the only one who can save the day. Government agent and disease expert Jonathan Smith (Stephen Dorff) is the Bauer-esque character who defies authority to save the world and expose government corruption, fleeing the military base despite lockdown, pursuing truth above all else. As in the book of the same name by Robert Ludlum and Gayle Lynds (originally published in 2000), an unknown Ebola-like virus begins to spread rapidly across the United States, but unlike Ebola, it is airborne and has a 90 percent kill rate, amping up the drama. The miniseries features several significant changes to the original story, most obviously the addition of Al Qaeda as the terrorist organization behind the outbreak, likely an attempt to make the story more current. However, the "othering" here is more complicated, primarily because the terrorists are not acting alone but are in cahoots with upper-level American government personnel and rogue CIA agents. They also use biological weapons developed by the American government and tested illicitly on American soldiers. The conspiracy runs deep, and the miniseries defies easy resolution, ending with the government's involvement kept secret. Elwood Reid, writer of the screenplay, attributes inspiration to real-life conspiracy and corruption by the military-industrial complex in various illicit activities.

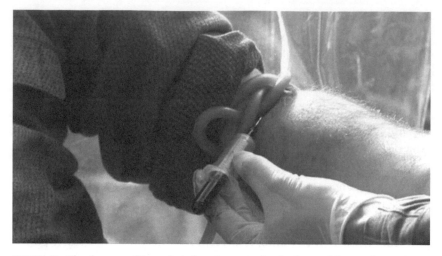

FIGURE 23 Blood extracted from the infected terrorist for the dispersal device, *Covert One: The Hades Factor* (CBS, 2006).

Reid elaborates, "There are countless examples, and what they all have in common is the military 'defense of country' excuse and the profit of corporations anxious to put potentially deadly things into the market place but doing so under the guise and guidance of military defense. It's a symbiotic relationship that the American public is, by and large, indifferent to. So that was the idea. The hypocrisy of the US military complex/business."[71] It is particularly telling that this portrayal of the US military and government corporations would appear on a broadcast network's primetime schedule, reflecting just how popular antigovernment narratives were to mainstream audiences in the years following 9/11.

All that aside, one of the most significant elements of *Covert One: The Hades Factor* is how it reinvents the very act of terrorism. In contrast, season 3 of *24* provides a traditional bioterrorist threat. When the terrorist eventually takes action, it is by leaving the virus in a detonation device within a hotel's ventilation system. In *The Hades Factor*, however, the virus replaces the traditional explosive device, and the threat is literally humanized. The "bomb" is the person. The infected terrorist is the carrier who smuggles the virus into the country before his symptoms start to show. Once he is sufficiently sick and infectious, his blood is taken and put into a detonation device, similar in design to the one used in *24* (see figures 23 and 24). The idea—never executed—is that his blood will spray innocent bystanders at Dulles International Airport and spread

FIGURE 24 Infected blood inserted into the dispersal device, *Covert One: The Hades Factor* (CBS, 2006).

the disease. Or as the army major (Fulvio Cecere) warns, "Suppose they are the weapon. Intentionally infected. Perfect patient zeros entering the country with the sole intent of infecting the populace." In *Global Effect* and the *Blacklist* episode "The Front" (NBC, Oct. 20, 2014), the threat becomes fully humanized. In those narratives, it is the intentionally infected person wandering the streets who spreads the virus passively, no device necessary, because the virus is aerosolized. These various reinventions of the trope of the "suicide bomber" combine already existing fears of healthy-looking carriers with fear of an unexpected (and impersonal) terrorist attack.

The trope of the "suicide bomber" is also given a viral twist in the "Desperate Remedies" (Apr. 10, 2016) episode of the CBS show *Madam Secretary* (2014–present). In this case, the suicide bomber *both* is infected with the virus—it is unclear if the infection happened accidentally or intentionally—and has explosives strapped to his chest. He enters a medical tent set up by the Americans to help with an outbreak of the Marburg virus in Cameroon, complaining of symptoms. When the medical staff move to treat him, the man sets off the explosives, blowing himself up. He kills seven people and infects most of the survivors with his blood and body parts. The man's suicide is part of an attempt to lash out at Western intervention in what is viewed as Boko Haram territory. Another unique element of this episode's viral plot is the way an experimental cure for

Marburg is used as a negotiation tool with Boko Haram. Hadi Bangote (Chukwudi Iwuji), the leader of the Boko Haram terrorist group, eventually falls ill with Marburg, and Secretary of State Elizabeth McCord (Tea Leoni) negotiates to get him a dose of an experimental cure in exchange for releasing 106 school girls that Boko Haram has captured in addition to letting the medical personnel treat the infected Africans safely.

One month after "Desperate Remedies" aired on CBS, "Reassortment" (May 24, 2016) aired, also on CBS. One of the final episodes of the television show *Person of Interest*, "Reassortment" would similarly use the terrorist-inflicted virus plot, adding its own unique twist. In typical terrorism outbreak narrative fashion, the protagonists—Finch (Michael Emerson) and Reese (Jim Caviezel)—are in a hospital when a military-grade version of H5N1 (avian flu) begins to spread in that hospital. Also, in typical outbreak narrative fashion, "patient zero" is international businessman James Ko (James Chen) working with US, British, and Chinese manufacturers. Much like Beth Emhoff in *Contagion*, his very job is a product of globalization. Also like Beth, James is traveling from Hong Kong, delivering the infection unknowingly to New York City. As Reese says, James is "a man who knows how to cross borders," or as his partner Finch says later in the episode, "Mr. Ko was waylaid, infected, and then turned into a weapon of mass destruction." A professional globetrotter, James is the ultimate viral threat: clean-cut, seemingly healthy, and spreading death in his wake.

Later in the episode, it turns out that the evil master-computer Samaritan—an artificial super intelligence designed after 9/11 by the American government to be a mass surveillance system—is behind the outbreak. The targets are hospital personnel who have noticed Samaritan's manipulation of the Network Inventory Database the hospital uses. Like in other outbreak narratives, the real problem becomes keeping people controlled and quarantined once the virus breaks out. When the hospital security guard (John Mondin) asks Reese under what authority they can stop people from leaving, Reese does not miss a beat: "The PATRIOT Act." The PATRIOT Act has become a catchall for allowing government powers to extend indefinitely under threat of terrorism.

The episode also provides a nod to intertextuality moments later, when one of the patients at the hospital overhears that a contagious virus is in the building. "Oh, hell no, that's how the zombie apocalypse starts!" he exclaims, bolting for the exit. Dr. Mason (Jenna Stern) soon discovers that the contagious virus is an implausible—but highly lethal—combination of avian flu and the human flu virus, combining the lethality of the former with the spreadability of the latter. Suddenly, every cough, every sneeze becomes suspicious; a hospital, ironically, is the last place anyone would want to be during this kind of outbreak. Fortunately, Root (Amy Acker) locates a cure, saving the lives of those infected—but that is only part of the story. Samaritan has an even more insidious agenda. Following the outbreak, the CDC requires everyone to be vaccinated, meaning that Samaritan will have all Americans' DNA in its National Healthcare Database. Mona (Rhonda "LaChanze" Sapp), observing the line of people outside the CDC, explains that "after 9/11, people were more than willing to allow the NSA to collect all of their personal data as long as it kept them safe." Security is, once again, prioritized over privacy. There is no explanation for what will happen to those deemed unfit, for how Samaritan will use the information it collects, but the implication is ominous.

This notion of infected bodies as weapons is increasingly popular, also showing up in the "Gone but Not Forgotten" (Sept. 18, 2016) episode of the FX show *The Strain* (2014–present). Villain Thomas Eichorst (Richard Sammel) brings together a small group of the infected "munchers," the vampire minions that serve the Master. If they can follow his simple instructions, he promises them a great feast: "The virgin blood of seventy humans." Sacrificing themselves will be "a great honor." This is a twist on the concept of martyrdom repurposed by many radical Muslims, who believe that if they sacrifice themselves for the cause, they will enter Paradise and receive seventy-two virgins. In this case, virgin *blood* is a more appealing reward. Eichorst chooses two from the group—both former employees of Councilwoman Justine Feraldo (Samantha Mathis)—and slices them open, placing C-4 explosives inside. He then sends the two "volunteers" to Feraldo's headquarters, where they easily slip inside, unnoticed, before exploding, sending millions of contagious white worms—the carriers for the strigoi "virus"—all over the workplace. Fet (Kevin Durand) saves Feraldo by killing the worm about to infect her, but sixty staff members are not so lucky.

The notion of infected bodies as weapons dates back to the fourteenth century, when the Black Plague was making its way through Europe, the Near East, and North Africa. History has it that the Mongol army threw plague-infected bodies into besieged cities in order to transmit disease to their enemies.[72] In these post-9/11 examples, however, unlike with early forms of biowarfare, the infected bodies are still alive, giving them the ability to move around and spread the virus to unknowing victims. The bomb has evolved from being an explosive, to being a virus, to being an infected person who may literally explode. Anxieties about contagious disease have combined with growing fears of terrorist attack to reinvent "the ticking time bomb" phenomenon and, therefore, redefine the paradigm of fear. The idea of terrorist as contagious threat is fully realized.

Combining fears of terrorism with fears of progress—and, specifically, overpopulation—is also a repeated plot point in this wave of the outbreak narrative. One example is *The Blacklist* episode "The Front," aired on October 20, 2014, on NBC. With Ebola getting ample news coverage at the time due to an outbreak in West Africa, "The Front" was perfectly synchronized with real-life events. In this episode, Maddox Beck (Michael Laurence) is an eco-terrorist who resurrects a dormant pneumonic plague virus and weaponizes it so that it operates at an accelerated rate. His goal is a worldwide epidemic that will kill off the entire human race, thereby supposedly saving the planet. "To preserve life on earth, we need to become extinct," Beck tells his cult-like followers, who then infect themselves with the virus so that they can spread it around the world. Sharon McManus (Freya Adams) is his first follower to infect herself (see figure 25) before heading to Washington, DC to spread the virus. In this case, it is an average-looking young woman with dark hair pulled back in a ponytail who spreads the

FIGURE 25 Eco-terrorist Sharon McManus (Freya Adams) infects herself with the virus, *The Blacklist*, "The Front" (NBC, Oct. 20, 2014).

virus to those unlucky enough to be near her (see figures 26 and 27). This technique contains echoes of the 2001 anthrax attack, emphasizing the seemingly facile ways with which terrorists can spread disease and the current power of ordinary social networks to harm us. It also reinforces another aspect of a terrorist attack: you can be killed anywhere through no specific action of your own. Just existing (at the wrong place, at the wrong time) is enough to kill you. Dressed inconspicuously in torn jeans, a striped sweater clutched around her, Sharon walks the streets, the pustules around

FIGURES 26 AND 27 Eco-terrorist Sharon McManus (Freya Adams) spreads the virus, *The Blacklist*, "The Front" (NBC, Oct. 20, 2014).

her nose and mouth ignored by passersby, spreading the virus merely by breathing. The virus is airborne and therefore requires no physical contact to spread. By the time she is identified as patient zero, roughly 2,300 people have been quarantined and given less than a day to live.

Almost exactly a year later, the *Blindspot* episode "Bone May Rot" aired on October 12, 2015, on NBC. It features two terrorists trying to release a virus to save the planet by killing off most of its human inhabitants. The only twist is that these two terrorists are also CDC scientists, again reinforcing the fear that the threat may lie within. Aptly, the plot thickens when former deputy director of the CDC, Dr. Walter Tunnel (Doug Barron), dies from a tear in his safety suit.

As if by clockwork, the movie *Inferno* was released a year later, on October 28, 2016. Based on the 2013 novel by best-selling author Dan Brown, and starring Tom Hanks and directed by Ron Howard, *Inferno* follows a similar idea. "Culling is God's Natural Order," says Bertrand Zobrist, the rogue terrorist (played by Ben Foster in the film). These are the new Dark Ages, and after a necessary culling, there will be a rebirth, a Renaissance, he declares. He even tries to convince the head of the WHO, Dr. Elisabeth Sinksey (Sidse Babett Knudsen), to support him, describing the human race as a cancer, its replicating out of control. He provides her with graphs depicting the skyrocketing rate of human population growth and the ensuing dearth of natural resources. "Did you know that if you live another nineteen years, until the age of eighty, you will witness the population *triple* in your lifetime? One lifetime—a tripling. Think of the implications."[73] The head of the WHO remains unconvinced, declaring him a terrorist and a murderer, but Zobrist continues with his plan.

The film *Global Effect* (Cunningham, 2002) also revolves around the concept that in order to save the world (most) humans have to go. Sasha (Rolanda Marais), the terrorist ringleader's girlfriend, infects herself with the virus, so that she can walk the streets of Cape Town, South Africa, infecting as many people as possible (see figure 28). There, too, the unlucky victims are infected through no act of their own, but merely by existing. The lead terrorist, Nile Spencer (Joel West), despises the fact that there are hundreds of languages and hundreds of religions on the planet, causing too many wars and too much destruction. Wiping the planet of most of that would be a benefit, Spencer insists, and having the cure in his possession will enable him to pick and choose whom to save.

FIGURE 28 Eco-terrorist Sasha (Rolanda Marais) infects herself with the virus, *Global Effect* (2002).

In a scene shortly after Spencer has captured the lead researcher for the Mungia virus (Mädchen Amick), the only one who has the cure, he explains to her how his plan will take effect. His words, however, could apply to any outbreak narrative. Pointing at a map of the world, Spencer says, "When you study the world, you can't help but draw parallels to the human body. See the veins? They are rivers. And people like blood cells, racing about, floating around, keep the world moving, doesn't it? 'Til the veins get poisoned, and the blood cells get weak and fail . . . Suddenly, the smallest molecule becomes the most feared." It is surely no coincidence that, in *Global Effect*, the white terrorist in Africa chooses to kill black Africans in order to cleanse the planet and that advisors to the American president repeatedly advocate blowing up all of Africa in order to protect the United States. These Americans seem to be the only ones in charge. There is never a mention of an African government that should be consulted or that Africans might have the last word on affairs in Africa. Instead, it is the *American* government that decides to quarantine Cape Town, the *American* government that decides to close African borders and airports, and the

American government that blows up Cape Town and even imagines what the map of the world would look like without Africa on it. Conrad Lee (Kirk B. R. Woller), the national security advisor, compares the outbreak to "a bodily infection." And when your toe becomes infected? "You cut it off to save your foot," he says, drawing a line through the southern tip of Africa, making the metaphor crystal clear (see figure 29). "Amputate early enough and the fear of spreading is alleviated," he continues. "That's forty million people!" is the shocked rebuttal. "Forty million to save six billion," he replies. The issue is not so much a question of mathematics, but the fact that Africa is not even consulted during the conversation. The white men (and one woman) in suits make all the decisions. The racial undertones are obvious, much as they are in many outbreak narratives.

Like in *Outbreak*, for instance, *Global Effect*'s Mungia virus begins in a remote African village, full of standing stagnant water and primitive huts, bodies of "primitive" Africans lying dead on the dirt. Also like in *Outbreak*, the American government must bomb this town in order to protect the world from contagion. Tourists, imports, and smuggling, the film tells us,

FIGURE 29 "Your toe becomes infected? You cut it off to save your foot." *Global Effect* (2002).

are the ways the virus will spread to the United States, Europe, and Asia, emphasizing that Africa is not a legitimate player in the world economy. In other words, the way the virus spreads is from tourists visiting exotic and primitive Africa, from Africa importing goods it cannot produce, and from illegal smuggling. During one of the briefings on the virus for top American political and military leaders, Spencer is described as the "new face of modern terrorism." More than that, it is that these outbreak narratives reflect the face of modern racism.

Throughout all these narratives, with the exception of the relentlessly patriotic *Madam Secretary*, there are distinct—and some more distinct than others—overtones of government and corporate conspiracy. This sense that the government either knows too much but does not do the right thing with that information or that the government is corrupt/broken/ineffective became stronger in the years following 9/11, after which many Americans were either disappointed in their government for allowing the attacks to happen or actively believed that the government had encouraged the attacks to happen.

However, the covert and untrustworthy nature of the American government was already brewing ten years earlier, as evidenced in most episodes of the Fox television show *The X-Files*. One of the longest-running science fiction shows on network television, *The X-Files* aired from 1993 to 2002 before returning with a reboot in 2016. One of the primary motifs of the television series is how many secrets the government keeps buried from the general public. For example, in the *X-Files* episode "F. Emasculata" (Fox, Apr. 28, 1995)—which tackles notions of bioterrorism, viral outbreak, pharmaceutical conspiracy, and government cover-ups—corporations working with the government are villains—specifically, pharmaceutical corporations who spread viruses intentionally for their own greedy motives. The episode follows a typical outbreak narrative arc, where we discover a deadly and unknown virus, watch as it is introduced to the general public, and then follow our heroes as they try to contain it. Of particular significance is the way the virus is spread (via mail, foreshadowing the later anthrax attacks), and the culpability of the CDC—working hand-in-glove with Pinck Pharmaceuticals, a corrupt pharmaceutical company—to bypass FDA regulations by testing new drugs on unknowing prison inmates. Mulder demands that Skinner (Mitch Pileggi) and the Cigarette Smoking Man (William B. Davis) reveal to the public what Pinck is doing, but the Smoking Man refuses, arguing that this kind of knowledge would only cause panic. And so the episode ends, leaving us with feelings of unease, a lack of resolution, and concerns about government conspiracies. As Monahan writes—about *24*, but equally applicable here—"just when the characters and viewers long for—and expect—resolution and safety; the best that can be hoped for is temporary management, containment, or postponement of the indiscriminate annihilation of civilian populations."[74] A happy and satisfying resolution is a thing of the past.

A similar plot, only this time using doctors rather than pharmaceutical companies, surfaced that same year with the NBC television movie *Formula for Death* (May 8, 1995), in which a group of doctors intentionally unleashes Ebola at select HMO hospitals in major American cities with the express purpose of making HMOs look risky.

Even before 9/11, there were feelings that neither the government nor the health industry could be trusted to protect the American people. This theme grew in popularity during the early years of the twenty-first century, as evident in the terrorist wave of the outbreak narrative. As Leger Grindon explains, in his essay "Cycles and Clusters," in order for a film cycle to remain relevant, it is common for subordinate and dominant traits to switch positions.[75] So while elements of government and military conspiracy can be seen as early as Romero's original *Crazies*, this theme moved from the realm of fringe, camp, and paranoia (à la *The X-Files*) to mainstream significance, showing up frequently even on CBS, which is known for having the most conservative viewership out of the main broadcast networks.

The idea of pharmaceutical cover-up—and the fundamental and relentless pursuit of profit—also plays a part in the *World War Z* novel (Crown, 2006), where author Max Brooks seems to provide a critique of capitalism and/or the pharmaceutical industry with his depiction of the drug Phalanx. Phalanx is a vaccine marketed as a solution to the "rabies virus" behind the zombie outbreak. Despite a lack of thorough testing, the drug is pushed to market (we also see this scenario happen in *The Hades Factor*) in order to provide the pharmaceutical company (and its investors) with significant profits and the general public with a sense of calm, even though it turns out that the drug can do nothing to prevent the zombie outbreak. Breckenridge Scott, the character behind Phalanx, justifies his ruse by explaining that, in addition to the false sense of security the drug provided, the success of the drug also brought profits to the biomed sector, jump-starting the stock market, and giving the country "the impression of recovery." The notion that a pharmaceutical company could be conspiring against us—more concerned with profit than our lives—further reinforces the threat that things (and people) that are supposedly good for us could actually kill us.

Another recent example of pharmaceutical conspiracy is *Toxic Skies*, a Canadian–American coproduction, starring Anne Heche as Tess Martin, a specialist with the Global Health Organization. She discovers that the underlying cause of an epidemic in Spokane, Washington, is reduced immunity caused by Kellor, a pharmaceutical company that is tampering with the jet fuel, adding metals to the fuel. The metals yield contaminated chemtrails that cause diminished immune response, leading to an increased dependency on the very same drugs the company is producing. Due to their reduced immunity, hospitals fill up with victims of an unknown viral strain that appears to be spread through touch and is referred to as "the plague." The outbreak, which is rapidly spreading among the immune-deficient residents of Spokane, was brought over from Malaysia by Professor Dylan Corbin, who is dead before we even get to meet him. This outbreak causes symptoms Tess has only seen in "rural Asian countries." Interestingly, this virus has many overt (although unmentioned) similarities to HIV: red spots that resemble Kaposi's sarcoma; a compromised immune system; initial symptoms are flu-like; the course of the disease can be documented with a rapidly decreasing antibody count; and the virus will not respond to any existing medications. The sick patients do not respond to conventional treatment because their antibody counts are dangerously low. As the virus spreads to other cities, it soon becomes clear that the military is affiliated with the pharmaceutical cover-up. People keep dying until rogue hero Tess Martin exposes the scheme.

Her "rogue nature" is evident early in the film, when she stands up to the mayor of Spokane (Kevin McNulty), the CEO of Kellor (Barclay Hope), and Major Stein (Tobias Slezak), all three of whom are, inexplicably, on a panel while she testifies about the outbreak. The three of them refuse to allow for the quarantine Tess requests, telling her that she will need more proof before they take her seriously. This combination of corporate America, political America, and military America thwarts Tess at every turn, despite the growing death toll. Tess even discovers that Kellor already has a vaccine for the outbreak, but the company does not want to release it because it would prove their link to the contaminated jet fuel. Nonetheless, Tess, with the assistance of rogue journalist Jack (James Tupper), does manage to obtain the vaccine and save the remaining patients. The mayor now praises her resolve, proclaiming in a press conference that "it is times like these when heroes rise to the occasion." However, his enthusiasm is empty, since the conspiracy with Kellor will not be made public, and the film ends with another pharmaceutical company being invited to work with the military, the motives and agenda questionable. When Tess asks Major Stein why Kellor would tamper with the jet fuel, the answer is "Money, Dr. Martin." In this scenario, corporate America, just like political and military America, is most concerned with the bottom line; greed is prioritized over people.

These various narratives all reflect the different ways that America, both pre- and post-9/11, feels itself to be under attack while also depicting how the forms of that attack have changed. While 9/11 may have brought fears of terrorism to the fore, temporarily alleviating our distrust in our own government, feelings of disillusionment—that the very establishments constructed to protect us are actually only looking out for their own interests—soon returned with a vengeance. Threats, both of viral outbreak and terrorist attack, could no longer be naively projected upon distant countries. Viruses—much like terrorism—now lurk next door. Internal threats are just as realistic as external ones, and our own government is as likely to let us die as the unknown Arab—or so the sound bites tell us.

The opening moments of the first episode of the ABC television show *Quantico* ("Run," Sept. 27, 2015) echo these sentiments as Miranda Shaw (Aunjanue Ellis), the assistant director of the FBI Training Division, tells the new students, "The state of this country is the most precarious it's ever been. Not only are there more threats than ever before, but the majority of those threats don't come from known organizations or extremist groups but our own backyard—a neighbor you grew up next to, a one-night stand you had, perhaps even a family member." We are under siege by enemies we cannot see.

These ideas can also be seen in the film *Contaminated Man* (Hickox, 2000), which portrays, rather than the infectious impact of other countries on America, the infectious impact of America on other countries, as well as the tragic consequences of bioweapons production. When an American company begins producing bioweapons in Hungary, Josef Muller (Peter Weller) accidentally blows up the lab (the "necessary accident" at play). Everyone else dies, but Muller manages to escape, albeit infected with a virus produced by the company. While the virus does not kill him, everyone with whom he interacts dies quickly and horrifically. As Ruth Mayer, points out, in this film, "the categories of 'foreign' and 'familiar' no longer make sense," with the United States "associated both with a contaminating influence *and* with the source of therapeutic intervention."[76] Chillingly, at one point, Muller puts a sample of his blood into a Coca Cola bottle in order to infect a water reservoir. What more American symbol is there than a bottle of Coke?

This film, like so many others, raises the question of "whether the threat from within is as great as the threat from without."[77] Ruth Mayer argues that, even though "the phobic rhetoric of othering" continues to be used with vigor, and "the blunt logic of 'us' versus 'them' is far from defunct," what remains most alarming is how difficult it can be to distinguish between self and other.[78] That which is within us may be trying to kill us. As *The Agency* episode "The Plague Year" demonstrates, a Jihadi radical might even have blue eyes and light skin. French sociologist and philosopher Jean Baudrillard observed that the events of 9/11 "brought to the fore a new, fantastical enemy and an antagonism that 'is everywhere and . . . in each of us.'"[79] Those that look like us may suddenly turn against us. It is with this in mind that Richard N. Haas, from the US Department of State, references President Bush's argument from October 2001 that "we are now engaged in . . . 'a different kind of war. It's not the kind of war that we're used to in America.'"[80] In a world where terrorists are increasingly difficult to identify, it becomes just as hard to know whom to trust as it is to know whom to fear, and the terrorist wave of the outbreak narrative reflects this.

The "internal threat" does not only come from unseen terrorist factions or from the occasional renegade patient zero. This threat, as these narratives depict over and over, can also come from the American government, the American military, and American corporations. Pharmaceutical companies, whose very purpose should be to cure us and keep us healthy, are seen to prioritize profits over patients, and the military, meant to protect us, is in on the take. The compounded impact of all these various conspiracies—terrorist, government, or corporate—results in a lack of safety in the very place where it should be resolute: our homes.

Without traditional signifiers, like meaningful geographic boundaries or race, gender, language, or cultural differences, it becomes increasingly difficult to determine who deserves suspicion. Instead, terrorism is more of a "contagion that circulates throughout society and may, theoretically, adhere to anybody (though certain bodies—brown, Arab, Muslim—remain more susceptible)."[81] This fear that the terror may come from the inside—that the evil is not only within our borders but that we cannot even identify it—is what truly keeps us up at night.

4

The Postapocalypse Outbreak

Every generation wants to be the last.
—Chuck Palahniuk, *Lullaby*

The proliferation of zombies in our dystopia is neither coincidental nor a fluke of timing.

Zombie cinema is known for exploring what the end of the world might look like, with its widespread infections, biological warfare gone haywire, uncontrollable violence, chaos, and looting, all images that resonate in a post-9/11 America. The chilling aspect is not that the world might fall apart but that it is already happening. This is a crucial component in recent zombie outbreak narratives; they depict a world that, while fantastical, still seems plausible, if not inevitable. In fact, an article in *Rolling Stone* from August 2015 was titled ominously "Apocalypse Soon: 9 Terrifying Signs of Environmental Doom and Gloom," and listed reasons—like rising sea levels, earthquake threats, and oil spills—that the world as we know it might be ending.[1] Against a real-life backdrop of economic crises, never-ending war, increasingly obvious climate change, environmental pollution, and corrupt politicians, it can often feel as if the only viable alternative is a zombie apocalypse.

Zombies have been lurking on the peripheries of American culture since the publication of William Seabrook's *The Magic Island*, a journalistic expose of Haitian voodoo culture, in 1929. Directly inspired by the book, Victor Halperin's *White Zombie* was released in 1932, bringing zombies to American movie screens. Both the book and the movie aim to ground the horror in a certain amount of plausibility and authenticity. For instance, both emphasize that the zombie is not merely a fantasy but an entity enshrined in the Penal Code of Haiti, article 249: "Also shall be qualified as an attempted murder the employment which may be made against any person of substances which, without causing actual death, produce a lethargic coma more or less prolonged. If after the administering of such substances, the person has been buried, the act shall be considered murder no matter what result follows."[2] In the film, not only was this excerpt from the penal code read out loud in its entirety by one of the characters, but it also was printed on promotional posters. The use of this terminology, as well as the adaptation of an otherwise "journalistic" text, allowed *White Zombie* to blur fact and faction in ways that would become common to outbreak narratives. As the first zombie film, *White Zombie* also goes to great lengths to make sure audiences understand what was at play. Not only do the "opening titles launch the word across the screen a letter at a time: Z-O-M-B-I-E," but one of the characters explains, "They are not men, monsieur. They are dead bodies. The living dead. Corpses taken from their graves and made to work."[3]

It took about a decade, and the onset of World War II, but other zombie films followed: *The Ghost Breakers* (Marshall, 1940), *King of the Zombies* (Yarbrough, 1941), *Revenge of the Zombies* (Sekely, 1943), *I Walked with a Zombie* (Tourneur, 1943), *Voodoo Man* (Beaudine, 1944), and *Zombies on Broadway* (Douglas, 1945). Some aimed to repeat the horror of *White Zombie*, some, like *Revenge of the Zombies*, stayed current by integrating evil Nazis with zombies—a combination that would continue to bear fruit, even recently with the Nazi Zombie game mode in various releases of the *Call of Duty* (Treyarch, 2008) videogame, starting in 2008, or with the film *Dead Snow* (Wirkola, 2009)—while others, like *The Ghost Breakers* went for parody.

After the end of World War II, however, there was a change in the representation of the zombie. The zombie was no longer "a lone figure or a gang of pitiful slaves under a single master. Instead, the zombies come in an anonymous, overwhelming mass," describes Roger Luckhurst.[4] This was a significant shift that continues to this day. Luckhurst ties this change to several key historical events. One was the discovery of the concentration camps by British and American forces, the horrifying sight of thousands of near-dead prisoners surrounded by thousands of unburied corpses. While the existence of the camps was known, this was the first time many actually saw them.[5] Primo Levi, author and Holocaust survivor, describes the "anonymous mass" he experienced at Auschwitz as "endless . . . continually renewed and always identical . . . non-men who march[ed] and labor[ed] in silence, the divine spark dead within them . . . One hesitates to call them living."[6] The second historical event that fed horrific images of near-dead (or dead) hordes into the brains of Americans came about during the Korean War. Luckhurst describes a tactic long advocated by Mao Zedong in which "thousands of barely armed infantry [were sent] to overwhelm better equipped professional armies through sheer force of numbers . . . It was even speculated that the piles of corpses mown down as they advanced were meant to demoralize the Americans, who would be disgusted by their own slaughter."[7]

Another key event that impacted American horror films was when nuclear bombs were used by the Americans on Japan in August of 1945. Luckhurst argues that "the atom bomb realized the prospect for the first time in history of a weapon with genuinely global reach. There was nowhere on the planet left to escape its deadly technological embrace . . . Fantasies of destruction—of New York or Chicago leveled within 30 minutes of a declaration of war—flooded the American imagination."[8] Suddenly, it was not just that Americans could imagine their own destruction but that they could visualize exactly how it could happen. Horror movies—such as *Godzilla* (Honda, 1954) or *Them!* (Douglas, 1954) or *The Incredible Shrinking Man* (Zugsmith, 1957)—began to integrate radiation or nuclear bombs into their plots, as well as deadly and out-of-control technology, both as an explanation for the source of the monster, as well as yet another threat. In *Teenage Zombies* (Warren, 1960), for example, a mad scientist backed by foreign agents turns kidnapped teenagers into zombies using an experimental nerve gas. In *Night of the Living Dead* (Romero, 1968), the zombies are caused by radiation from a fallen space satellite.

Inspired both by Richard Matheson's novel *I Am Legend*, published in 1954, as well as by its first filmic adaptation, *The Last Man on Earth* (Salkow and Ragona, 1964), Romero's film replicated those earlier works' dark atmosphere, the theme of isolation, and the image of an undead horde trying to get at a barricaded Robert Neville (played by Vincent Price in the film), the last remaining survivor of a worldwide epidemic. In the book, the virus—to which Neville is mysteriously immune—has turned everyone into vampires. Romero freely admits to "ripping off" Matheson, but explains that he could not use vampires, since Matheson had already done so: "I wanted something that would be an earth-shaking change. Something that was forever, something that was really at the heart of it. I said, so what if the dead stop staying dead? . . . And the stories are about how people respond or fail to respond to this. That's really all [the zombies] ever represented to me."[9] Other than that, Romero stuck close to Matheson's work, replicating the claustrophobia and helplessness of being trapped in a house, surrounded by monsters who want you dead.

Despite the fact that Romero's film was initially met with outrage and disgust—largely because it was inadvertently screened to young children, audiences not knowing what to expect—*Night of the Living Dead* went on to earn twelve million dollars at the American box office, as well as eighteen million dollars internationally.[10] In 2017, that translates to a worldwide box office gross of approximately $213,000,000. Zombies were in the zeitgeist, bigger and badder than ever. Romero went on to make *The Crazies* (1973), about the accidental release of a military biological weapon on a small American town. The inhabitants are forced to contend not only with those driven crazy by the weapon but also the military, which is trying to contain and conceal the outbreak by killing off residents—establishing tropes of military and government conspiracy and malfeasance that have resurfaced in countless outbreak narratives. In 1978, he released *Dawn of the Dead* (1978), cowritten with notorious Italian horror director Dario Argento. Far larger in scope, it portrayed an America decimated by zombies, with most cities totally overrun.

The 1980s featured not only Romero's next zombie feature—*Day of the Dead* (1985), a depiction of a world overrun with zombies—but more zombie movies than any previous decade.[11] However, many of these were cheaply and quickly made—such as *Bloodsuckers from Outer Space* (Coburn, 1984), *I Was a Teenage Zombie* (Michalakis, 1987), and *Beverly Hills Bodysnatchers* (Mostow, 1989). It was only in 1996, with Capcom's release of the video game *Resident Evil* (1996), that zombies finally became a big-budget affair and that the latest wave of the outbreak narrative was launched. Fittingly, Romero's zombie films were a key inspiration for the game, which also drew on the plot of *The Crazies*.[12] Originally called *Baiohazādo*, which translates literally to "Biohazard," more than twenty different versions of the game have since been released, as well as comic books, novels, and action figures (six films, seven novels, twenty-three games, and two CGI films, just for starters). The highest-grossing film series based on video games of all time, the combined box office gross of all the films is $1.233 billion worldwide.[13]

So far, the twenty-first century has been full of horror films—remakes, reboots, and originals—and the preoccupation with zombies and the apocalypse now fills both television and movie screens. To say the last two decades have mainstreamed zombies is an understatement. In 2005, Steven Wells from the *Guardian* exclaimed that "there were zombies everywhere," while the *New York Times* declared a "zombie literary invasion" in 2006.[14] The invasion continued, with more than forty-one films listed for 2008 alone, and the debut of the most popular basic cable drama of all time—*The Walking Dead*, AMC's contribution to the zombie canon—in 2010. The Internet Movie Database (IMDb) has a list of the fifty most popular zombie films from 2015. Focusing only on the "most popular," the list is not exhaustive, implying that there were many from which to choose.[15] There are now too many to count.

As these various narratives demonstrate, we have become increasingly fond of zombies and the postapocalyptic narrative. A term that sounds inherently contradictory, James Berger argues that the term apocalypse can mean a literal end to everything, but it can also refer to catastrophes that function as "definitive historical divides, as ruptures, pivots, fulcrums, separating what came before from what came after."[16] It is in this respect that I use the term "postapocalypse" to describe the latest and most popular incarnation of the outbreak narrative. Movies like the *Dawn of the Dead* remake (Snyder, 2004) and *I Am Legend* (Lawrence, 2007), the most recent filmic adaptation of Neville's book, as well as television shows like *The Walking Dead* (AMC, 2010–present), *Fear the Walking Dead* (AMC, 2015–present) and *The Last Man on Earth* (Fox, 2015–present), play into our fascination with the idea of a postapocalyptic world devoid of humans, governments, and technology, forcing survivors to adopt a ruthless neoliberal ethos. These narratives look at what happens *after* an unstopped infection, *after* social order has broken down, *after* cities have been devastated and deserted. They play on the tension of what might be possible, preparing us for what may occur in a way that our families and our governments do not.

Zombie narratives, by their very conventions, speak to present-day America precisely because of how well they capture what feels like an eventual future (if not the actual present). Kyle William Bishop argues that "the aftereffects of war, terrorism, and natural disasters so closely resemble the scenarios depicted by zombie cinema . . . Scenes depicting deserted metropolitan streets, abandoned human corpses, and gangs of lawless vigilantes have become more common than ever, appearing on the nightly news as often as on the movie screen."[17] Zombie narratives play out the dystopia that already seems to be occurring. The empty streets, the packs of zombies, and the fetishization of guns, in particular, have now become tropes for a twenty-first century where war and the need for security feel just as ubiquitous as the threat of socioeconomic collapse and environmental crisis.

Another reason contemporary zombie narratives speak to present-day America has to do with their portrayals of networks with indeterminable centralized figures, with their emphasis on diminishing individuality and diminishing individual agency, and with their fusion of disease with fears of a terrorist attack. Even though the world was overrun with zombies in *Day of the Dead*, *World War Z* (Forster, 2013) is generally considered to be the first global zombie narrative because of its depiction of a worldwide fight to stop the outbreak. In the film, Gerry Lane (Brad Pitt) flies from New York to South Korea to Israel to Wales to Nova Scotia. The original book, *World War Z: An Oral History of the Zombie War*, written by Max Brooks and published in 2006, was a critical and commercial success, selling more than one million copies by November 2011. The film adaptation is the most expensive zombie movie to date, with a production budget of $200 million and a worldwide box office of $540 million.

However, the impact of globalization and a networked world could already be seen in the earlier *Resident Evil* franchise. The narrative arc of the franchise revolves around the global health industry, with a stronger emphasis on bioterror following 9/11. The central plot depicts a set of characters and their battle with zombies, caused as a result of exposure to the t-Virus, created by the Umbrella Corporation. The original *Resident Evil* film opens with a description of how the Umbrella Corporation has become the largest commercial entity in the United States: "Nine out of every ten homes contain its products. Its political and financial influence is felt everywhere. In public, it is the world's leading supplier of computer technology, medical products, and health care. Unknown, even to its own employees, its massive profits are generated by military technology, genetic experimentation, and viral weaponry." This prologue already establishes a global capitalistic world where one "umbrella-like" company impacts almost every aspect of contemporary life, hearkening to Galloway and Thacker's description of a world where the "networks of FedEx or AT&T can be seen as more important than that of the United States."[18] While the first film and the sequel, *Resident Evil: Apocalypse* (Witt, 2004), both take place in Raccoon City, by the third film, *Resident Evil: Extinction* (Mulcahy, 2007), the destruction has gone global. In fact, one of the tag lines for the fifth film, *Resident Evil: Retribution* (2012, Anderson), is "When Evil Goes Global." Not only does the series reflect fears of overly powerful corporations using overly powerful technology and biowarfare to have their way, but it also demonstrates the way infected individuals are reduced to "animalistic, subhuman threats."[19] After all, the dehumanized are disposable, and the disposable are dehumanized.

Yet another reason for the zombie's increased contemporary resonance also has much to do with its lack of centralized agency and control. In early Haitian incarnations of the zombie figure, as seen in *White Zombie*, a voodoo master controls and creates the early zombies. Similarly, Dracula is known for his ability to exert mind control over his victims. In contrast, the modern zombie terrifies because "no singular agent acts to possess the victim's mind."[20] The zombie's individuality and mind are both blank, replaced only with an insatiable appetite. Modern zombies drift aimlessly and mindlessly, driven only by their search of food, an appropriate shift considering that decentralized networks have become "the most common diagram of the modern era."[21]

The lack of centralized agency in an era of networked and global capitalism also results in a loss of individuality. Stephanie Boluk and Wylie Lenz, coeditors of *Generation Zombie: Essays on the Living Dead in Modern Culture*, argue that, in an era of cloud computing, bots, and avatars, the possibilities for agency and individuality are "ever more restricted," our subjectivity limited to "various network protocols of control."[22] Zombies embody fears of no longer being discrete entities (as people or countries), of losing freedom, identity, and agency. After all, the zombie is, as Marina Warner describes, "a body which has been hollowed out, emptied of selfhood."[23] Unlike Frankenstein or Dracula, zombies are stripped of their personal identity, losing their individuality as well as their connections to others. While vampires and werewolves can be seen as representing attractive states of being—primal, sexual, emotional, intense, and charismatic—becoming hyperbolic versions of themselves, zombies become empty versions, with no identity or consciousness. Zombies are fueled by a desire to consume vacantly, eating their way to the end of civilization, infecting us with their emptiness.[24] Zombies are us, hollowed out. They emphasize what we can become when only a body is left.

An additional reason for the zombie's contemporary resonance is that the zombie, especially in its current incarnation, fuses current fears of disease with fears of terrorism. In his book *Post-9/11 Horror*, Kevin J. Wetmore observes that, since their minds are blank, "zombies cannot be reasoned with, they seek only to replicate themselves, to contaminate, which also makes them an excellent metaphor for terrorists."[25] The zombie, after all, is the terrorist who infects, an embodiment of *both* terrorism and infection. The zombie is also the *obvious* terrorist—refreshingly easy to identify and kill. There is no ambiguity about who the zombie is or whether it is acceptable to attack it. In fact, hesitation to do so could be deadly. Nick Muntean and Matthew Thomas Payne, in their essay "Attack of the Livid Dead: Recalibrating Terror in the Post–September 11 Zombie Film," take the terrorist argument further, comparing zombies to "domestic terrorists within one's own private and public borders . . . Like the 'sleeper-cell' terrorist, the zombie can potentially be anyone at any time."[26]

For example, the title sequence for the *Dawn of the Dead* remake begins with a shot of a temple-like room packed with praying Muslim men. The sequence ends with a reporter on a balcony in what looks to be Turkey, the Hagia Sophia in the distance. While he is giving his report, the camera swings to the side, showing us a pack of zombies invading the room. The final shot of the title sequence is of a seemingly Middle Eastern zombie attacking the camera. Even if the outbreak is global, it still seems to be centered—inexplicably—in the Middle East. This is an interesting shift from traditional outbreak narratives, which blame the origin of the virus on Africa or Asia. It is not just that the zombie–terrorist connection is made literal during this title sequence but that the terrorist–Middle Eastern connection is made literal as well.

Another connection between zombies and terrorists is that, at least until they turn, they are ordinary people. Like the sleeper-cell terrorist, the zombie can also be *anywhere* at any time. The horror of the zombie ravaging "picture perfect suburbia" is portrayed within the first few minutes

FIGURE 30 Monsters show up in the most unexpected places, *Dawn of the Dead* (2004).

of the *Dawn of the Dead* remake. The film begins with Ana (Sarah Polley) heading home to her boyfriend and her manicured-to-within-an-inch-of -its-life suburban neighborhood. This suburban neighborhood, however, is soon overrun with zombies, tearing it and its residents apart. The first zombie we see is the sweet little blonde girl from next door (Hannah Lochner), the least threatening figure we could imagine (see figure 30), and the first place we get a zombie attack is in the suburban bedroom, one of the most private and supposedly "safe" of all spaces. Director Zack Snyder uses this juxtaposition for maximum impact. The fact that this little blonde girl is the first zombie we see makes the experience all the more jarring, and interestingly, the first zombie we see on *The Walking Dead* is also a small blonde girl. There is something doubly horrifying about being attacked by what should be the most angelic and least threatening of creatures, and it is even worse that it happens in what should be the least threatening of environments. When Ana flees, we see that her perfect neighborhood has become a war zone (see figure 31). A neighbor in a bathrobe points a gun at her, and seconds later, an ambulance runs him over; surrounding houses go up in smoke; helicopters dot the horizon. People on a bus are eaten alive while Ana takes off in her white Toyota Corolla. This is not what should happen in Small Town, USA. The mundane meets the monstrous. The terror literally hits home.

Another reason for the increasing popularity of narratives that visualize humanity's demise has nothing to do with fear at all. We are genuinely curious to see what the end of the world will look like, to imagine how quickly social order will deteriorate and what will cause it to happen. As Robert Kirkman, creator of *The Walking Dead* comic and television show,

FIGURE 31 The terror hits home, *Dawn of the Dead* (2004).

puts it, "Apocalyptic storytelling is appealing when people have apocalyptic thoughts. With the global economic problems and everything else, a lot of people feel we're heading into dark times. As bad as it is for society, I'm benefiting greatly."[27] When confronted with the question of how the world may likely end, a pandemic continues to feel like a legitimate possibility in the current climate, or so politicians, journalists, and Hollywood continue to emphasize. As the title communicates, twenty-eight days is all it takes for social order to collapse in *28 Days Later* (Boyle, 2002). Selena (Naomie Harris) describes the process in detail:

> It started as rioting. But right from the beginning you knew this was different. Because it was happening in small villages, market towns. And then it wasn't on the TV any more. It was in the street outside. It was coming through your windows. It was a virus, an infection. You didn't need a doctor to tell you that. It was the blood. Or something in the blood. By the time they tried to evacuate the cities, it was already too late. The infection was everywhere. The army blockades were overrun. And that's when the exodus started. The day before the TV and radio stopped broadcasting there were reports of infection in Paris and New York. You didn't hear anything more after that.

After she recounts the chain of events for Jim (Cillian Murphy), who has been in a coma, he asks her about the government. "What are they doing?" he wants to know. Selena tells him there is no government. Jim replies that this is impossible. "Of course there's a government. There's always a government. They're in a bunker or a plane." Mark (Noah Huntley) shakes his head. "No, there's no government, no police, no army. No TV, no radio, no electricity." Twenty-eight days was all it took for everything to fall apart (see figure 32).

Ironically, many of the films discussed in this chapter were shot during or immediately following real-life outbreaks, or had their release date postponed due to a real-life outbreak—or both. For instance, while *28 Days Later* was in production, there was an outbreak of foot-and-mouth disease in England. Affecting mainly hoofed animals, like sheep, cows, and pigs, it was discovered in February 2001 in Essex but quickly spread across the country. The highly infectious disease "plunged the agricultural industry into its worst crisis for decades," and government contingency plans (which were based on a maximum of only ten affected farms) were woefully underprepared.

The film's American release also coincided with the SARS (Severe Acute Respiratory Syndrome) epidemic in 2003. SARS initially surfaced in November 2002, in the Guangdong province of China, near Hong Kong. The WHO issued a global alert on March 12, 2003, declaring Hong Kong "a city under siege," with overrun hospitals, quarantined apartment complexes, and deserted "restaurants and bars in one of the most crowded cities in the world."[28] Many Hong Kong residents wore masks, and public service announcements reminded people to bow rather than shake hands, to wash properly, and to be aware of contagion. SARS quickly spread around the world, hitching rides on travelers who left Hong Kong, intensifying fears already exacerbated by the recent memories of 9/11 and by initial suspicions that bioterrorism might be to blame. The remake of *Dawn of the Dead* was shot during this SARS outbreak. Originally planned for an October 2003 release, the release of *Resident Evil: Apocalypse* was delayed almost a year, to September 2004, due to the same SARS outbreak.

These real-life outbreaks had to have impacted the production of these films, however implicitly, as well as serving as organic promotion for the films' releases. Hollywood may have been responding to the zeitgeist by greenlighting these pictures, but the seemingly constant series of real-life outbreaks only confirmed the public's fears and the films' box office potential. Snyder, director of the *Dawn of the Dead* remake, said he could not help but notice the parallels between his film—which portrays the fear and uncertainty that would be likely to occur during a viral outbreak—and news media reports on the SARS outbreak, "as both were fraught with panic and misinformation."[29]

FIGURE 32 *28 Days Later* (2002) movie poster.

Offscreen, zombies may not be roaming the streets, and social order may still (somewhat) exist, but the world knows what it is like to have continuous war, threats of terrorism, random shootings, and police violence. It is not merely that war has become a constant in the distant Middle East but that war has invaded domestic territories as well. Both zombies and terrorists hit close to home rather than on distant battlefields, ignoring any "rules" or "protocols" of war. This constant fear of attack has translated into a fear of primitive, irrational humans hell-bent on destroying humanity (in real life) and primitive, irrational zombies hell-bent on destroying humanity (on-screen). Steven Pokornowski acknowledges in his essay "Burying the Living with the Dead: Security, Survival and the Sanction of Violence," that the "same generation of people who grew up playing 'survival horror' video games like the transmedia *Resident Evil* franchise is now, in the adult world, faced with the implication that everyday life is like survival horror: we must be prepared, we must be secure."[30] Zombies have become a celluloid substitute for terrorists, and postapocalyptic narratives a hyperbolized reaction to everyday fears.

While the classic outbreak narrative template, as seen in *Outbreak* (Petersen, 1995) or *Contagion* (Soderbergh, 2011), may most closely resemble the science fiction genre, the postapocalyptic outbreak narrative fuses the science fiction element of plausibility with the horrors of a world gone mad, combining the outbreak narrative's proclivity for viral infection with our fetish for postapocalyptic visions. Unlike the original Haitian voodoo zombie, who could only be created by a nonzombie, and unlike the zombie incarnation of the 1950s, where the zombie outbreak would often be blamed on radiation, the contemporary zombie, as seen in the narratives I discuss in this chapter, is frequently created via infection. Columnist Ezra Klein writes for the *Washington Post* that if "werewolves represent our fear of the wild, aliens our fear of the unknown and vampires our fear of sex, zombies represent our fear of infectious disease."[31]

This evolution of fear can be traced through the various adaptations of Richard Matheson's novel *I Am Legend*, published in 1954. The original book blames the initial outbreak on mosquitos spawned by dust storms caused by weapons used in a massive war—appropriate for its time of publication, several years after World War II and one year after the end of the Korean War. The pandemic turned ordinary humans into vampires. While its first filmic adaptation, *The Last Man on Earth* (Ragona and Salkow, 1964), remained fairly faithful to the book, in *The Omega Man* (Sagal,

1971), released during the Cold War, the cause of the zombies is a bio-weapon bomb and, specifically, biological warfare between China and Russia. Significantly, in *I Am Legend*, released in 2007, the cause comes from scientific alterations of existing viruses, and the result is a curious mix of both vampire and zombie. Limited to nighttime exposure due to an aversion to sunlight, the nameless/faceless quality of the horde still has more in common with zombies than vampires. Each time, the outbreak reflects anxieties relevant to that specific time period. While *I Am Legend* is the latest filmic adaptation, the Fox television network debuted a television show in 2015 inspired by the book's fundamental premise. Its title is *The Last Man on Earth*, a nod to the 1964 film. In this latest case, the world's population is still wiped out by a virus (with the exception of a handful of survivors), and there is no specific explanation or causality beyond "the virus." Our fears have grown so abstract that specifics are no longer needed. The end of the world feels inevitable, even without a medical diagnosis.

These fears have trickled their way into the current popularity of American zombie and apocalyptic narratives. Wetmore argues that genres like drama and action "fail to present 9/11 in a manner that captures the experience and the understanding of that experience."[32] Instead, the fears and shock of 9/11 are best co-opted by the science fiction and horror genres. Cultural theorist Douglas Kellner writes that it is a fusion of science fiction and horror, in particular, that most accurately depicts the "allegories of disaster and visions of social catastrophe" that emerged during the Bush-Cheney era.[33] In turn, it has been science fiction and horror—in the form of the postapocalyptic outbreak narrative—that have continued to depict our visions of social catastrophe in the years since. Additionally, Susan Sontag suggests, in her essay "The Imagination of Disaster," that by grouping science fiction and horror movies together as modes of disaster film, the complicity with the abhorrent is shared, even if only to neutralize it.[34] So it is not just that these narratives depict the experience but that they help us cope with it, making it seem more manageable.

It is not as simple as blaming 9/11 and terrorism for this shift, however. The years following 9/11 have included a variety of other catastrophes, both terrorist and natural, exacerbating a sense of vulnerability and fatalism. These have ranged from the anthrax attack of 2001 to Hurricane Katrina in 2005, the economic meltdown of 2008 to the Gulf oil spill in 2010, the seemingly endless wars in Iraq, Afghanistan, and Syria, to the devastating earthquakes in Chile, New Zealand, Japan, and Haiti. Max Brooks, writer of *World War Z* and *The Zombie Survival Guide: Complete Protection from the Living Dead* (Three Rivers Press, 2003) and, explains, "Since 2001, people have been scared. There's been some really scary stuff that's been happening . . . I think people really feel like the system's breaking down . . . It's neighbors knifing each other for food, women being raped, the cops not showing up, children dying of starvation, an old lady dying in a wheelchair."[35]

Viruses are our current fear, the way the world now seems most likely to end. For example, in "Splinter" (Jan. 16, 2015), the first episode of Syfy's *12 Monkeys* (2015–present), Dr. Cassandra Reilly (Amanda Schull) outlines a brief history of great epidemics in order to support her argument that it is only a matter of time until we have to confront the next one: "It's never been about 'if.' It's always been *when*," she declares. Terry Matalas, creator and executive producer of the show, explains the appeal of viruses: "You get on a plane and somebody sneezes, and you think, am I going to get that? Every year, the flu seems to be more aggressive. It's the next step in science gone awry. For a while, the threat was always about a nuke. And now it's about viruses. In a way, it's about absolute destruction."[36] Or, as journalist Andy Coghlan concludes in *New Scientist Magazine*, infectious diseases are "the new paranoia that's striking Western society."[37]

While this fusion of zombies with viruses establishes a new wave in the outbreak narrative cycle, the unity is not unprecedented, on- or offscreen. On-screen, in *White Zombie*, Bela Lugosi plays Murder Legendre, a voodoo master who turns his victims into zombies via potions that are little more than primitive pharmaceuticals. Pokornowski, in his article "Insecure Lives: Zombies, Global Health, and the Totalitarianism of Generalization," recounts a scene from the film in which Legendre describes zombification as a "curious medical experiment."[38]

Offscreen, zombies and viruses have even more commonality. Historically, during the early years of the HIV crisis, many believed that Haiti was the source for AIDS. The *Journal of the American Medical Association* even speculated, under the headline "Night of the Living Dead," that HIV might be "spread by Voodoo rituals using human blood."[39] Less fantastically, there are also biological justifications for the fusion of viruses with zombies. Molecular biology professor Luis P. Villarreal, in an article for *Scientific American*, observes that viruses occupy a netherworld between life and nonlife, allowing them to pull off some remarkable feats that may sound familiar to zombie aficionados. Villarreal writes, "Although viruses ordinarily replicate only in living cells, they also have the capacity to multiply, or 'grow,' in dead cells and even to bring them back to life. Amazingly, some viruses can even spring back to their 'borrowed life' after being destroyed . . . Viruses are the only known biological entity with this kind of 'phoenix phenotype'—the capacity to rise from their own ashes."[40] Similarly, Wendell Stanley, a Nobel Prize–winning virologist, describes viruses as "neither living nor dead," placing them in "the twilight zone between the living and the nonliving."[41] Much as it seems inevitable that viruses and terrorism would come together in the second wave of the outbreak narrative, it also seems inevitable that zombies would permeate the third wave of the outbreak narrative, embodying, as they do, the virus writ large.

Linking the zombie condition to a specific scientific or biological cause, as many of these recent narratives do, further reinforces the connection between science and zombies. The specificity of the connection also emphasizes anxieties about microbiological health interventions, as well as about the dissemination of pharmaceuticals without proper vetting and research. In *Resident Evil*, for example, the zombies are a result of the Umbrella Corporation's t-Virus. Danny Boyle, director of *28 Days Later*, describes his film as "a warning for us as well as entertainment."[42] In *28 Days Later*, it is the Rage Virus—a manufactured virus similar to rabies, somehow caused or triggered by televised images of violence that monkeys are forced to watch—that causes the zombie outbreak. In *Resident Evil: Extinction* (Mulcahy, 2007), Dr. Sam Isaacs (Iain Glenn), the head of Umbrella Corporation's science division, creates the zombie in his laboratory, defying regulations and accidentally turning himself into a monster in the process. In *I Am Legend*, the Krippin Virus—a manufactured virus based on measles—produces the zombies. In the novel *World War Z*, the vaccine for the zombifying "rabies virus" is pushed to market too soon. Robert Rodriguez's *Planet Terror* (2007) also ascribes a scientific cause to the zombie outbreak. When one of the first men to catch the "zombie virus" goes to a hospital, the doctor (Josh Brolin) originally describes the symptoms as "chronic viral lesions" in advanced stages of gangrene and containing epidermal rot, with a "black abscessed tongue," all of which reshape the zombie as literally diseased and infected (see figure 33). As the doctor reports to his patient, "What I'm seeing here is a deep impact wound with several virals and secondary bacterials and that, by the accumulation of denuded tissue around the incision marks, indicates that you've had this bite for over fourteen days." The zombies in *Zombieland* (Fleischer, 2009) are the result

FIGURE 33 "Black abscessed tongue," *Planet Terror* (2007).

of a mutated strain of mad cow disease that became "mad zombie disease." While there is no specific virus in *The Walking Dead*, in season 1, episode 6 of AMC's *The Walking Dead* ("TS-19," Dec. 10, 2010), Dr. Edwin Jenner (Noah Emmerich) documents how the walkers came to be using the words "microbial," "parasitic," and "fungal," ascribing biological qualities to the walkers and their "infection." He explains that the virus "invades the brain like meningitis." Even Richard Preston, author of *The Hot Zone: A Terrifying True Story* (Anchor Books, 1994), describes Ebola as triggering "zombie-like behavior."[43]

The CW television show *iZombie* (2015–present) dramatically rethinks the zombie paradigm. Not only does it envision how zombies would manifest in everyday life, without the requisite apocalypse, but it also subverts the antiquated gender politics common to the genre by providing viewers with a female zombie protagonist, Olivia Moore (Rose McIver). Moore, through whose eyes the story is told, absorbs personality traits and memories belonging to the brains she eats, from frat boy to alcoholic, stripper to housewife. And yet, despite this reinvention of the template, *iZombie* digs even deeper into the contemporary zombie text's reliance on the trope of infection, portraying "zombie-ness" (also referred to on the show as "zombie-ism" and "the big z") as a chronic contagious illness with many similarities to HIV. For instance, there is much conversation on the show about how to have sex without spreading the zombie virus. Olivia insists that even people with HIV have sex without infecting their partners, while

Ravi Chakrabarti (Rahul Kohli), her boss and the medical examiner, insists that condoms will not protect against the transmission of the zombie virus because it is "a hundredth the size of a typical virus." ("Max Wager," Nov. 10, 2015). Rob Thomas, cocreator and executive producer of the show, explains that another aspect of HIV that is important to the show is "the sense that it's a condition in which people suffering from it wouldn't want to tell anyone. Zombies are very much in the closet." Thomas also addresses the fact that the zombie virus is worse than HIV in the sense that condoms cannot stop it from spreading: "We chose to go this route because we wanted to be able to create a tragic scenario where the couple at the base of the show couldn't be together, or at least they couldn't be together on a sexual level."[44] Contagion fosters isolation.

Both infected and infectious, these new zombies are modern-day lepers, hyperbolic manifestations of the real-life viruses that lurk behind the television set or off the movie screen. Some, as in *iZombie*, avoid infecting others, while most zombies only know how to feed and infect. Fascinatingly, the trope of the infected carrier willfully and sadistically spreading disease actually played out in the early days of the AIDS epidemic. In her book *Bodies: Sex, Violence, Disease, and Death in Contemporary Legend*, Gillian Bennett repeats a real-life tale from Bielsko, Poland: "There is a huge concentration of infected people here. They are terribly aggressive . . . It is like a vacationland that attracts infected visitors, and the city becomes really dangerous. Last year they supposedly became so aggressive that they were going after people with their needles, especially children." Bennett also recounts stories of HIV-infected gays on both sides of the Atlantic "who were deliberately spreading (or threatening to spread) the virus among the straight as well as gay population."[45] The most terrifying part of this kind of willful infection is that, in real life, the carrier most likely looks healthy. Like viral contagion, zombies contaminate—if not destroy—what they encounter, but unlike viral contagion, you can see them coming.

And they are coming faster. Viral infection typically creates fast zombies. Infection results in a state of superanimation as if, media scholar Gwyneth Peaty writes, they are "infected with life, as much as with death."[46] In contrast, in the original *Night of the Living Dead*, a journalist asks, "Are they slow-moving, chief?" The cop answers, "Yeah. They're dead." Even in the 1990 remake of *Night of the Living Dead* (Savini), the heroine describes the horde of zombies as "so slow" that "we could just walk right past them. I wouldn't even have to run." Now, however, zombies are "a bunch of high-strung car chasers."[47] For example the first rule of survival in *Zombieland* is cardio: "When the virus struck, for obvious reasons, the first ones to go were the fatties." This rule is told to viewers via voice-over as a zombie sprints across a football field after an overweight victim who is barely able to breathe, much less run. Modern zombies move so quickly, in fact, that some traditionalists argue they are too fast to be zombies.[48]

Not only do these modern zombies move quickly, but they transform quickly as well. They can become the living dead without being dead at all. For example, in *World War Z*, the time between being bitten and becoming a zombie is fewer than fifteen seconds. As Dawn Keetley argues in the introduction to her book, *We're All Infected: Essays on AMC's "The Walking Dead" and the Fate of the Human*, the infected "simply don't have time to die."[49] The increased speed of contemporary zombies reflects the increased speed of the twenty-first century, where everything seems to happen at an accelerated speed. Or, as Commander Tom Chandler (Eric Dane) observes in *The Last Ship* episode "It's Not a Rumor" (TNT, June 28, 2015), "Everything moves a lot faster in the apocalypse."

Speed is not the only defining characteristic of the contemporary zombie narrative. Guns also permeate every aspect, much as they appear to be an inescapable part of contemporary America. This obsession with guns reflects American's unrelenting emphasis on security and protection, and the fact that, in whatever society the characters build, these factors must come first.[50] In zombie narratives, there is inevitably a hyperbolization of physical structures: building walls, fortifying existing walls, and barricading windows. In fact, quite literally, the central characters take shelter in the West Georgia Correctional Facility during season 3 of *The Walking Dead*. Unlike the Mad Max movies, where the battlements are used to preserve resources, in zombie narratives there is a constant emphasis on the need to barricade, to isolate and protect in order to keep others at bay. This arguably reflects our anxiety over our inability to contain things. We cannot contain within the media body or within the physical body. Boundaries are increasingly porous, and zombies, like terrorists, do not respect the rules of containment.

In spite of their fetishization of guns, however, zombie narratives are not patriotic odes to government supremacy, military power, or "the establishment." Quite the contrary. Not only has the zombie narrative evolved from reflecting fears of the Cold War and potential nuclear disaster to more contemporary fears of viral outbreak and the ensuing social breakdown, but it also echoes concerns about overly strong and opportunistic governments, an out-of-control military, as well as the increasingly dominant realms of science and technology. For instance, when Steven Kane and Hank Steinberg adapted William Brinkley's novel *The Last Ship* for their television show of the same name (TNT, 2014–present), they were drawn to "the concept of a lone war ship surviving a global catastrophe." However, they discarded the "cold war aspects of the book, trading a nuclear holocaust for a global pandemic."[51] And one result of this global pandemic was out-of-control authority, politicians and criminals using the situation for their own personal gain. Even while it fetishizes guns, *The Walking Dead* does not celebrate the constant need for violence but, rather, asks at what cost it comes. *28 Days Later* questions the dangers of science and technology. *World War Z* questions the repercussions of too much fighting and too many wars. *Resident Evil* questions what happens when corporations have unlimited monopolies and no oversight. *I Am Legend* questions the repercussions of playing God. Each of these stories is cautionary, if not outwardly critical. Each of these narratives emphasizes the direct culpability our civilization plays in its own demise.

For example, the Syfy network show *12 Monkeys* uses a time travel device to jump back and forth between the apocalyptic future and a dangerous present in order to try to stop the outbreak that will wipe out humanity. Similar to the movie on which it is loosely based, James Cole (Bruce Willis in the film, Aaron Stanford in the show), is sent back in time to the "present" to stop the plague from happening. Season 1 executive producer Natalie Chaidez explains that the significance of the time travel element speaks to a yearning to being able to go back in time to fix our problems: "It's the sense of the world being in jeopardy and that we long to be able to go back to a time [where we could fix it]. If we could just go back and fix it, if we could just go back and stop global warming, if we could just go back and stop any of the threads that we see leading to the threats that we have now, I think people long for that idea."[52] This revisits the issue of blame that I discussed in chapter 1, and the notion that we know our culpability in our own destruction. It is also a commentary on our failure as a society to look to the long term, our preference for short-term fixes, and the pessimistic certainty that—without a magical twist—the world is doomed.

Civilization is also culpable in its own downfall in *World War Z*. The book, in particular, emphasizes that those in power ignored initial warnings about the zombie threat, just one of many government mistakes in a world full of greed, arrogance, and ignorance. The American military had also been weakened by too much fighting, by endless wars on drugs and terror, and as such, Travis D'Ambrosia, the supreme allied commander, recounts in the book, "no amount of incentives could fill our depleted ranks, no payment bonuses or term reductions, or online recruiting tools . . . This generation had had enough, and that's why when the undead began to devour our country, we were almost too weak and vulnerable to stop them."[53]

In stark contrast to the pro-America, promilitary narratives so common after 9/11, the military—and authority figures in general—are often portrayed as dangerous and/or out of control in the postapocalypse outbreak narrative. For example, as in *28 Days Later*, the primary villains in *Planet Terror* are not zombies but military thugs.[54] In *The Walking Dead*, the real threat may have become other humans, but we also see at the beginning of episode "TS-19" (AMC, Dec. 5, 2010), in a flashback to the initial outbreak, military personnel shooting doctors, nurses, patients—anyone in the hospital. The evil antagonist in seasons 3 and 4 of *The Walking Dead*, known as "The Governor" (David Morrissey) is much more threatening than any zombie. He rules the town of Woodbury with sadistic brutality, killing anyone he deems a potential threat. Even Rick (Andrew Lincoln), the protagonist, declares at the end of *The Walking Dead* season 2 finale ("Beside the Dying Fire," Mar. 18, 2012) that "this isn't a democracy anymore." Negan (Jeffrey Dean Morgan) becomes the new evil antagonist in seasons 6 and 7. As the leader of a group of survivors called "The Saviors," Negan is ruthless and cruel, maintaining his control through vicious methods, forcing local communities to give him supplies with the threat of death, and eventually taking over Rick's group. Similarly, even though it is done in a comedic fashion, in *The Last Man on Earth* (FX, 2015–present), Phil (Will Forte) appoints himself president via a rigged election. He uses his self-appointed title as a way to justify various efforts to maintain order in the new society, including almost murdering two of the other characters. These types of situations propel conflicts between self-interest and public interest, between short- and long-term needs, between democratic action and authoritarianism. When survival is at stake, there is no time for negotiation, and yet absolute power can still corrupt absolutely.

When military figures and authority are not presented as dangerous or corrupt, it is because they do not appear at all—or because they are totally useless. The uselessness of the CDC—a representative of the government in that it is a federal agency under the Department of Health and Human Services—is also emphasized in the title sequence for the *Dawn of the Dead* remake. Interspersed with rapidly edited shots of burning buildings, stampeding mobs, masked military personnel, and animations of cells spreading, there is a CDC press conference where the repeated answer is "We don't know." ("Is it a virus?" "We don't know." "How does it spread? Is it airborne?" "That is a possibility. We don't know." "Is this a health hazard or a military threat?" "Both." "Are these people alive or dead?" "We don't know.") This sequence is significant for its fusion of health hazard and military threat (after all, a zombie is emphatically *both*) and its depiction of a CDC and a government that is unable to help.

At the end of season 1 of *The Walking Dead*, the lead characters finally reach their destination, the Atlanta offices of the CDC, in episode "TS-19" (AMC, Dec. 5, 2010). They assume that the CDC will have answers and will be able to provide assistance and protection. The first shocking realization, upon arrival, is that the entire agency is deserted. Dr. Jenner is the only scientist left, and his response to their arrival is a curt: "Why are you here? What do you want?" There is no offer of welcome or assistance. Instead, the CDC is little more than a fortress. Ironically, as the door closes and the group rushes inside, a map of the world is displayed on the wall in front of them behind the CDC logo. This proves an unsettling reminder of how an organization once driven to disseminate information and assistance globally has become little more than a deserted, useless, and isolated prison.

The second shocking realization is that Dr. Jenner, as the CDC's sole representative, has no explanation for the zombie outbreak. Jenner plays out our nightmare that, when the big outbreak hits, the CDC will not be able to stop it or even know what to stop. "I did the best I could in the time I had," he says, defeated and defensive. Not only is the CDC unable to help, but the characters survive *in spite* of the CDC—the building that is supposed to protect them almost kills them.

Jenner introduces the characters to Vi, the CDC's supercomputer that controls the building's systems and functions. Vi activates high-impulse thermobaric fuel-air explosives to destroy the building and everything inside it following a power outage, ensuring that no infectious diseases can escape the facility. This is referred to as a "full decontamination." In a sequence that appears to be a clear reference to the original *Andromeda Strain* (Wise, 1971), the clock ticks downward as the team is trapped, locked in by Jenner and unable to halt the inevitable technologically induced and controlled decontamination.

In the *Andromeda Strain*, the virus causes the lab's seals to deteriorate, which activates the nuclear self-destruct countdown. Dr. Mark Hall (James Olson) manages to disable the bomb that was going to "decontaminate" the laboratory in the nick of time. In the remake, aired on A&E in May 2008, a similar succession of events occur, only this time they are triggered by Colonel Ferrus (Louis Ferreira) blackmailing Dr. Barton (Viola Davis) to keep a sample of the Andromeda virus. The casing around Barton's sample disintegrates, causing the contamination sensor to set off the lab's self-destruct sequence. In an attempt to deactivate the sequence, Keane (Ricky Schroder) and Chou (Daniel Dae Kim) both die, deaths that do not occur in the original. However, in both movies and the book, someone reaches the control panel and deactivates the sequence with seconds to spare, saving the lab from a nuclear blast. In *The Walking Dead*, however, there is no deactivation. Jenner eventually relents and opens the doors to the underground. Rick then blasts out one of the CDC building's windows with a grenade handed to him by Carol, enabling them to escape. The building erupts into flames behind them.

Vi, the supercomputer, seems also to reference the Red Queen, the supercomputer at the heart of the Umbrella Corporation in *Resident Evil*. "You're all going to die down here," the Red Queen tells her similarly trapped survivors, refusing to release them. In order to prevent the t-Virus from spreading, she locks everyone inside while trying to flood the laboratories and kill everyone with Halon gas. The survivors have to outsmart her in order to escape, much like in *The Walking Dead* and both versions of *The Andromeda Strain*.

Another notorious supercomputer and source of inspiration could be HAL (Douglas Rain) from the film *2001* (Kubrick, 1968). HAL (a Heuristically programmed ALgorithmic computer) is, much like Vi and the Red Queen, an all-knowing computer that controls the Discovery One spacecraft. Our association with him is primarily auditory rather than visual, much as it is with Vi and the Red Queen. We hear his calm voice, cool and conversational, as he orchestrates the demise of the astronauts on board, his visual presence limited to a blinking red camera eye. Rather than have his malfunction reported, HAL attempts to destroy the humans he is meant to protect and assist, all in the interest of preserving the mission. *2001*, with the character of HAL, became a seminal depiction of our worst fears of technology gone mad, of what happens when technology is given too much power. This fear, of technology and artificial intelligence turning on its creator, is also the central plot in the film *Westworld* (1973), written and directed by Michael Crichton (author of the novel it is based on, as well as *The Andromeda Strain*) and remade for HBO in 2016 by Jonathan Nolan and Lisa Joy. In the book, the film, and the television show, robots literally turn on their human masters as a result of an infectious disease. In the earlier book and film, the disease is clearly biological in spirit, as the notion of computer viruses had still not yet emerged. *The X-Files* episode "Ghost in the Machine" (Fox, Oct. 29, 1993) deals with a similar premise, as a sophisticated computer begins to engineer the deaths of those who might threaten its control over the infrastructure of an office building, demonstrating the continued currency of this particular brand of fear.

During the 1980s and 1990s, the AIDS outbreak portrayed just how inept and inadequate the science and medical communities could be at finding a cure, and how inept and inadequate governments could be at looking after their citizens. It continues to be clear that the American government, military, and health departments cannot protect their citizens, as evidenced by incidents like 9/11, Katrina, and the Flint water scandal. This has been a pattern during the end of the twentieth century and the beginning of the twenty-first, and it is one that continues to resonate in film and television. Max Brooks admits that one of the key inspirations for *The Zombie Survival Guide* was the HIV outbreak and the lack of response it received: "I watched this horrible virus just murder millions of people, and our government did nothing."[55] The failure of the government to keep its own citizens safe only reminds us of how vulnerable and alone we truly are.

In other outbreak narratives, like *28 Days Later*, *Resident Evil*, *Contaminated Man* (Hickox, 2000), *I Am Legend*, and *Toxic Skies* (Erin, 2008), science is not just missing in action but explicitly condemned for developing the virus that leads to the inevitable outbreak.

The CDC plotline does not exist in the original *Walking Dead* comic, and its insertion into the television show provides a telling critique not only of science but of technology, as well. The high-tech fortress initially offers comfort and safety, but beyond that, the elaborate technological equipment cannot do anything to help our characters.[56] In fact, technology seems out to destroy our heroes in narratives such as *The Andromeda Strain*, *Resident Evil*, or *The Walking Dead*—and this theme is a pervasive one.

Much as we may fear the impact of too much technology, it is the loss of technology that seems to be the tipping point that turns an urban center into a dystopian wasteland, sending us back to the natural world. When technology fails (or goes rogue), protagonists are forced to get by in a world without electricity, computers, televisions, or information networks. The loss of technology speaks to a lack of control over the environment, nature, or the world around us, depicting, instead, a return of the natural world, a world we thought we had captured and controlled. Mary Anne Doane portrays catastrophe as the "conjecture of the failure of technology and the resulting confrontation with death."[57] For instance, the loss of technology figured significantly into the trauma of 9/11, when cell phones did not work, planes were grounded, and television broadcasting was interrupted. In our technologically reliant world, it is when the Internet stops working, when technology fails, that the gravity of a disaster hits close to home. Without technology, there is no communication, no safety net, no one at the other end of the line, much like the inactive 9-1-1 service in *Containment* (CW, 2016). There is only disconnect, a collapse of the network, a further reminder of how vulnerable and alone we truly are.

This loss of technology is especially significant because it is so integrally tied to contemporary life and social interaction. Twenty-first century culture depends on technology so much that it turns us into metaphorical zombies. A popular Internet meme shows a group of adolescents walking side by side, headed in the same direction. All of them have the now familiar posture—elbows bent, hands raised, heads tilted downwards, attention focused on their phones. The text reads, "What's the point of being afraid of the zombie apocalypse when you're already a zombie?" We are already detached and de-individualized, shuffling in groups toward some unclear purpose, connected via our online networks, making it all the more traumatic when that technology fails, when Facebook crashes, when the Wi-Fi network does not load, when Netflix refuses to play. We have become zombies without the guiding voice of a master to lead us.

In the title sequence to the zombie parody *Shaun of the Dead* (2004), director Edgar Wright portrays with alarming accuracy the seeming equivalence between actual zombies and those of us on handheld devices or trudging through repetitive labor, with little awareness of our actions or surroundings. The sequence, in particular, emphasizes the zombifying characteristics of working-class life. A series of shots features an average morning—a man pushing shopping carts, cashiers swiping products at the register, a line of people staring at their phones while waiting for the bus—everyone emotionless and robotic. Wright emphasizes not only the lack of individuality inherent in modern-day life but also the mind-numbing repetition that consumes much of our daily routines, especially due to our reliance on technology rather than actual craftsmanship and labor.

The difference between zombies and low-wage workers is, in this *Shaun of the Dead* sequence, intentionally difficult to determine, emphasizing that we may already be partially zombified. This resonance is nothing new. Zombies originated as slave labor during a time when American marines used forced labor to perform menial tasks during the American occupation of Haiti at the start of the twentieth century. Fred Botting compares zombies to symptoms of "modern mechanical processes," with living labor having the life sucked out of it, "rendering workers the mere appendages—puppets, automata—to the mechanisms of production."[58] Steve Beard describes zombies as the "disenfranchised underclass of the material world . . . a projection of postmodern capitalism's anxiety about itself."[59] It is not only low-wage work that turns us into zombies but modern life itself. *Shaun of the Dead* plays on Shaun's (Simon Pegg) utmost devotion to routine such that he does not even notice that his village has been overtaken by zombies, so blind is he to the world around him. Similarly, Shaun's best friend and roommate Ed (Nick Frost) spends his days staring with glazed eyes at the television, playing video game after video game. In fact, at the end of the film, even though Ed has since become a zombie, he continues to play video games, merely chained up in a shed in Shaun's backyard. Little has changed. In the final sequence of the film, we also see that zombies have been absorbed into the workforce, taking over low-paying jobs based on mindless repetition. This seems like a reference to the original Haitian zombies, who were created to be slaves working in the fields. Based on these films, the fear is not that we will one day turn into zombies but that we have already become them. As French philosopher Gilles Deleuze predicted in 1990, we no longer need to be separated and disciplined because we discipline ourselves through routine (and are even encouraged to do so).

These tropes are so familiar that they were even repurposed for an episode of Nickelodeon's *SpongeBob SquarePants* that aired on September 29, 2006 ("Once Bitten," season 4, episode 73b). In the episode, SpongeBob's neighbor Squidward walks outside to find that his yard is covered in slime from SpongeBob's pet snail, Gary. "This isn't the first time you've soiled my yard with your revolting excretions," Squidward shouts at Gary. Squidward tries to keep Gary out by building a tall fence around his yard. "Now I feel safe," he sighs happily, reclining inside his new fort (see figure 34). Unfortunately, like with every other outbreak narrative, borders are porous, and Gary still manages to climb over the fence and drip his excretions on Squidward's head. To everyone's surprise, Gary also bites Squidward. "This isn't like you!" SpongeBob exclaims, and they both agree that something appears to be wrong with Gary. Squidward says that he hopes Gary has had all his shots: "For rabies?" "Yup." "Snail pox and softshell dance?" "Yupie." "Bronchitis, lumpy-bump trump, teen angst?" "Yup, yup, yup." But then Patrick suddenly appears and says, "Well, let's not forget the worst of them all: Mad Snail Disease."

It turns out Gary has *not* been vaccinated for this, and now it seems Squidward has caught it as well. Patrick delivers the bad news: "This disease will ravage your body with bloodshot eyes, loss of balance, messy pants, ticklish rib cage, severely untrimmed toenails, and finally, the bite from that infected snail will turn you into . . . a zombie." Panic breaks out all over town, as random citizens exclaim that they, too, have been bitten.

FIGURE 34 "Now I feel safe," *SpongeBob SquarePants*, "Once Bitten" (Nickelodeon, Sept. 29, 2006).

"Mad snail on the loose! If he bites you, he'll turn you into a zombie!" Everyone races around, screaming in total hysteria. At this point, a "News Blast" entitled "Terror in a Shell" interrupts the episode. The voice-over proclaims that "fear and disease is spreading like wildfire as a killer snail has been biting the citizens of Bikini Bottom, infecting them with Mad Snail Disease. Ask any old fish on the street, and they'll tell you that germs enter through the bite radius, traveling upstream until the entire host body is full of Mad Snail Disease!"

We then cut to Action News Reporter Perch Perkins, who interviews Squidward, the "first victim of the epidemic." Perkins asks him when he suspected he was a zombie. Squidward begins to detail his symptoms, which prompts another local resident to declare that he, too, is infected and that it must be spreading through the air, since some people with symptoms have not been bitten. Perkins shouts out that everyone is doomed "to a horrible demise," all because of a "diseased snail." The townspeople turn into zombies and chase after SpongeBob who flees to the safety of a local restaurant. At first, the employees do not want to let him in, asking, "How do we know you're not one of those voracious flesh-eaters?" He is forced to convince the others that he is not a zombie because he has a photo of his best friend in his wallet. The hysteria spreads to such an extent that Old Man Jenkins asks, "Who's to say we're not all zombies?" Everyone screams.

Gary slithers onto the scene, and SpongeBob says to him, "All those people think you're a monster. But I know you're just a snail." Unfortunately, Gary chooses that moment to bite SpongeBob, causing Harold to freak out and declare that Gary must be quarantined immediately before he bites everyone. The citizens gang up and try to wrest Gary away from SpongeBob—"Seize the snail!"—while SpongeBob tries to protect his beloved pet. At just that moment, Dr. Gill Gilliam orders everyone to halt, presenting himself as snail disease expert. He tells them that Mad Snail Disease does not actually exist, that it is an urban legend. "Does that mean we're not zombies?" Patrick asks. "Of course not," he replies. "No one is. It's just mass hysteria . . . All the supposed symptoms are just common ailments." Gary's strange behavior was merely the result of a splinter. As soon as the splinter is removed, Gary goes back to normal. However, Squidward's zombie-esque behavior continues. SpongeBob reminds Squidward that he is not a zombie, and Squidward nods before replying in a monotone, "Oh, yes I am." Getting behind the cash register, Squidward goes back to work. Robotically, he utters the familiar lines: "Welcome to the

Krusty Krab. May I take your order?" And so the episode ends, reminding us of the dangers of misinformation and hysteria as well as the incurable zombie disease known as low-wage work.

I Am Legend also looks at the difference between humans and the "other," however, the book and the film do this in significantly different ways. Near the end of the 2007 film adaptation, Anna (Alice Braga) arrives, disrupting Neville's solitary existence. She is not infected and, along with a child, plans to make her way to a survivors' camp in Vermont. It turns out that Neville's blood contains the cure, so he gives her a vial of his blood moments before he blows himself and a horde of zombies up, thus allowing her to escape. This, naturally, makes his character sympathetic and admirable, reinforcing whatever tenuous distinction there was between him and the zombies.

The film's original ending—referred to as the "alternate ending"— however, is quite different. Neville, Anna, and the child are in the underground lab as the zombies invade, just as in the official version. However, in this case, the leader of the zombies, who had been pursuing Neville ever since Neville captured a female zombie for his experiments, draws a butterfly on the wall of the lab. Neville remembers that the female zombie has a butterfly tattoo and makes the connection. He wheels the female zombie out into the main room. The leader and the female subject have a loving reunion, and then all the zombies leave. Neville looks at the photos of all the zombies he has killed in the guise of research, as if realizing the repercussions of his work, realizing that the zombies were not as dehumanized as he made them out to be.

The differences between the two endings are significant because the alternate ending humanizes the zombies and complicates Neville's "heroic" status, reinforcing the blurring between the two types of being. This echoes the conclusion of Matheson's book, where, after having killed hundreds of the infected vampires, Neville realizes that "many of the infected are still very much sentient, rational beings, however transformed by vampiris, . . . [and] it is he who is the Dracula-like monster in this new world . . . still clinging to a nonexistent world of property and privilege."[60] Matheson collapses the traditional distinction between protagonist and monster, giving us zombies with consciousness and community rather than what we might expect, questioning both what it means to be human and whether being human is better. However, test audiences did not like the original ending, prompting the studio to replace it with the current "theatrical ending," thus changing the moral thrust of the story.

By proposing that we are not that different from—or better than—zombies, clear-cut definitions of monster versus human fall apart, much like clear-cut definitions of life versus death. For example, in the original *Dawn of the Dead* (1978), when one of the characters is asked what the zombies are, he responds, "They're us, that's all." This blurring between "us" and "other," infected and uninfected, is dramatized in *28 Days Later*, when American soldiers instructed to shoot the infected end up shooting everyone because they cannot tell who is sick and who is not. Similarly, in *I Am Legend*, Neville's wife initially fails the eye scan, incorrectly demarcated as infected. She is about to be dragged off to the infected zone, but Neville insists she get checked again. Luckily for her, the eye scan is correct the second time, but in most cases, when in doubt, when the possibility of viral or zombie infection lurks, elimination is the only sure option. This inability to determine friend or foe, infected or healthy, is compounded when friends and family become infected, and the threat they create is not immediately apparent. It might not become apparent, in fact, until it is too late, which is why the only safe course of action is to be quick and ruthless.

On *The Walking Dead*, the fact that all humans contain the "zombie virus," that those who are not yet zombies already have the zombie virus within them, blurs whatever binary there might have been between zombie and human. Everyone is either already a zombie or will become one after death. Escaping infection is impossible since everyone is infected, thus emphasizing the difficulty of trying to defend one's self against what is already inside. As Bishop writes, "If the early twenty-first century ushered in the viral zombie (notably in *28 Days Later*), it has also, in *The Walking Dead*, introduced the viral human."[61]

The viral human confuses distinctions between human and monster, living and dead. As Rick says in the final episode of *TWD* season 2 ("Beside the Dying Fire," Mar. 18, 2012): "We're all infected." At the end of volume 4 of the graphic novel, Rick goes even further, "You *know* that when we die—we *become* them. You think we hide behind walls to protect us from *the walking dead*? Don't you get it? We *are* the walking dead!"[62] This blurring is literalized in season 1, episode 2 ("Guts," Nov. 7, 2010) when Rick and Glenn smear zombie guts on themselves to make themselves smell like zombies so that they can slip undetected through a horde of zombies, a technique used often on the show. If the zombie complicates rules of internal and external—functioning even as body parts dangle and limbs are lost—Rick and Glenn complicate rules of external and internal by rubbing zombie guts on their bodies. In that same episode, before Rick chops up a zombie, he looks at the man's wallet to see who he used to be. While showing the group the man's driver's license, Rick says, "He used to be like us. Worrying about bills, the rent, or the Super Bowl." In this case, the horror comes not from the monsters roaming the earth but from the realization that these monsters were once human, and that those still human will one day become monsters, both literally and metaphorically.

Shane (Jon Bernthal), in the episode "Pretty Much Dead Already" (Nov. 27, 2011), says the walkers are not people because "all they do is kill." And yet, our protagonists do an awful lot of killing. In fact, at the end of the episode "Twice as Far" (Mar. 20, 2016), Carol (Melissa McBride) exiles herself from the town of Alexandria because she is not up to the task of being one of its residents. The town, as a desirable location, is under constant threat of attack. Carol must leave because, as she puts it, "I cannot love anyone because I cannot kill for anyone." She says this even though she has already killed, many times. In *The Walking Dead* universe, if you care for anyone, you must be able to kill to protect them. Ironically, in the episode "Heads Up" (Nov. 22, 2015), Sam (Major Dodson) asks Carol, "If you kill people do you turn into one of the monsters?" Carol replies, "The only thing that keeps you from becoming a monster is killing." At the very end of the season 2 finale of *The Strain* ("Night Train," Oct. 4, 2015), the professor declares: "In order to defeat the Master, we must be as cold and ruthless, as savage as he is—and yet, without becoming monsters ourselves."

Language may set humans apart from the zombies, as do rituals, rules, and guidelines, but all of these feel pointless in a world without order. So what happens as language and time disappear? Dale (Jeffrey DeMunn), for example, winds his watch every day at the same time, this routine providing him with a sort of solace and structure. However irrelevant the action might now be, it helps him hold onto a vestige of his former life, affirming his difference from the zombies. In season 1, episode 4 ("Vatos," Nov. 21, 2010), Andrea (Laurie Holden) holds her sister's dying body and cries that she does not know what to do. Traditional rituals and guidelines for dealing with the dead and the dying no longer apply when the dead do not stay dead. The zombies force a disrespect for bodies, for death, and for life by questioning what it means to be alive.

Humans will also become monsters if the definition of monster is "an abject part of the self."[63] As decaying bodies that will not hide, zombies remind us of the ugliness and terror of death. The more we try to distance ourselves from the mortality of our bodies, the more zombies provide an unpleasant reminder. We, too, will one day rot. Zombies pursue us, much as death does. Normally, we manage to shield ourselves from both death and infection—the former relegated to crematoriums, mortuaries, and grave-yards, the latter to hospitals and quarantine zones—but zombies make the two very real and present. As philosopher Julia Kristeva puts it, "Corpses show me what I permanently thrust aside in order to live."[64] What is a zom-bie but a walking corpse determined to turn you into one, too? Sociolo-gist Chris Schilling explains that death is especially disturbing to modern individuals because it represents "the precise point where human control ends in a world which is orientated to the successful achievement of con-trol."[65] And zombies are, as the title goes, the walking dead. Simon Pegg, writer of *Shaun of the Dead*, explains that zombies embody our fear of "our own death, personified. The physical manifestation of that thing we fear the most."[66]

In the *Dawn of the Dead* remake, Kenneth (Ving Rhames) asks about Fort Pastor, a nearby US Army base, and whether everyone there is dead. Steve's (Ty Burrell) response is that everyone is "dead-ish." Zombies are *both* alive and dead, alive in terms of being a threat, but dead in terms of being "excluded from the polis and the fortifications of security and politi-cal order."[67] This echoes Primo Levi's description of the "anonymous mass" he experienced at Auschwitz. People who were once human had become "non-men who march and labor in silence," arguably alive but without a voice, either literal or symbolic. The zombies represent the indistinguish-able masses who can be counted—in terms of statistics and numbers—but do not "count." Italian philosopher Giorgio Agamben argues that the concentration camps were "the place in which the most absolute *condi-tio inhumana* ever to appear on Earth was realized" precisely because the inhabitants were divested of political status and reduced to bare life.[68] Alive enough to be a threat, but too dead to matter. Or, as political theorist Han-nah Arendt describes, the horror of the concentration camps "can never be fully embraced by the imagination for the very reason that it stands outside of life and death."[69]

Significantly, the release of *Night of the Living Dead* coincided with a change in the medical definition of death. Professor Luckhurst describes how the invention of the Intensive Care Unit (ICU), combined with a new generation of more effective artificial respirators, would mean that patients with a complete absence of cortical activity—who were "brain dead"—could continue "to live on within the biotechnical apparatus of the ICU." Death was shifted "from a decisive moment to an ongoing process." Beyond the fact that these medical innovations complicated the determination of when, exactly, someone was dead, Luckhurst also points out just how many times the plot of a zombie narrative "is launched from the recovery room of an abandoned ICU."[70] *28 Days Later* and *The Walking Dead*, for instance, both begin with very similar hospital sequences: Jim and Rick wake up postcoma to see the wreckage around them.

As zombies blur the boundary between life and death, so, too, do they blur the boundaries between self and other, echoing the same kind of blurring happening offscreen. Globalization and technology have caused a process of de-differentiation and homogenization; corporate logics and networks have replaced cultural diversity and individuality. The more technology and software quantify and shape our everyday lives, the more standards have become unified, reducing individuality and turning consumers into little more than dots on a curve. Similarly, the tearing apart of skin, the consumption of bodies, and the exchange of infectious fluids common in a zombie movie convert everyone not only into zombies but into a homogeneous mass. This mass, with its permeable bodies and unstable categories of "otherness," is at the heart of both viral outbreaks and zombies.[71]

To illustrate, zombies, when they appear in *The Walking Dead* comic, are often drawn with a grey wash that renders them "as one grim mass," further distinguishing them from the more individualized human characters.[72] The zombies are faceless and forgettable. They exist as the despecified, the ultimate multitude. One zombie is interchangeable with the next, while it is our individuality that defines us and makes us human.

Another example of this loss of individuality—the human replaced with the despecified mass—occurs in *Resident Evil: Extinction* (Mulcahy, 2007), where there are countless Alice clones, each one an identical physical match. The most disturbing part about them may not be that Dr. Isaacs (Iain Glen) created them in a lab, but how identical they are—and how disposable. A few minutes into the film, we see piles of them, discarded and dead in a ditch, failures in Isaacs's experiments. While they are not zombies, the impact comes from the sheer quantity, the disposability, much like with zombies.

The loss of individuality can be seen offscreen in the contemporary treatment of people as "populations," aggregated numbers rather than individuals. This shift reflects Michel Foucault's theory of biopolitics, which he describes as "a set of processes such as the ratio of births to deaths, the rate of reproduction, the fertility of a population, and so on."[73] This kind of disciplinary administration of populations entails a reliance on categorization and statistics, all of which favors the mass over the individual. James A. Tyner argues that the specific emergence of biopolitics was, in fact, "predicated on the institutionalization and standardization of censuses and population-related concepts . . . New technologies of power—including population forecasts, statistical estimates, and various other demographic measures and concepts—were applied not to individual bodies, but to a 'global mass,' collectivities and aggregates, or, simply put, populations."[74] The process of homogenization encouraged by globalization and technology has been further facilitated by the treatment of people as populations, as aggregated numbers and statistics.

Timothy J. Reiss, in an essay entitled "Calculating Humans: Mathematics, War, and the Colonial Calculus," traces the process of how "mathematics could become such a constructive, manipulating, and instrumentalist knowledge—notably of *people*" back to the sixteenth century, where "the idea of calculation . . . gave *true understanding* of the physical world and human actions." Calculation of people would become an essential component of military strategy and management, for instance, where "a strict calculus" would determine the "distribution of human bodies on the battlefield, in camp, or on the march."[75]

Once the initial counting is complete, then comes the task of "creating divisions between different groups and sacrificing (or abandoning) some to secure others." This technique relies heavily on impersonal statistics and categories, a limited visibility that "results in the erasure of the individual."[76] The shift to population-thinking involves a shift from a mode of power predicated on discipline and repression—Foucault provides the example of "the ancient *patria potestas* that granted the father of the Roman family the right to 'dispose' of the life of his children and his slaves"[77]—to one predicated on "fostering life." To foster life most efficiently may require the deaths of those who pose a "risk" to the population's health and well-being. As risks are always only potential, however, this means individuals may be punished for what they *might* do or what they *represent*. It is about probabilities and risk minimization, rather than "punishment" or "correction."

Thus, for example, the harsher sentences for crack cocaine versus regular cocaine use in the 1990s were not about differences in the nature of the offense or any individual offenders but about differences in populations. It was about minimizing the risks to society posed by a group of people presumed to be dangerous. Correction was not the point; corralling and containing risk was.

During a viral outbreak, not only are the infected lumped together, individuality abandoned, but they are also considered less worthy, less human, and more expendable. The infected, along with anyone deemed potentially infectious, are dehumanized in the interests of security.[78] This echoes the core tenant of necropolitics, which, as outlined by philosopher and political theorist Achille Mbembe, emphasizes that "the ultimate expression of sovereignty resides, to a large degree, in the power and the capacity to dictate who may live and who must die."[79] In the *World War Z* novel, for example, under the infamous Redeker Plan, not only are uninfected citizens routinely killed in order to be certain that the infected have been eradicated, but they are even used as bait. Their purpose is specifically to distract the undead so that others can escape. Once you have been infected, or once you are within the proximity of someone who is infected, or even once your death can somehow serve the "greater good," your traditional rights as a citizen evaporate. Redeker even devises calculations for who is worthy of being saved and who is not, based on criteria which includes IQ, geography, military capability, and fertility.[80] The Redeker Plan was omitted from the movie.

Biopolitical thinking finds a visual analogue in the zombie horde, but the shambling horde is also a reminder that life in such a society has no guarantees. We are all equally expendable if the health and well-being of the masses requires it. For example, in season 4 of *The Walking Dead*, Carol kills Karen (Melissa Ponzio) and David (Brandon Carroll) and burns their bodies after they both come down with the flu—even though they had been quarantined—in an attempt to keep the flu from spreading. In the episode "Indifference" (AMC, Nov. 3, 2013), Carol tells Rick when he confronts her about the killing, "I stepped up. I had to do something." Rick points out that even though he, too, has killed people to save the group and himself, he has never killed a member of their surrogate family. Carol points out that he did, in fact, do so, referring to Shane. "He was going to kill me," Rick explains. "So were they," she responds. "They were going to kill all of us." Rick tells her that she did not know that, but while it may not have been a certainty—and the flu ends up spreading anyway—Carol did what she felt she had to do in order to minimize the risk.

Alternatively, we are all equally complicit in the murder of others—whether real, symbolic, or social murder—to save ourselves and our way of life. Neoliberalism is a regime that fosters self-discipline, self-control, and self-protection; in other words, it involves a competition for survival.[81] Our ability to thrive (our very survival) may depend on the selective murder/torture/suppression of "others" (those who do not fit into the aggregate, who are not members of the population that count), an ever-evolving group—sometimes Japanese, sometimes Africans, sometimes Muslims, sometimes Jews, always the poor. Biopolitics requires necropolitics; the zombies seem a walking reminder of that connection.

Another way to look at the division between "those who must be protected" (the elite) and "those they must be protected from" (the masses) is by imposing the parable of the 1 percent. The target of the "Occupy Wall Street" movement that began in 2011 was the wealthiest 1 percent of the United States, a small percentage of people who control nearly half the wealth of the country. Carlo Rotella posits the argument that many of the changes made to the original *I Am Legend* book for its 2007 film adaptation—such as the conversion of the vampires from the book into the zombies of the film—were to retrofit the text for the twenty-first century by incorporating elements of the tensions between the "1 percent" and the "99 percent." Vampires, after all, are "cosmopolitan, cerebral, queer, often grown rich over their extended lifespans," while zombies are "local, dimwitted, gruntingly conventional in their desire for living flesh, and utterly without possessions over the course of their brutish existences," Rotella maintains. Vampire narratives put hunger in the hands of the elite, whereas the recent crop of zombie narratives depicts the conflict of "the special few against the undifferentiated and perpetually hungry many." Unlike the modest, average Neville of the book, Will Smith's Neville is a well-educated and wealthy doctor, surrounded by pricey art in his multimillion-dollar home, forced to defend himself from the ravenous masses outside.[82] The movie *I Am Legend* also reimagines the typical zombie paradigm by situating the conflict as one man against many zombies, rather than a team of survivors versus an attacking horde, a reimagining that supports the parable of the 1 percent. Luckhurst points out a similar dynamic during a scene in *World War Z*, where the infection breaks out in the crowded economy seats of an aircraft before making its way toward first class. Naturally, the diseased poor are to blame.[83]

The parable of the 1 percent also plays a part in the TNT series *The Last Ship*. In the episode "No Place Like Home" (Aug. 24, 2014), when Dr. Scott (Rhona Mitra) discovers Granderson (Alfre Woodard) is killing those she deems unworthy, Granderson retorts that "the Plague killed indiscriminately. The artists, scientists, thinkers, so few and precious to begin with, were wiped out. It upended the social order and prolonged the Dark Ages a hundred and fifty years. I cannot let that happen here . . . It is my duty to help the right people first. The people whose survival will ensure the future of our entire society and all that we hold dear." By the "right people," she means those artists, scientists, and thinkers she deems part of her 1 percent. The elite few gather behind protective walls, while those outside fall ill. However, as Commanding Officer Tom Chandler realizes moments later, they do not fall ill by chance. They are injected intentionally, killed by whatever "medicine" they are being given by the men in gas masks. Trucks then move the bodies to a nearby factory where they are burned for power to fuel the city. Granderson not only decides which members of the human race are worth keeping, but she turns the rest (the 99 percent) into fuel. Some individuals are arguably "more human" or "better humans" than others.

So the question is this: Is the zombie narrative commenting on neoliberal capitalism's particular *way* of fostering life (its emphasis on self-discipline and competition)? Is it a critique aimed at initiating a shift in the regimes of biopower? Or is it advocating this life strategy, since, after all, these narratives show us—over and over—what happens without self-discipline, self-control, or self-protection: death. Much like how horror films condemn promiscuity, killing off the most sexual character first, zombie narratives teach us to remain vigilant, to look out for ourselves, and not to hesitate to leave the weakest link behind (or dead).

The seminal portrayal of what happens after the end of the world, where survivors are forced to adopt a ruthless neoliberal ethos to survive, may be hit television show *The Walking Dead*. James Hibbard, *Entertainment Weekly's* editor at large, tries to explain just how big ratings are for *The Walking Dead*. They are "23 percent bigger among adults 18–49 than NBC's *Sunday Night Football* (8.4), which is broadcast's top rated weekly telecast . . . You know ABC's *Scandal* (4.8)? One of the biggest hits on TV, right? Well, *The Walking Dead* doubles its rating."[84] While these numbers may only factor in viewers between eighteen and forty-nine years old, the television show is still the most-watched drama in basic-cable history, and the premiere of its spin-off, *Fear the Walking Dead* (2015), was also record-breaking for a cable show. American television reviewer Alan Sepinwall writes that, according to AMC, "the spin-off's 90-minute debut drew 10.1 million viewers in its initial airing, 6.3 million of whom were adults 18–49. Both are records for a cable series premiere."[85]

Based on a comic series that began in 2003, *The Walking Dead* originated, as young adult author Ned Vizzini writes, "between our era's two most compelling apocalyptic fantasies: 9/11 and the 2008 financial crisis."[86] How appropriate for a show devoted to the end of everything that we once thought safe and secure. On this show, everything civilized—including the government, the military, science, and technology—is long gone, with no possibility of return. This absence of government to discipline marks another shift toward Deleuze's control society, in which we willingly discipline ourselves. As the first serialized TV zombie narrative, *The Walking Dead* immediately signaled a break with tradition. In the words of creator Robert Kirkman, the initial concept behind *The Walking Dead* was, for it to be "the zombie movie that never ends."[87] In very simplistic terms, that is exactly what it is. Literally a story without end, we are deprived of the reassuring conclusions common to cinematic narratives. The show, instead of crafting resolution, focuses on the human survivors and "their struggle to reconstitute something that looks like a viable social order in the postapocalyptic world."[88]

The Walking Dead also signifies a paradigm shift for making it especially clear that "the show about zombies" is not really about zombies. In fact, the zombies are referred to as "walkers," because no one in the show knows what zombies are, so that term is never used.

Another demonstration of the fact that it is not a show about zombies is the amount of screen time they get. For example, during the pilot episode, after the initial shot of a zombie, we do not see any other zombies for twenty-three minutes. This is in marked contrast to a movie like *Dawn of the Dead* (2004), where the first zombies arrive fewer than five minutes into the film and then never leave. In *The Walking Dead*, zombies are also conspicuously absent from the show's title sequences, arguably responsible for setting the tone of the show. The title sequence for seasons 1 and 2 only show broken photographs of the central cast, interspersed with images of urban and rural devastation. The photographs are behind broken glass, often covered with dirt, rocks, and dust. The images, as they flash by, are all different representations of postdisaster detritus: a house, a trailer, a teddy bear, a water tower, an empty and trash-filled downtown street, two different empty cityscapes, an abandoned hospital, another empty street, an abandoned government building (the King County sheriff's department) with the American flag billowing beside an overturned car, abandoned railroad tracks, an abandoned bus, crows eating a dead cat, and a final shot of more broken-down cars on an abandoned highway, a city on fire in the background. Transportation is defunct, civilization is defunct, any illusion of safety and warmth is defunct, even without a glimpse of zombies.

Bloodshot eyes make an appearance in the title sequence for seasons 3 and 4, but it is unclear if they belong to zombie or human. Vegetation and decay are more pronounced in this newer title sequence, objects that used to have power in an earlier life now covered with grass or vines. Even the American flag, which billowed proudly in the original title sequence, is now in tatters. There are hints of threatening figures with the bloodshot eyes but also a figure pacing behind a door. The editing has also sped up, and in the title sequence for season 5, it speeds up even more, reflecting the increasing speed of contemporary life, even during the apocalypse. The human objects, by this point, look decayed and unnatural. We see fingers prying from behind a locked door, reminiscent, if not identical, to the hand clawing at a barricaded door in the early minutes of the pilot episode ("Days Gone Bye," Oct. 31, 2010). But there are still no clear shots of zombies.

The pilot episode opens with a shot of small town deputy sheriff Rick Grimes driving his sheriff's car down a street blocked by an assortment of abandoned vehicles. He makes his way through the cars and trucks to an abandoned gas station, hoping to siphon gasoline. The only sound is the distant chirp of birds. Rick scans the insides of the cars grimacing at the dead bodies. It appears to have been a makeshift campsite. Rick spots movement—it is a little girl with long blonde hair, a pink bathrobe, and a teddy bear. "Little girl, little girl, I'm a policeman," are the first words we hear in the episode. He tells her not to be afraid as she turns to face him. The bottom quarter of her face is missing, her eyes shadowed, blood dripping out of her mouth. She faces the camera straight on, allowing us to stare back at her. This is the first zombie we see, and the juxtaposition of pale-pink pajamas, pale-pink robe, long blonde hair, and a teddy bear with exposed flesh and dripping blood makes it even more jarring. The camera tracks closer, and we can see the redness around her pupils and the braces on her teeth. She shuffles toward Rick, who does not know if he should shoot or run—or both. He shoots her point blank, the bullet entering the center of her forehead. The force of the impact sends her flat onto the pavement, while the camera moves above her, the spray of blood surrounding the outline of her body. Not even five minutes into the episode and the writers of *The Walking Dead* have already conveyed how screwed up this new world has become: cops are shooting angelic little girls who have blood dripping off their face.

After the title sequence, the episode flashes back to the days before the zombie outbreak, showing us the accident that landed Rick in the hospital, his coma, and then his eventual awakening in an abandoned hospital. In a sequence remarkably similar to one near the start of *28 Days Later*, where London bike courier Jim also wakes from a coma in an abandoned hospital, all Rick finds, as he drags himself out of his hospital bed, are lights that do not work, phones that do not work, an elevator that does not work, trashed hallways, a half-eaten dead body on the floor, bullet holes in the walls, and wires hanging from the ceiling. Like a Neanderthal, he staggers through a dark stairwell, matches providing brief and limited illumination. He makes his way outside into the blinding daylight only to discover row after row of rotting bodies covered by sheets, flies swarming in the air. Rick stumbles past abandoned military equipment, including a helicopter (the only sign of the military throughout the whole series), and toward a nearby suburban neighborhood. He finds his first zombie (twenty-three minutes into the episode) in a neighborhood park and escapes from this zombie via bicycle. Rick makes his way back to his former home, searching desperately for his wife and son. He calls their names over and over in desperation, before curling into a fetal position on the floor. This is his first breakdown. Significantly, meeting a zombie only causes him confusion and alarm but losing his family causes utter despair. This is one of many crucial signs that this show is not about zombies. It is about people confronted with impossible situations, about trying to maintain a semblance of domestic civility in a world determined to crush it.

Rather than seeking cheap thrills or B movie horror, the show aspires to show how these protagonists endure their circumstances as well as evolve because of them. In the introduction to volume 1 of *The Walking Dead, Days Gone Bye*, Kirkman describes his attempt to depict what would happen once the world as we know it falls apart: "I hope to show you reflections of your friends, your neighbors, your families, and yourselves, and what their reactions are to the extreme situations in this book."[89] Similarly, Frank Darabont, creator of *The Walking Dead* television show, explains that the show is about "a group of people who are forced to survive together, be a family together, and endure very, very difficult circumstances."[90]

It quickly becomes clear that the walkers are not the real danger. The show provides, instead, an examination of humanity's propensity for aggression and destruction. Contrary to traditional concepts, where the diseased (and contagious) person is the enemy, in this narrative, the healthy and noncontagious people are the real threat. The fear becomes not of the mindless monsters but of the damage humans can do to each other when they are competing for their very survival. Scott Kenemore warns that, "For humans to survive . . . they must become killers."[91] If typical monster narratives depict the struggle to protect the home from the evil that lurks without, to keep the monster at bay, in *The Walking Dead*, the monster is both within and without. This theme echoes that which has been in outbreak narratives all along but gained dominance following the terrorist attacks of 2001. Traditional techniques of othering, containment, and quarantine do not apply because the enemy is already inside the gates. Appropriately enough, the tag line for season 3 is "Fight the Dead, Fear the Living."

Rick eventually manages to find his wife, Lori (Sarah Wayne Callies), and son (Chandler Riggs) amid a group of other survivors, including his best friend, Shane, another former member of the police force. Rick and Shane have frequent conflicts over leadership strategies, as Rick still clings to the ideal of moral integrity, whereas Shane prefers quick and ruthless violence. Rick becomes the group leader and unofficial cowboy sheriff, his trademark cowboy hat and police uniform a frequent part of his attire. By preserving his uniform, he preserves himself as a figure of authority, echoing traditional power structures and implying that they still have a resonance in this new world (see figure 35). The tropes of the Western extend beyond Grimes's cowboy hat and boots. For example, in "Guts" (season 1, episode 2), Glenn sarcastically compliments Rick Grimes when he says, "Nice moves there, Clint Eastwood." As Rick's son, Carl, grows up, he, too, begins wearing a sheriff-style hat given to him by his father. P. Ivan Young, in his essay "Walking Tall or Walking Dead? The American Cowboy in the Zombie Apocalypse," argues that it was clear before *The Walking Dead* even began "that the story was steeped in cowboy lore."[92]

FIGURE 35 Sheriff Rick (Andrew Lincoln), *The Walking Dead* (2010–present).

It is not only that *The Walking Dead* is steeped in cowboy lore but that it actively reinvents and repurposes tropes of the Western genre. Anna Froula writes that the American national narrative "has historically cast US corporate and imperial interests as a fantasy of rugged, masculine individualists fighting for the establishment of white civilization against savage, dark heathens; for unregulated freedom to consume natural resources; and for the imagined manifest destiny of global military dominance." Froula goes on to make direct comparisons between this rugged narrative and the AMC television show, mentioning Rick's hat and six-shooter, the frequent dinners around a campfire, as well as the constant search for a new frontier that might offer the opportunity for safety and regeneration. A crucial difference between the show and the genre it so often references is the replacement of the mythological rugged hero with "tribe-like groups warring over shrinking resources—namely food and shelter—on the ever-encroaching brink of extinction." Staying with a group becomes the only way to stay alive, "eschewing the western genre's adulation for the lone outlaw hero for the horror genre's insistence that to go it alone is to guarantee a horrible death."[93] This also reflects the trend of replacing individual heroes with networks, as seen in films like *Contagion* (2011).

Much like the male heroes discussed in the "Terrorism Outbreak" chapter, *The Walking Dead* both favors and complicates (white) masculine leadership. During the shows first two seasons, the women "keep house," cleaning (even if this means cleaning the guns), doing laundry, and cooking. They are, in fact, punished for defying gender roles, while the men go off on raids and rescue missions.[94] Rick, even with the occasional hiatus, is the show's unofficially official leader. Political writer and editor Kay Steiger, in her essay "No Clean Slate: Unshakable Race and Gender Politics in *The Walking Dead*," observes that the gender roles depicted on the show "would have been right at home in a John Ford western."[95]

However, Michonne (Danai Gurira), with her katana sword, dark skin, and aggressive demeanor, slashes her way through traditional gender expectations. Entering the show as "a hooded warrior who leads two armless, toothless zombies around by chains as camouflage," their scent concealing her own human odor, she is "the ultimate mash-up of inverted American slavery, Akira Kurosawa samurai remakes of classic westerns, and the exotic solitary woman warrior, always in a constant state of war preparedness."[96] One of the few original cast members still remaining on the show, Carol is another female character who defies the initial gender politics of the show. A cast member from the beginning, Carol was initially defined by her submissive relationship to an abusive husband. However, after his death—she impales him repeatedly with an ax to prevent reanimation, a significant turning point for her for various reasons—she evolves into one of the toughest and most ruthless members of the cast and, along with Rick, one of the longest surviving. Maggie (Lauren Cohan) is another similar example of a character who initially fell into gender stereotypes, even arguing for compassion for the zombies, whom she felt were merely sick. However, after the destruction of her father's farm, followed by his death, and then her sister's death, she becomes increasingly colder and more forceful.

If *The Walking Dead* is any indication, traditional gender roles do not suffice in a postapocalyptic world, where any kind of individual hero is doomed, and teamwork becomes an essential component of survival. This is in contrast to real-life scenarios, at least as depicted by the media. For example, American journalist and author Susan Faludi, in her book *Terror Dream: Fear and Fantasy in Post-9/11 America*, describes the journalistic response during the post-9/11 era. Faludi observes the denigration of capable women, the magnification of manly men, and a "heightened call for domesticity."[97] For instance, in portrayals of 9/11 in the media, even though nearly three quarters of the victims were male, the media created the perception that "only men were involved in the response, rescue, and recovery efforts," with women relegated to the role of victims and/or widows.[98] As Kevin Wetmore writes, summarizing Faludi's argument, "The immediate media consensus was that feminism was no longer relevant or even useful in the wake of 9/11."[99] The odd example—*I Am Legend*, *World War Z*—may still favor the rugged individual hero, but television narratives that delve deeper into the day-to-day survival in a decimated world—like *The Walking Dead* or *The Last Man on Earth*—reflect the reality that sustained survival requires a team, because sometimes it is a child (Carl) who will save you, sometimes it is an African American woman waving a sword (Michonne), and sometimes it is a blonde with a shotgun and perfect marksmanship (January Jones as Melissa on *The Last Man on Earth*).

In these various narratives—the ones that focus on the day-to-day as well as the ones that focus on tying up loose ends, Hollywood style—the same question remains: How does one embrace a life strategy built on self-discipline, self-control, and self-protection without becoming a monster? Where does the line lie between human and monster? Rene Descartes famously declared, "I think therefore I am." So if one keeps thinking, does one stay human? If one becomes infected, does one become a monster? If one is infectious, does one become a monster? Are there categories of "monster," much like categories of "infected"? Brendan Riley, in his essay "Zombie People," writes, "It wasn't so long ago that upstanding members of society argued vigorously about whether certain human beings were, in fact, people." In fact, classifying people of other races, faiths, or geographic heritage as subhuman was a way of fulfilling the economic and social needs of the expanding European states and America.[100] For instance, slaves were deemed property, not people, while those trapped in vegetative states also fuel debates over who is and who is not worthy of life, over what makes one human.

The horror of these zombie narratives is not merely about turning into a monster; it is also about a fear of losing one's self, of being reduced to a grim mass. Echoing many a terrorist, in season 1, episode 7 of *12 Monkeys* ("The Keys"), Adam Wexler (Ari Millen) proposes that maybe the world *needs* a plague: "The liars die out, the living forget the lies. Society's great reset switch." Cole responds by saying that this would not reset anything; it would just turn us "back into animals." As much as it may be romanticized, the end of the world will turn us into animals and zombies and monsters, bringing with it a loss of self, the inevitable dehumanization common to so many of these narratives. The pilot episode of *12 Monkeys* ("Splinter") opens with the following voice-over: "Where are you right now? Somewhere warm? Safe? Next to someone you love? Now what if all that was gone? And the only thing you could do is survive? You would, right? You'd try? You'd do things. Horrible things. Until you lose that last thing you have left. Yourself."

There is a line that runs straight through the zombie template: that humans are already zombies, just not quite as abjected. We see it in *Dawn of the Dead* (1978)—"They're us, that's all"—in the infamous *Shaun of the Dead* opening sequence, even in the *SpongeBob SquarePants* episode. Contemporary life, with its constraints and conformity, with its repetitive labor and incessant responsibility, may have turned us into zombies. As Kirkman describes, "A hundred years ago, we were living in houses we built, growing food we ate, interacting with our families. That's a life that makes sense. Now we're doing jobs we don't enjoy to buy stuff we don't need. We've screwed things up."[101]

And so, ironically, at the same time that we are struggling to define what sets human apart from zombie, one of the primary appeals of the zombie apocalypse is that it is only when society collapses that we begin to come alive, to de-zombify. Ned Vizzini, in his essay "The Objectivist Hero in *The Walking Dead*" writes that the biggest draw of the apocalypse is the way it absolves us of our responsibilities. In the twenty-first century, our lives are "burdened by crushing metastasizing obligations: to our bodies, our clothes, our homes, our cars, our jobs, our kids, our Internet presence."[102] Or as poet Henry David Thoreau said, "Men talk of freedom! How many are free to think? Free from fear, from perturbation, from prejudice? Nine hundred and ninety-nine in a thousand are perfect slaves." From a romantic perspective, the apocalypse strips all this away, releasing us from slavery and leaving us with only one responsibility—staying alive—and with one reality—the "real" one.[103] On the back of the first *Walking Dead* graphic novel is the following description: "The world as we know it is gone. The world of commerce and frivolous necessity has been replaced by a world of survival and responsibility . . . In a matter of months, society has crumbled, no government, no grocery stores, no mail delivery, no cable TV. In a world ruled by the dead, we are forced to finally start living."[104] As this quote indicates, it is contemporary life that prevents us from living. In a world burdened by omnipresent debt and mundane responsibility, the end of the world symbolizes liberation. As Camilla Fojas believes, "There is no outside to capitalism before the apocalypse. The economic order atomizes, instrumentalizes, and denatures. The zombie apocalypse occasions an alternative, an outside to this order and its institutions . . . The eradication of money seems to signify freedom from its structural logic of valuation."[105] In other words, before the apocalypse, there is no escape from capitalism, from the economic system. However, the zombie apocalypse provides a way out. If money is gone, so, too, is financial responsibility and obligation. In place of capitalism, there is freedom.

In his book *Haunted Media: Electronic Presence from Telegraphy to Television*, Jeffrey Sconce posits that, "One might even say that violent disasters and catastrophes evoke a certain exhilaration in that they promise momentary liberation from the mass-mediated social order."[106] It is when in conflict with the zombie (the metaphorical abject other), when confronted by fear, that one finally feels alive, or so we imagine. Carol, in *The Walking Dead* episode "The Same Boat" (Mar. 13, 2016), when describing herself now versus herself before the world collapsed, says, "I'm still me but better. I lost everything and it made me stronger." In their article "A Zombie Manifesto: The Nonhuman Condition in the Era of Advanced Capitalism," Sarah Juliet Lauro and Karen Embry remark that "fear heightens our awareness of ourselves as individuals because our individuality is endangered in life-threatening situations."[107] So if globalization and technology have eroded our individuality, perhaps the zombie apocalypse is the only suitable antidote.

When confronted with the possibility of losing one's mind, one's body, and one's identity, one becomes acutely aware of all three—a refreshing contrast to the numbness created by everyday contemporary life. Douglas Kellner argues that, prior to 9/11, French sociologist Jean Baudrillard wrote repeatedly about "the destruction and disappearance of the real in the realm of information and simulacra, and the subsequent reign of illusion and appearance."[108] However, the popularity of movies and television shows like *The Walking Dead*, that strip away this simulacra and illusion, demonstrates a desire for authenticity and a return to a primal real.

In a world that emphasizes and rewards standardization, that turns consumers into data and dots on a curve, that homogenizes experience, flushing it through the same algorithms to achieve maximum efficiency, the postapocalypse outbreak narrative provides a mark of rebellion. In a world where almost everyone has been lost, the actions of a few take on added gravitas. Small gestures are now loaded with significance, potentially impacting your fate and the fates of those you love. It is no longer about a life of monotony. It is no longer about a life tethered to social and financial upkeep. It is a life where every day could be your last, where an impulsive decision could mean the end. Perhaps narratives like *The Walking Dead* are merely retaliation against a world where networks have overshadowed individuals, where borders have become ephemeral and irrelevant. They represent a world where, instead, borders are everything, and individuality is celebrated, where class, education, and nepotism are meaningless, and you are judged solely on your own merits. The desire to see what would happen after the end of civilization is not merely about a desire to return to the Wild West or to celebrate white male patriarchy. It is about a desire to feel alive, to be reborn.

Conclusion

> If we didn't fundamentally misunder-
> stand the risk, we probably wouldn't
> watch.
> —Marc Siegel, *False Alarm*

After a nine-season run, *The X-Files* television series wrapped in 2002, only to return to the Fox network as a six-episode revival in 2016. That season's finale, entitled "My Struggle II" (Fox, Feb. 26, 2016), revolves around a mysterious outbreak of the Spartan virus. Bearing remarkable parallels to the AIDS virus, Spartan works by removing a gene from your DNA, thus causing your immune system to simply vanish—or, as rogue journalist Tad O'Malley (Joel McHale) declares it, "a fast-moving AIDS without the HIV." Dr. Rubell (Julian Christopher) warns that once your immune system is wiped out, you will then be vulnerable to a variety of contagions, much like with AIDS, and the threats are not limited to conventional fatal diseases. Agent Einstein (Lauren Ambrose) points out that "pathogens are virtually everywhere. Every cough, every sneeze, every cut on the finger—deadly." Even vaccines can now be deadly, attacking the systems of those with compromised immunities. Soldiers, in particular, who have been given anthrax vaccines to protect them in the event of biological warfare, are now dying of anthrax. This, Agent Scully (Gillian Anderson) explains, is only "a harbinger of infections to come. Measles, mumps, rubella, the flu.

We're all going to be exposed." In fact, the origin of the Spartan virus lies within the smallpox vaccine. So rather than it being something you "catch," the Spartan virus is already within us, triggered by a release of aluminum in the atmosphere through chemtrails—à la *Toxic Skies* (Erin, 2008)—or by microwave radiation, calling to mind horror narratives from the 1950s. The premise echoes that of *The Walking Dead* (AMC, 2010–present) in that everyone is already infected. Hospitals are flooded. The CDC is at a loss. Scully tells Einstein that they are witnessing "what may be the advent of a global contagion."

Global. Contagion. Pathogens. Vulnerability. Outbreak. AIDS. Immunity. Biological warfare. Chemtrails. Conspiracy. Infections. Buzzwords that should now be familiar. Buzzwords that reflect a new and heightened awareness of the increasingly ineffective boundaries between personal bodies and national bodies, between bodies and microbes, and between good and bad bodies. As depicted by this episode, the collapse of our immune system has occurred in tandem with the collapse of political borders, the failures of both to protect and quarantine. While studies of the immune system have always been concerned with how the body defends itself from foreign antigens, it had previously been easy to distinguish between self and other. Now, however, as a result of autoimmune diseases and HIV/AIDS, as well as the blurring of borders facilitated by globalization and a shift to a more horizontal and networked social structure, this distinction has grown increasingly murky. There is no longer a single recognizable enemy.

As the Spartan virus would indicate, it is not that we are afraid of getting sick. It is not even that we are afraid of "catching a bug." It is that we are afraid we are *already* sick, that our compromised immune system will not be able to protect us, that we are living in a world that cannot protect us and that will most likely make us sick. We are afraid that the things we do—or things we cannot avoid doing—will make us sick, like traveling or breathing or using a microwave or getting a shot at the doctor's office. It is that things that are packaged as "for our own good" will actually lead to our own death. It is that when something is seriously wrong, the media will not tell us and our politicians will lie to us. It is that when we get sick, no one will be able to help us.

We are afraid of discovering, as Todd Haynes said about the memorable protagonist from his film *Safe* (1995), that "we all have a little Carol White in us."[1] When White first develops multiple chemical sensitivity, her symptoms include nosebleeds, weakness, coughing, vomiting, and convulsions. An inherently controversial diagnosis, multiple chemical sensitivity is officially seen to be a reaction to chemicals found in everyday products. As defined by the US Department of Labor, MCS is an "adverse physical reaction to low levels of many common chemicals . . . Proposed theories to explain the cause of MCS include allergy, dysfunction of the immune system, neurobiological sensitization, and various psychological theories."[2] MCS is what happens when your immune system becomes dysfunctional, arguably defined as an allergic response to the contemporary world. MCS is what happens when your world makes you sick.

In the twenty years or so since *Safe* was released, anxieties about contagion and infiltration have continued to swirl through American news and entertainment media. In contrast to fears from earlier decades, which reflected vulnerabilities of nations as a whole, these latest threats reflect risk for the individual. Depending on the moment, we have been alternately afraid of AIDS, swine flu, Zika, Ebola, Al Qaeda, ISIS . . . just fill in the blank. What all these fears have in common is that they are not isolated events but, rather, inevitable consequences of the way we live now, results of porous and ineffective barriers. As Peter Knight, a senior lecturer in American culture, argues, they also are all threats over which centralized and antiquated governmental systems cannot protect us: "If life-threatening world-wide phenomena such as global warming or the AIDS epidemic can be neither traced back to a single cause nor confined to a single location, then individual national governments are unlikely to be able to bring them under control . . . We now need to think in terms of clusters of causes, convoluted feedback mechanisms, syndromes, and decentered agency."[3]

Unfortunately, thinking in terms of clusters of causes and decentered agency lacks reassurance. And so, as a way to restore a sense of agency and responsibility, there has been a rise in conspiracy thinking. In an article from 2011, author and British screenwriter Nick Harding looks at the recent rise of conspiracy theories, blaming the increase on how easy the Internet has made it to propagate rumor and supposition on a global scale.[4] However, in this case, the medium is not the message. The medium just transmits the content. While the Internet facilitates transmission, the crux of what is being transmitted emphasizes that it is more comforting to imagine that there is *someone* in control rather than no one in control, that things happen for a reason, even if that agenda is not a noble one. As Knight explains about the current proliferation of conspiracy theories: "Even as they draw attention to the people's lack of power (since the conspiracy controls everything), they offer a compensatory fantasy that at least things are still controllable by an all-powerful individual or group . . . in short, to put a name and a face to otherwise unrepresentable and impenetrable systems." This notion—that there is a greater agenda and a greater purpose—appears in *The X-Files* finale's opening sequence, as relayed via an Agent Scully voice-over. Scully acknowledges that there is, in fact, "a larger conspiracy" behind all the mysteries explored on *The X-Files,* that there *is* "a conspiracy of men hiding science for almost sixty years," and that there *are* "secrets kept from the American people by a self-interested cabal intent on the consolidation of power both at home and on a perilously global scale." We are pawns and puppets at the mercy of this cabal, or so some of us want to believe, because it is easier than believing that there is no one in charge, that there is no greater purpose.

A persistent theme throughout *The X-Files* has always been this notion of shadowy men in shadowy corners pulling the strings to further their agenda while concealing the truth, and this episode is no exception. However, when Agent Mulder (David Duchovny) confronts the Cigarette Smoking Man (William B. Davis), the truth proves to be more complicated. Yes, the Cigarette Smoking Man, as "the most powerful man in the world," is behind the Spartan outbreak. However, as he puts it, he just changed the timetable. Mankind was still headed toward self-extermination, even without the Cigarette Smoking Man and his shadowy cabal. "I didn't set out to destroy the world," he tells Mulder, "People did . . . We have just had the hottest summer on Planet Earth. I didn't do that. I'm not responsible for the 40 percent loss of birdlife or the decimation of the megafauna."

In this episode, much like in many recent outbreak narratives, the conceit of the primitive other, the "dirty immigrant" spreading infection, has been removed. Even the conceit of the "shadowy cabal" engineering our doom has been complicated. Emerging infectious diseases are not the fault of Muslims or Africans or Asians or the cabal. Emerging infectious diseases are the products of globalization, and we are culpable in our own destruction, or so the episode would like us to believe. As the saying goes in the Walt Kelly poster for Earth Day in 1970, "We have met the enemy and he is us." In the poster, Pogo the possum looks sadly at us as he prepares to clean up the trash littering his planet (see figure 36).[5] The writing is on the wall. The Cigarette Smoking Man just sped things up.

FIGURE 36 Walt Kelly's poster for Earth Day 1970: "We have met the enemy and he is us."

It is not difficult to appreciate the appeal of the "eco-terrorist plot" evident in the *Blindspot* episode "Bone May Rot" (NBC, Oct. 12, 2015) or *The Blacklist* episode "The Front" (NBC, Oct. 20, 2014), or *Inferno* (Howard, 2016), all of which depict attempts to create a pandemic in order to reduce the world's population, thereby saving the Earth. At least, in these narratives, there is a sense of agency, a sense of purpose, a sense that *something* is being done. What *The X-Files* has always tapped into has been this lack of trust in traditional outlets and traditional institutions, the notion that there are secrets and conspiracies behind almost every government door. And now we see that the conspiracy theory, rather than being the worst possible option, is actually the best one, because it implies that someone is in control.

Elaine Showalter, in her book *Hystories: Hysterical Epidemics and Modern Media*, brings up an important point as she defines the significant difference between infectious diseases—which are spread by ecological change, modern technology, urbanization, jet travel, and human interaction—and infectious *epidemics*—which are spread by the media, "by stories circulated through self-help books, articles in newspapers and magazines, TV talk shows and series, films, the Internet, and even literary criticism."[6] While infectious diseases are the result of, among other things, globalization and environmental destruction, infectious epidemics are the true cause of unnecessary panic. It is this crucial difference, between the outbreak of a disease and the outbreak of hysteria, which is integrally linked metaphorically and literally to the "viral" spread of digital communication. Infectious epidemics are the hyperbolic narrative imposed upon infectious diseases.

Whether the outbreak narrative depicts the cultural and social impact of globalization, the increased fear of bioterrorist attack, or the uncomfortable realization that twenty-eight days is all it takes for society to collapse, it continues to provide allegorical (and sometimes literal) reflections of our world, both in the current moment and for the future. While the various fictional texts I have discussed construct versions of reality that perpetuate certain biases in our culture in ways that may demand critique or condemnation—our anxieties about marginalized groups such as women, gays, and immigrants, for instance—the outbreak narrative, in all its incarnations, still reflects an awareness of viral threats, and the inability of immune systems or national borders to protect us, in ways that can be constructive and enlightening to examine. This awareness is compounded by a pervasive lack of trust in government and medical institutions to save us, as well as by hyperactive digital communication reminding us of death and danger at every turn. Disease metaphors speak profoundly not only to the connections between bodily threats and threats to the body politic but also to the way the world has been reimagined—and marketed—in terms of containment, protection, and vulnerability.

Fictional texts are especially useful at mapping out this world, at portraying significant cultural and social changes, for a variety of reasons. One, because they "address dimensions of the political unconscious that more solution-oriented political and journalistic approaches to the same phenomena tend to reason away or repress."[7] And two, because they teach viewers about this reimagined world and how to act within it. Professor John L. Sherry, whose research focuses on media theory and the effects of mass media, argues that viewers intentionally use the media in this way. In his article on media saturation and entertainment-education, he points out that these effects are not the result of a single message, "or even a message repeated a number of times," but rather the consequence "of a flood of consistent themes about social reality across multiple television programs."[8] And since these narratives are teaching so many viewers so many things, it is instrumental to look at what is being taught and in what ways. Tellingly, Kyle Bishop, in his book *American Zombie Gothic*, recounts the tale of a law student who survived 9/11 and claimed "that he had been emotionally prepared for the tragedy, not by his family, community, or government, but by the zombie movies of which he had been a long-time appreciator."[9] While this is a fascinating extrapolation, the attacks of 9/11 were also not a zombie attack. Monsters in the street were not the threat. No one was being eaten alive. While the event was a tragedy and a horror, to describe it as a zombie movie also demonstrates the hyperbolic response to danger and disaster. Ironically, the CDC actually has a fictional "Zombie Apocalypse Defense Plan" on their website as a means of better educating the public about mass disaster and contagion, implying that a total apocalypse is something for which to prepare.

To return to Ulrich Beck, it is not that risks have intensified; it is that *perceptions* of risk have intensified. It is that, in an increasingly media-savvy world, headlines must be hyperbolic in order to get attention. Skye Cooley, professor of public relations at Mississippi State University, laments in an editorial for the *Huffington Post* how little attention the media was paying to the disastrous floods in Louisiana in 2016: "In order to be worthy of attention the very fabric of societal order has to have been sheered away; news media requires scenes that look like a zombie apocalypse."[10] The media reminds us of death, bringing it to our phones and our living rooms, amplifying portrayals of outbreaks into dramatic life-or-death situations—or not covering them if such amplification is not possible. We have become so used to the hyperbolic din that we cannot hear anything else.

Exacerbating this amplification is the fact that alterations in media, spectatorship, and representation have led to an intermedial phenomena in which the news becomes the films becomes the news becomes the television shows becomes the video games. Is it any wonder that public responses to real-life outbreaks are so affected by fictional narratives when the "factual" narratives may be just as hyperbolic as the fictional ones? The threat of plague transcends medium: the cover of *Rolling Stone* ominously warns of apocalypse as you download the latest version of *Plague Inc.* for your phone, the latest *Walking Dead* episode hits your television while

Fight of the Living Dead: Experiment 88 (YouTube Red, 2016) streams on your computer and the latest *Resident Evil* video game launches on your Xbox. As Lynn Spigel wrote in her article "Entertainment Wars: Television Culture after 9/11" following the events of 9/11, "The difference between real wars and 'made-for-TV' wars hardly mattered."[11] Life imitates art imitates life in a dizzying and self-nurturing circle.

There are even numerous examples of current Hollywood practices that intentionally blur the boundaries between fact and faction, continuing a trend that began with Seabrook's *The Magic Island*. For example, the *NBC Nightly News* integrated clips from two Hollywood films, *And the Band Played On* (HBO, Sept. 11, 1993) and *Outbreak* (Petersen, 1995), into a story on the 1995 Ebola breakout in Zaire, with "no verbal mention of the origins or fictive nature of the film segments."[12] Conversely, shows often feature news footage running within the episode, using staged news footage with real news logos. For example, the television show *24* (Fox, 2001–10) features not only multiple TVs tuned to Fox News, running staged Fox News footage with the real Fox News logos during its series run, but the characters on the show also frequently watch the news, "exuding the heightened state of alert that viewers share (both in watching *24* and the real Fox News)."[13] It is also common for films and television shows to use real reporters appearing as themselves in order to lend "a certain authenticity," says Hollywood producer Kim Sherrell.[14] In other words, to make the fictional narrative appear less fictional. Some of the biggest names in television news have appeared on the Netflix drama *House of Cards* (2013–present), for instance. Another blurring of reality and fiction occurs when actors with memorable characters perform real-life endorsements based not on their real-life persona but on their *fictional* personas. For example, Kiefer Sutherland filmed a recruitment spot for the navy following the success of *24*, while *Alias* (ABC, 2001–2006) star Jennifer Garner filmed a recruitment spot for the CIA. In its press releases, the CIA describes Garner as embodying the "integrity, patriotism, and intelligence the CIA looks for in its officers."[15]

In another surreal partnership, the University of Southern California's Institute for Creative Technologies unites government officials with Hollywood creators, like directors David Fincher or Spike Jonze, in order to set the "best minds of the entertainment industry to the task of creating state-of-the-art training exercises for soldiers and to create possible terrorist scenarios for government consideration."[16] So in this case, Hollywood shapes government scenarios and military strategies rather than vice versa. As I mentioned in the "Terrorism Outbreak" chapter, another example of fictional scenarios influencing real-life policy occurred when President Clinton intensified military measures against bioterrorism after reading Richard Preston's biothriller *The Cobra Event* (Random House, 1998), as well as recommending the book to his advisors and high-ranking Pentagon officials.[17] This is the same book that Secretary of Health and Human Services Donna Shalala would use to open her article on bioterrorism for the CDC's *Emerging Infectious Diseases* journal.

Yet another example of Hollywood intentionally blurring fact and fiction occurs on the season 3 box set for *24*. The box set includes a featurette entitled "Bio Threat: Beyond the Series." This featurette offers interviews with a variety of scientists, doctors, and government officials meant to provide an air of legitimacy to the season. Jennifer Gillan, in her book *Television and New Media: Must Click TV*, argues that the featurette "leaves viewers with the impression that the weaponizing of a virus is not only possible, but probable." She points out that Joel Surnow, creator of *24*, makes a case for the imminent threat of bioterrorism, "despite the overwhelming evidence to the contrary."[18] As Surnow himself says in his interview for the featurette, "Unfortunately, what you can imagine is usually true. As outrageous as some of the stuff that we come up with is, there is always something there to support it."

He is not alone in that belief. After the season 6 premiere of *24*, which includes the detonation of a small nuclear bomb over Los Angeles, John Gibson, host of Fox News's *The Big Story* declared, "Well, it may be fiction for now. But *24*'s Jack Bauer has it right. People need to wake up to the possibility of nuclear attack." Gibson later asked, "Is *24*'s faux suitcase nuke bomb a real wake-up call for America? Should we take this as an early warning sign that something like this could happen here?"[19] Similarly, in his January 30, 2007, syndicated column, Cal Thomas urged his readers to watch *24* "for what could be our prophetic and imminent future with a nuclear device exploding in major cities."[20] Apparently, when fictional texts "address dimensions of the political unconscious that more solution-oriented political and journalistic approaches to the same phenomena tend to reason away or repress,"[21] they are also able to predict the future.

Some even use the fictional as justification for government and military action. For instance, on January 17, 2007, Neil Cavuto, host of the Fox News show *Your World*, interviewed private investigator Richard "Bo"

Dietl, a former detective with the New York City Police Department. The topic was a group of forty American Muslims who had recently been barred from boarding a Michigan-bound plane in Frankfurt, Germany. Dietl justified the action by replying, "A bunch of Irish guys are not going to get on a plane now and blow themselves up or put themselves into buildings. The fact of the matter is—I mean, you don't watch *24* on Fox TV? They're out there. They're out there. There are cells out there. We have to protect ourselves against it, as Americans."[22] *24*, much like *The Cobra Event*, was used as justification for action without acknowledgement of its fictional status.

However, it is no longer only television and radio that bring sounds, images, and horrors into our homes, feeding our fears and fueling our emotions. With contemporary events like 9/11, our exposure is immediate and global and often uncensored. As E. Ann Kaplan writes, "The phenomenon of 9/11 was perhaps the supreme example of a catastrophe that was experienced globally via digital technologies (Internet, cell phone) as well as by television and radio."[23]

While part of the original appeal of television revolved around its "liveness," watching television live is becoming an antiquated procedure. Instead, it is the Internet that relies on its liveness for its relevance, for its immediate delivery of content. Thanks to handheld devices, we are always "in touch," just as M describes to Bond in *Casino Royale* (Campbell, 2006). Exposure is instantaneous and mass-oriented but also personal and private. We can watch the horrors from the intimacy of our homes, or the checkout line at the supermarket, united and isolated at the same time. Thanks to this new media immediacy, standard rules of temporality and geography no longer apply. For example, news of the terrorist attack in Paris on November 13, 2015, initially spread primarily via social media, with more than 10.7 million tweets posted about Paris between November 13 and November 14.[24]

Significantly, voice-of-the-truth journalist Tad O'Malley on season 10 of *The X-Files* broadcasts via the Internet. Rather than flipping on the television to catch his latest news, the agents flip open a laptop. The implication, when O'Malley skewers the mainstream news for ignoring the real story, is that the renegade on the Internet is the one who has the truth. The corporate suits on the corporate networks are too busy toeing the party line. In terms of being a renegade, O'Malley echoes the character of Alan Krumwiede in *Contagion* (Soderbergh, 2011). In 2016, however, the Internet provides the truth, the only truth, rather than being "graffiti with punctuation," as Dr. Ellis Cheever describes Krumwiede's website. Much has changed in five years. The truth, or what so many believe to be the truth, is now to be found online. The truth does not need the voice of an authority figure (or an authoritative network) to vouch for it. To the contrary, it works better without either. Alison Bashford, in her essay on "Panic's Past and Global Futures," describes the digital world as "a new world for panic, disease, communication, and containment," where "the presence of disease, or suspected disease, can be communicated instantly and by anybody, bypassing experts, and with little heed for verification or authorization."[25]

The digital world may be a new world, but it works in tandem with the world that exists offscreen. The current popularity of images and narratives of contagion—online and off—has resulted in anxiety both displaced and exacerbated, as evidenced by the Ebola panic of 2014, which bordered on hysteria even though it was never a significant threat to America. While some theorists argue that watching a film of something awful decreases one's sensitivity, these narratives serve to *increase* our awareness of infectious disease and our vulnerability to it. Media portrayals of both terrorist attacks and viral outbreaks legitimize and sensationalize the events themselves. How a society responds to disease—especially epidemic disease—can illuminate its relationship not only to science and medicine but also to illness, fear, death, and identity. Public responses to real-life outbreaks like Ebola and AIDS reflect cultural fears of contagion and disease, as well as the power and internal logic of film and television to construct and shape those fears. Fear is no longer merely a response but a cultural state of being.

As explored throughout this book, the purpose of the outbreak narrative is to contain, control, and ultimately obliterate the contagion, whether it be a microbe, a terrorist, a zombie, or a combination of the three. It is not friendly to contagion, and contagion is not friendly to it. After all, contagion welcomes the thing—microbe, terrorist, or zombie—that the outbreak narrative aims to contain, control, and obliterate. In order to succeed, contagion requires the services of a microbe, terrorist, or zombie. Contagion is also unfriendly to the protagonists of these narratives, to the hero or team trying to save the day. It does not want them to persevere. It wants, instead, to contaminate and spread. Contagion is a threat to the subject and, in turn, a threat to the story about the threat to the subject, because without protagonists, without a subject, traditional narrative stumbles. In a traditional narrative, there must be at least one key power-ful figure that prevails. Such is the narrative arc. And yet, in our increas-ingly anonymous and automatized society, everyone seems to be a pawn in the machine. There are fewer and fewer powerful figures. Instead, there are powerful networks.

First there was the death of God, and then the death of the author, and now it appears to be the death of Man. The individual is no longer a key agent in history. After all, viral propagation does not require the individual. It does not require an authority figure or a guiding voice. It only requires a network. And so the outbreak narrative becomes a last ditch effort to save the subject, to save the story, to overcome the propagation of the viral with an insertion of a traditional narrative structure. During a time that feels like the end of days, with the convergence of one catastrophe after another, the outbreak narrative, perversely, provides a glimmer of hope. Maybe, as the world falls apart, there will be a voice, a figure to show the way.

Acknowledgments

Writing a book is a solitary process, as every author knows. Lots of self-doubt coupled with hours spent staring at a computer monitor or scribbling furiously on endless pages. For making this process less solitary and more survivable, I extend infinite thanks to Melody Sandoval (who always seemed able to track down a rare zombie movie when my efforts failed) and to Stacy Takacs, whose comments and critiques pushed me to be a better writer and (I hope) a better thinker. Without Leslie Mitchner, this book would not be in your hands.

Thank you to Denise Mann, for being willing to step up for me, as well as Tom Schweitzer, Toby Miller, Vivian Sobchack, John Alberti, Jonathan Allen, Eric Levy, and Tandy Philip Franciosa.

Notes

Introduction

1 Alison Bashford, "Panic's Past and Global Futures," in *Empires of Panic: Epidemics and Colonial Anxieties*, ed. Robert Peckham (Hong Kong: Hong Kong University Press, 2015), 205.

2 Frank Furedi, "The Only Thing We Have to Fear Is the 'Culture of Fear' Itself," *Spiked*, April 4, 2007, http://www.spiked-online.com/index.php?/site/article/3053/.

3 Peter Knight, *Conspiracy Culture: From Kennedy to "The X-Files"* (London: Routledge, 2000), 177.

4 Todd Haynes, interview by Scott Tobias, *The Dissolve*, December 18, 2014, https://thedissolve.com/features/interview/856-todd-haynes-on-the-unsafe-world-of-safe/.

5 Michael D. Lemonick, "The Killers All Around," *Time*, September 12, 1994, http://content.time.com/time/magazine/article/0,9171,981430,00.html.

6 Ibid.

7 Richard Preston, "The Vaccine Debacle," *New York Times*, October 2, 1994, D-17.

8 Nicholas B. King, "The Scale Politics of Emerging Diseases," *Osiris* 2.19 (2004), 64, 65.

9 Ibid., 66.

10 Harrison Blackman, "Crisis in West Africa: Richard Preston on Ebola," *Affairs Today*, August 9, 2014, accessed May 19, 2017, https://web.archive.org/web/20141026122830 http://affairstoday.co.uk/crisis-west-africa-richard-preston-ebola/.

11 Richard Preston, "Crisis in the Hot Zone," *New Yorker*, October 26, 1992, 80, 81.

12 King, "Scale Politics," 71.

13 Stephen S. Hall, "Panic Everywhere," *New York Times*, October 30, 1994, http://www.nytimes.com/1994/10/30/books/panic-everywhere.html?pagewanted=all.

14 David Hughes, *Tales from Development Hell: The Greatest Movies Never Made?* (London: Titan Books, 2012), 169–170.

15 King, "Scale Politics," 67.

16 Elizabeth Fee and Theodore M. Brown, "Preemptive Biopreparedness: Can We Learn Anything from History?," *American Journal of Public Health* 91 (2001): 722.

17 Handwritten talk circa 1978, Alexander D. Langmuir Papers, Alan Mason Chesney Medical Archives of the Johns Hopkins Medical Institution, Box no. 1, Folder, "JHV Honorary Degree 1978," quoted in Amy L. Fairchild and David Merritt Johns, "The 'Excited and Terrified' Public Mind," in *Empires of Panic: Epidemics and Colonial Anxieties*, ed. Robert Peckham (Hong Kong: Hong Kong University Press, 2015), 172.

18 Handwritten notes, Alexander D. Langmuir Papers, Alan Mason Chesney Medical Archives of the Johns Hopkins Medical Institution, Box no. 5, Folder, "Lecture Notes, Miscellaneous History CDC," quoted in Amy L. Fairchild and David Merritt Johns, "The 'Excited and Terrified' Public Mind," in *Empires of Panic: Epidemics and Colonial Anxieties*, ed. Robert Peckham (Hong Kong: Hong Kong University Press, 2015), 172.

19 Fee and Brown, "Preemptive Biopreparedness," 722.

20 Ibid.

21 "What You Should Know about Biological Warfare," *Johns Hopkins Science Review*, WAAM, Baltimore, MD, April 3, 1951. The video is available to view here: https://archive.org/details/WhatYouS1952.

22 Fee and Brown, "Preemptive Biopreparedness," 722, 723.

23 William Schaffner and F. Marc LaForce, "Training Field Epidemiologists: Alexander D. Langmuir and the Epidemic Intelligence Service," *American Journal of Epidemiology* 144.8 (Apr. 1996): S16.

24 Martin A. French, "Woven of War-Time Fabrics: The Globalization of Public Health Surveillance," *Surveillance & Society* 6.2, 104.

25 Fee and Brown, "Preemptive Biopreparedness," 723.

26 Donna Shalala, "Bioterrorism: How Prepared Are We?," *Emerging Infectious Diseases* 5.4 (July/Aug. 1999): ftp://ftp.cdc.gov/pub/eid/vol5no4/ascii/vol5no4.txt.

27 King, "Scale Politics," 75.

28 Janet Heinrech, "Bioterrorism: Public Health and Mental Preparedness," in *Bioterrorism and Public Health*, ed. Vitali Mellehovitch (New York: Nova Science, 2004), 109.

29 Crystal Boddie, Tara Kirk Sell, and Matthew Watson, "Federal Funding for Health Security in FY 2015," *Biosecur Bioterror* 12.4 (Aug. 2014): 163, 164, http://pubmedcentralcanada.ca/pmcc/articles/PMC4106388/.

30 Eugene Thacker, "Cryptobiologies," *Artnodes*, no. 6 (2006), 4.

31 Tara Kirk Sell and Matthew Watson, "Federal Agency Biodefense Funding, FY 2013–2014," *Biosecurity and Bioterrorism: Biodefense Strategy, Practice, and Science* 11.3 (Sept. 2013): 196.

32 Jennifer Cooke, *Legacies of Plague in Literature, Theory and Film* (New York: Palgrave Macmillan, 2009), 183.

33 Ruth Mayer, "Virus Discourse: The Rhetoric of Threat and Terrorism in the Biothriller," *Cultural Critique* 66 (Spring 2007): 17.

34 John Murlowski, e-mail message to author, August 6, 2015.

35 Bruce Dorminey, "Ebola as ISIS Bio-Weapon?," *Forbes*, October 5, 2014, http://www.forbes.com/sites/brucedorminey/2014/10/05/ebola-as-isis-bio-weapon/.

36 Kelley Beaucar Vlahos, "Could Ebola Become 'Bioterrorist Threat'?," *Fox News*,

October 17, 204, http://www.foxnews.com/politics/2014/10/03/could-ebola-virus
-become-bioterrorist-threat.html.

37 Fred Lucas, "GOP Congressman: Ebola as a Terrorism Tool 'Should Be on the
Radar Screen," *Blaze*, October 17, 2014, http://www.theblaze.com/stories/2014/
10/17/gop-congressman-ebola-as-a-terrorism-tool-should-be-on-the-radar-screen/.

38 King, "Scale Politics," 68.

39 Lawrence K. Altman, "The Doctor's World; Infectious Diseases on the Rebound in
the U.S., a Report Says," *New York Times*, May 10, 1994, http://www.nytimes.com/
1994/05/10/science/the-doctor-s-world-infectious-diseases-on-the-rebound-in
-the-us-a-report-says.html?pagewanted=all.

40 Ibid.

41 Peter Piot, quoted in Michael D. Lemonick and Bruce Crumley, "Return to the
Hot Zone," *Time*, May 22, 1995, 62.

42 Lemonick and Crumley, "Hot Zone," 62.

43 Ibid.

44 Lemonick, "Killers All Around."

45 Ibid.

46 King, "Scale Politics," 68.

47 Laurie Garrett, *The Coming Plague* (New York: Penguin Books, 1994), 618.

48 Stephen A. Morse, "The Year 2000: Only a Plane Flight Away from Disaster?,"
Public Health Reports 110.2 (Mar.–Apr. 1995): 223.

49 Richard Preston, *The Hot Zone* (New York: Anchor-Doubleday, 1995), 420.

50 Ibid., 16.

51 N. S. Galbraith, "Reviewed Work: *The Hot Zone* by Richard Preston," *BMJ: British
Medical Journal* 309.6962 (Oct. 29, 1994): 1169.

52 Robert J. Howard, quoted in Malcolm Gladwell, "The Plague Year," *New Republic*,
July 16, 1995, https://newrepublic.com/article/62521/the-plague-year.

53 Robert J. Howard, "Perspective: Media Coverage of Emerging and Re-Emerging
Diseases behind the Headlines," *Statistics in Medicine* 20 (2001): 1357.

54 Brigitte Nerlich and Christopher Halliday, "Avian Flu: The Creation of Expectations in the Interplay between Science and the Media," *Sociology of Health and
Illness* 29.1 (2007): 48.

55 Ibid., 54.

56 Ibid., 54, 56.

57 Dorothy Nelkin, "Managing Biomedical News," *Social Research* 52.3 (Autumn
1985): 625, 626.

58 Robert J. Howard, "Getting It Right in Prime Time: Tools and Strategies for Media
Interaction," *Emerging Infectious Diseases* 6.4 (Aug. 2000): http://wwwnc.cdc.gov/
eid/article/6/4/00-0422.

59 Vicki Freimuth, Huan Linnan, and Polyxeni Potter, "Communicating the Threat of
Emerging Infections to the Public," *Emerging Infectious Diseases* 6.4 (Aug. 2000):
http://wwwnc.cdc.gov/eid/article/6/4/00-0403.

60 Ibid.

61 Ibid.

62 For a more in-depth analysis of *The Eternal Flight*, see Nicholas B. King, "Mediating
Panic," in *Empires of Panic: Epidemics and Colonial Anxieties*, ed. Robert Peckham
(Hong Kong: Hong Kong University Press, 2015), 190, 191, 192.

63 Peter N. Stearns, *American Fear: The Causes and Consequences of High Anxiety* (New York: Routledge, 2006), 210.

64 Craig Silverman and Jeremy Singer-Vine, "Most Americans Who See Fake News Believe It, New Survey Says," *Buzzfeed*, December 6, 2016, https://www.buzzfeed.com/craigsilverman/fake-news-survey?utm_term=.urzy8yar0#.vnkMxM42L.

65 Sheldon Ungar, "Hot Crises and Media Reassurance: A Comparison of Emerging Diseases and Ebola Zaire," *British Journal of Sociology* 49.1 (Mar. 1998): 41.

66 Ibid., 42, 43.

67 Douglas Kellner, *Cinema Wars* (West Sussex: Wiley Blackwell, 2010), 4.

68 Hughes, *Development Hell*, 172.

69 Rebecca Ascher-Walsh, "Crisis in the Plot Zone," *Entertainment Weekly*, March 24, 1995, http://www.ew.com/article/1995/03/24/crisis-plot-zone.

70 "Outbreak (1995)," Box Office Mojo, accessed May 19, 2017, http://www.boxofficemojo.com/movies/?id=outbreak.htm.

71 According to Box Office Mojo, the domestic gross was $57,141,459 and the total worldwide gross $168,839,459. "12 Monkeys (1995)," Box Office Mojo, accessed May 19, 2017, http://www.boxofficemojo.com/movies/?id=twelvemonkeys.htm.

72 Kellner, *Cinema Wars*, 14.

73 Stearns, *American Fear*, 41.

74 Melissa Leach, "Time to Put Ebola in Context," *Bulletin of the World Health Organization*, World Health Organization 88.7, http://www.who.int/bulletin/volumes/88/7/10-030710/en/.

75 Josh Gardner, "How Ebola Doctor Roamed New York," *Daily Mail*, October 23, 2014, http://www.dailymail.co.uk/news/article-2805673/Ebola-panic-Brooklyn-Doctor-treated-patients-West-Africa-visited-hip-bowling-hotspot-ONE-DAY-rushed-hospital-103F-fever.html#ixzz3H3Pv6fLZ.

76 Dana Blanton, "Fox News Poll: More than 6 in 10 Worried about Ebola Spreading to US," *Fox News*, August 14, 2014, http://www.foxnews.com/politics/2014/08/14/fox-news-poll-more-than-6-in-10-worried-about-ebola-spreading-to-us.html.

77 Paul Bedard, "American Fear: 74% See 'Catastrophic Terrorist Attack' inside United States," *Washington Examiner*, January 7, 2015, http://www.washingtonexaminer.com/american-fear-74-see-catastrophic-terrorist-attack-inside-united-states/article/2558294.

78 Kevin J. Wetmore, *Post-9/11 Horror in American Cinema* (New York: Continuum, 2012), 109.

79 Roger E. Kasperson and Jeanne X. Kasperson, "The Social Amplification and Attenuation of Risk," *Annals of the American Academy of Politics and Social Science*, no. 545 (1996): 97.

80 "On a Wing and a Prayer," *Nature: International Weekly Journal of Science*, May 25, 2005, http://www.nature.com/nature/journal/v435/n7041/full/435385a.html.

81 Michael T. Osterholm, "Preparing for the Next Pandemic," *New York Times*, June 21, 2005, http://www.nytimes.com/cfr/international/20050701faessay-v84n4_osterholm.html?pagewanted=all&_r=0.

82 Wendy Orent, "Chicken Little," *New Republic*, September 11, 2005, https://newrepublic.com/article/64264/chicken-little.

83 Marc Siegel, *False Alarm* (Hoboken, NJ: John Wiley & Sons, 2005), 145.

84 Orent, "Chicken Little."

85 Hillary Evans and Robert E. Bartholomew, *Outbreak! The Encyclopedia of Extraordinary Social Behavior* (San Antonio, TX: Anomalist Books, 2009), 52.

86 Grey Szymanski, "Avian Flu May Come to America," *American Free Press*, October 1, 2005, http://www.americanfreepress.net/html/avian_flu.html.

87 Evans and Bartholomew, *Outbreak!*, 52.

88 Orent, "Chicken Little."

89 "Human Death Toll from Bird Flu Tops 100," Live Science, March 21, 2006, http://www.livescience.com/659-human-death-toll-bird-flu-tops-100.html.

90 Frank Furedi, *Culture of Fear Revisited* (London: Continuum, 2006), 30.

91 David Quammen, interview by Michaleen Doucleff, "How *The Hot Zone* Got It Wrong and Other Tales of Ebola's History," *NPR*, November 11, 2014, http://www.npr.org/sections/goatsandsoda/2014/11/11/362379449/how-the-hot-zone-got-it-wrong-and-other-tales-of-ebolas-history.

92 Ungar, "Hot Crises," 43.

93 Amy L. Fairchild and David Merritt Johns, "The 'Excited and Terrified' Public Mind," in *Empires of Panic: Epidemics and Colonial Anxieties*, ed. Robert Peckham (Hong Kong: Hong Kong University Press, 2015), 169.

94 Gerald Ford, quoted in Richard E. Neustadt and Harvey Fineberg, *The Epidemic That Never Was: Policy-Making and the Swine Flu Affair* (New York: Vintage, 1983), 46.

95 Editorial, "Light on Swine Flu," *New York Times*, July 20, 1976, 30.

96 Editorial, "Doubts about Swine Flu," *New York Times*, August 9, 1976, 16.

97 Harry Schwartz, "Swine Flu Fiasco," *New York Times*, December 21, 1976, 33.

98 Siegel, *False Alarm*, 127–128.

99 Orent, "Chicken Little."

100 Ibid.

101 Diane Chun, "Experts Dismiss Scare over Bird Flu," *Gainesville Sun*, November 1, 2005, http://www.gainesville.com/news/20051101/experts-dismiss-scare-over-bird-flu.

102 Vivian Sobchack, *Screening Space: The American Science Fiction Film* (New Brunswick, NJ: Rutgers University Press, 1987), 19, 88.

103 Nerlich and Halliday, "Avian Flu," 54.

104 Ulrich Beck, *Risk Society: Towards a New Modernity* (London: Sage Publications, 1992), 55.

105 Mads P. Sorensen and Allan Christiansen, *Ulrich Beck: An Introduction to the Theory of Second Modernity and the Risk Society* (London: Routledge 2013), 12–13, 15.

106 Kai Erikson, *A New Species of Trouble: The Human Experience of Modern Disasters* (New York: W. W. Norton, 1995), 106.

107 Ibid., 144.

108 Stearns, *American Fear*, 3, 9.

109 Oliver Laughland, "The Ministering of Fear: Dystopia and Loathing at the Republican Convention," *Guardian*, July 23, 2016, https://www.theguardian.com/us-news/2016/jul/23/republican-convention-cleveland-donald-trump-fear.

110 Dylan Matthews, "Donald Trump's Convention Speech Was an Overwhelming Victory for Fear," *Vox*, July 22, 2016, http://www.vox.com/2016/7/22/12254826/donald-trump-convention-speech-rnc-fear.

111 Danny Boyle, quoted in Kyle William Bishop, *American Zombie Gothic* (Jefferson, NC: McFarland & Company, 2010), 28.
112 Stearns, *American Fear*, 19.

Chapter 1   The Outbreak Narrative

1 Amanda Ann Klein, *American Film Cycles: Reframing Genres, Screening Social Problems, and Defining Subcultures* (Austin: University of Texas Press, 2011), 3–4, 6, 13.
2 Leger Grindon, "Cycles and Clusters," in *Film Genre Reader IV*, ed. Barry Keith Grant (Austin: University of Texas Press, 2012), 55.
3 John T. Caldwell, "Welcome to the Viral Future of Cinema (Television)," *Cinema Journal* 45.1 (2005): 91, 92.
4 Klein, *American Film Cycles*, 6.
5 Nicholas B. King, "Mediating Panic," in *Empires of Panic: Epidemics and Colonial Anxieties*, ed. Robert Peckham (Hong Kong: Hong Kong University Press, 2015), 196.
6 Ibid., 197.
7 Bill Albertini, "Contagion and the Necessary Accident," *Discourse* 30.3 (Fall 2008): 462, 444.
8 Alexandra Alter, "Updating a Chronicle of Suffering: Author of *The Hot Zone* Tracks Ebola's Evolution," *New York Times*, October 19, 2014, http://www .nytimes.com/2014/10/20/books/the-hot-zone-author-tracks-ebolas-evolution .html.
9 Sheldon Ungar, "Hot Crises and Media Reassurance: A Comparison of Emerging Diseases and Ebola Zaire," *British Journal of Sociology* 49.1 (Mar. 1998): 50.
10 Donna Haraway, "The Biopolitics of Postmodern Bodies: Determinations of Self in Immune System Discourse," in *American Feminist Thought at Century's End*, ed. Linda S. Kaufman (Cambridge: Blackwell, 1993), 219.
11 Laura Seay and Kim Yi Donne, "The Long and Ugly Tradition of Treating Africa as a Dirty, Diseased Place," *Washington Post*, August 25, 2014, https://www .washingtonpost.com/news/monkey-cage/wp/2014/08/25/othering-ebola-and-the -history-and-politics-of-pointing-at-immigrants-as-potential-disease-vectors/.
12 Ibid.
13 Alan M. Kraut, "Foreign Bodies: The Perennial Negotiation over Health and Culture in a Nation of Immigrants," *Journal of American Ethnic History* 23.2 (Winter 2004): 5.
14 Louis Jacobson, "Rep. Phil Gingrey Says Migrants May Be Bringing Ebola Virus through the U.S.–Mexico Border," *Politifact*, July 18, 2014, http://www.politifact .com/truth-o-meter/statements/2014/jul/18/phil-gingrey/rep-phil-gingrey-says -migrants-may-be-bringing-ebo/.
15 Louis Jacobson, "Are Illegal Immigrants Bringing 'Tremendous' Disease across the Border, as Trump Says? Unlikely," *Politifact*, July 23, 2015, http://www .politifact.com/truth-o-meter/article/2015/jul/23/are-illegal-immigrants-bringing -tremendous-diseas/.
16 Geddes Smith, *Plague on Us* (New York: Commonwealth Fund, 1941), 23.
17 Thomas R. Feller, "World War Z," *Science Fiction Film and Television* 7.3 (Autumn 2014): 447.

18 Elizabeth Goren, "Society's Use of the Hero following a National Trauma," *American Journal of Psychoanalysis* 67 (2007): 44.

19 Jacqueline Foertsch, *Enemies Within: The Cold War and the AIDS Crisis in Literature, Film, and Culture* (Urbana: University of Illinois Press, 2001), 28.

20 "Trump: I'll Build the Wall and Mexico's Going to Pay for It," *CNN* video, July 31, 2015, http://www.cnn.com/videos/us/2015/07/31/trump-mexico-border-foster-new-day.cnn.

21 "Great Again TV Spot," Donald J. Trump for President, January 4, 2016, accessed May 18, 2017, https://www.youtube.com/watch?v=itsSDhgKwhw.

22 In an interview with WGIR radio that was captured by the New Hampshire Democratic Party, Brown was asked whether he favored travel restrictions on some passengers in and out of West Africa. He replied: "We need a comprehensive approach and I think that should be part of it. I think it's all connected. For example, we have people coming into our country by legal means bringing in diseases and other potential challenges. Yet we have a border that's so porous that anyone can walk across it. I think it's naive to think that people aren't going to be walking through here who have those types of diseases and/or other types of intent, criminal or terrorist. And yet we do nothing to secure our border." Quoted in Greg Sargent, "Scott Brown: Anyone with Ebola Can 'Walk Across' Our 'Porous' Border," *Washington Post*, October 14, 2014, https://www.washingtonpost.com/blogs/plum-line/wp/2014/10/14/scott-brown-anyone-with-ebola-can-walk-across-our-porous-border/.

23 E. Ann Kaplan, *Trauma Culture* (New Brunswick, NJ: Rutgers University Press, 2005), 9.

24 Robin Cook, *Invasion* (New York: Berkley Publishing, 1997), 238.

25 Kirsten Ostherr, *Cinematic Prophylaxis: Globalization and Contagion in the Discourse of World Health* (Durham, NC: Duke University Press, 2005), 50.

26 Ibid., 123–124, 131.

27 Frank Furedi, *Culture of Fear Revisited* (London: Continuum, 2006), xiv.

28 Richard Preston, *The Hot Zone* (New York: Anchor Books, 1994), 405, 406.

29 Allison Fraiberg, "Of AIDS, Cyborgs, and Other Indiscretions: Resurfacing the Body in the Postmodern," *Postmodern Culture* 1.3 (May 1991): 6.

30 Alexander R. Galloway and Eugene Thacker, *The Exploit: A Theory of Networks* (Minneapolis: University of Minnesota Press, 2007), 86.

31 Peter Christian Hall, "How the *Contagion* Virus Was Born," *Reuters*, September 13, 2011, http://www.reuters.com/article/idUS57323549020110913.

32 Geoffrey Cowley "How Progress Makes Us Sick," *Newsweek*, May 4, 2003, http://www.newsweek.com/how-progress-makes-us-sick-137163.

33 Torin Monahan, "Just-in-Time Security," in *Reading "24": TV against the Clock*, ed. Steven Peacock (London: I. B. Tauris, 2007), 109.

34 Geoffrey Crowley, "Outbreak of Fear," *Newsweek*, May 21, 1995, http://www.newsweek.com/outbreak-fear-183188.

35 Heather Schell, "The Sexist Gene: Science Fiction and the Germ Theory of History," *American Literary History* 4.4 (Winter 2002): 823.

36 Frederic Jameson, *The Geopolitical Aesthetic: Cinema and Space in the World System* (Bloomington: Indiana University Press, 1992), 3.

37 Peter Knight, *Conspiracy Culture: From Kennedy to "The X-Files"* (London: Routledge, 2000), 208.

38 Ruth Mayer, "Virus Discourse: The Rhetoric of Threat and Terrorism in the Bio-thriller," *Cultural Critique* 66 (Spring 2007): 2.

39 All categories are taken from table 1.10 in Richard Nowell, *Blood Money: A History of the First Teen Slasher Film Cycle* (New York: Continuum, 2011), 55.

Chapter 2 The Globalization Outbreak

1 Roland Robertson, *Globalization: Social Theory and Global Culture* (London: Sage Publications, 1992), 8.

2 Alexander R. Galloway and Eugene Thacker, *The Exploit: A Theory of Networks* (Minneapolis: University of Minnesota Press, 2007), 9.

3 Robert Gilpin, *The Challenge of Global Capitalism* (Princeton, NJ: Princeton University Press, 2002), excerpted in *New York Times*, https://www.nytimes.com/books/first/g/gilpin-capitalism.html.

4 Alexander Galloway, *Protocol* (Cambridge, MA: MIT Press, 2004), 31.

5 Jose van Dijck, *The Culture of Connectivity: A Critical History of Social Media* (New York: Oxford University Press, 2013), 5.

6 Manuel Castells, *The Rise of the Network Society* (Malden: Blackwell, 1996), quoted in Jussi Parikka, "Digital Monsters, Binary Aliens—Computer Viruses, Capitalism and the Flow of Information," *Fibreculture Journal* 4 (2005): par. 3, http://four.fibreculturejournal.org/fcj-019-digital-monsters-binary-aliens-%E2%80%93-computer-viruses-capitalism-and-the-flow-of-information/.

7 Jonathan Crary, *24/7* (London: Verso, 2013), 42.

8 Galloway and Thacker, *The Exploit*, 10, 25.

9 Ed Cohen, "The Paradoxical Politics of Viral Containment; or, How Scale Undoes Us One and All," *Social Text* 29.1 106 (Spring 2011): 17.

10 Steven Melendez, "What 'Safety Check' Reveals about Facebook's Changing Role," *Fast Company*, July 7, 2016, http://www.fastcompany.com/3061576/safety-check-facebook.

11 Priscilla Wald, *Contagious: Cultures, Carriers, and the Outbreak Narrative* (Durham, NC: Duke University Press, 2008), 22.

12 Stacy Takacs, *Terrorism TV: Popular Entertainment in Post-9/11 America* (Lawrence: University Press of Kansas, 2012), 67.

13 Ibid., 69.

14 Bonnie Noonan, *Gender in Science Fiction Films, 1964–1979* (Jefferson, NC: McFarland & Company, 2015), 81.

15 Ibid., 82, 83.

16 David Holloway, *Cultures of the War on Terror: Empire, Ideology, and the Remaking of 9/11* (Montreal: McGill-Queen's University Press, 2008), 83.

17 Bonnie Noonan, *Women Scientists in Fifties Science Fiction Films* (Jefferson, NC: McFarland & Company, 2005), 44, 48–49.

18 Eileen Pollack, "Why Are There Still So Few Women in Science?," *New York Times*, October 3, 2013, http://www.nytimes.com/2013/10/06/magazine/why-are-there-still-so-few-women-in-science.html?_r=0.

19 Noonan, *Gender in Science Fiction*, 109.

20 Laura Prudom, "*The X-Files*: Gillian Anderson Was Offered Half as Much as David Duchovny for Revival Series," *Variety*, January 22, 2016, http://variety.com/2016/

tv/news/gillian-anderson-pay-gap-x-files-david-duchovny-x-files-revival-salary
-1201686438/.

21 Kirsten Ostherr, *Cinematic Prophylaxis: Globalization and Contagion in the Discourse of World Health* (Durham, NC: Duke University Press, 2005), 6.

22 Ibid., 7.

23 Ibid.

24 Joshua Clover, "Fall and Rise," *Film Quarterly* 65.2 (Winter 2011): 8.

25 Brent Bellamy, "Contagion," *Science Fiction Film and Television* 6.1 (Spring 2013): 122.

26 Scott Z. Burns, interview with author, November 18, 2015.

27 Edward Douglas, "Interview: *Contagion* Writer Scott Z. Burns," *Coming Soon*, September 6, 2011, http://www.comingsoon.net/news/movienews.php?id=81596.

28 Peter Christian Hall, "How the *Contagion* Virus Was Born," *Reuters*, September 13, 2011, http://blogs.reuters.com/fanfare/2011/09/13/how-the-contagion-virus-was-born/.

29 Scott Z. Burns, interview with author, November 18, 2015.

30 Melinda Burns, interview with author, October 16, 2015.

31 Leonard A. Cole, *Clouds of Secrecy: The Army's Germ Warfare Tests over Populated Areas* (Lanham: Rowman & Littlefield, 1990), 80, 81.

32 George Wilson, "Army Conducted 239 Secret, Open-Air Germ Warfare Tests," *Washington Post*, March 9, 1977, https://www.washingtonpost.com/archive/politics/1977/03/09/army-conducted-239-secret-open-air-germ-warfare-tests/b17e5ee7-3006-4152-acf3-0ad163e17a22/.

33 Ian Sample, "Mutant Virus Experiments Risk Unleashing Global Pandemic," *Guardian*, May 21, 2014, http://www.rawstory.com/2014/05/mutant-virus-experiments-risk-unleashing-global-pandemic-study-warns/.

34 Frank Furedi, *Culture of Fear Revisited* (London: Continuum, 2006), 74.

35 Peter N. Stearns, *American Fear: The Causes and Consequences of High Anxiety* (New York: Routledge, 2006), 36, 40, 42–43.

36 Mary Ann Doane, "Information, Crisis, Catastrophe," in *Logics of Television: Essays in Cultural Criticism*, ed. Patricia Mellencamp (Bloomington: Indiana University Press, 1990), 230.

37 Daniel Yergin, "The Age of 'Globality,'" *Newsweek*, May 18, 1998, https://web.archive.org/web/20090323082216/http://www.newsweek.com/id/92486?tid=relatedcl.

38 Paul Virilio, quoted in Anne Friedberg, *The Virtual Window: From Alberti to Microsoft* (Cambridge, MA: MIT Press, 2006), 188.

39 Vivian Sobchack, "Comprehending Screens: A Meditation *in Media Res*," *Rivista di estetica*, n.s., 55 (Jan. 2014): 92.

40 Ibid., 88.

41 Editorial Board, "Fear Spreads Faster than Ebola: Our View," *USA Today*, October 14, 2014, http://www.usatoday.com/story/opinion/2014/10/14/ebola-aids-sars-fear-virus-cdc-facts-editorials-debates/17280073/.

42 Stacy Lu, "An Epidemic of Fear," *Monitor on Psychology* 46.3 (Mar. 2015): par. 1, http://www.apa.org/monitor/2015/03/fear.aspx.

43 Doane, "Information, Crisis, Catastrophe," 223.

44 Galloway and Thacker, *The Exploit*, 91.

45 D. M. Berry, *The Philosophy of Software: Code and Mediation in the Digital Age* (London: Palgrave, 2011), 4.
46 Galloway and Thacker, *The Exploit*, 10.

Chapter 3   The Terrorism Outbreak

1   "How Much Did the September 11 Terrorist Attack Cost America?," The Institute for the Analysis of Global Security, accessed May 19, 2017, http://www.iags.org/costof911.html.
2   Public Law 107–40 (2001), http://www.gpo.gov/fdsys/pkg/PLAW-107publ40/html/PLAW-107publ40.htm (emphasis added).
3   Michel Foucault, *Discipline and Punish: The Birth of the Prison* (New York: Random House, 1995), 195, 197–199, 231.
4   Michel Foucault, *Abnormal: Lectures at the Collège de France, 1974–1975* (New York: Picador, 2003), 41.
5   Foucault, *Discipline and Punish*, 195, 197–199, 195.
6   Foucault, *Abnormal*, 47.
7   Alexander R. Galloway and Eugene Thacker, *The Exploit: A Theory of Networks* (Minneapolis: University of Minnesota Press, 2007), 26.
8   Peter N. Stearns, *American Fear: The Causes and Consequences of High Anxiety* (New York: Routledge, 2006), 190.
9   Ibid., 190–191.
10 Alison Bashford, "Panic's Past and Global Futures," in *Empires of Panic: Epidemics and Colonial Anxieties*, ed. Robert Peckham (Hong Kong: Hong Kong University Press, 2015), 208.
11 Jonathan Metzl, interview by Harry Smith, "Psychological Effects after Terror Attacks," *MSNBC Live*, MSNBC, Nov. 21, 2015.
12 Ibid.
13 Kevin J. Wetmore, *Post-9/11 Horror in American Cinema* (London: Continuum, 2012), 173.
14 Art Spiegelman, *In the Shadow of No Towers* (New York: Pantheon Books, 2004), 1.
15 John Donne, *Devotions upon Emergent Occasions and Death's Duel* (New York: Vintage, 1999), 3.
16 Susan Sontag, *Illness as Metaphor and AIDS and Its Metaphors* (New York: Doubleday, 1990), 97.
17 Ibid., 105, 106.
18 Joanna Burke, *Fear: A Cultural History* (Emeryville, CA: Shoemaker & Hoard, 2006), 311.
19 Emily Martin, *Flexible Bodies: The Role of Immunity in American Culture from the Days of Polio to the Age of AIDS* (Boston: Beacon Press, 1994), 51, 53.
20 Christine Gorman, "Returning Fire against AIDS," *Time*, June 24, 1991, 44.
21 Randy Shilts, *And the Band Played On: Politics, People, and the AIDS Epidemic* (New York: St. Martin's Press, 1988), 518.
22 Paula Treichler, "AIDS, Homophobia and Biomedical Discourse: An Epidemic of Signification," in *AIDS: Cultural Analysis, Cultural Activism*, ed. Douglas Crimp (Cambridge, MA: MIT Press, 1988), 60.
23 George F. Kennan, quoted in Mark Neocleous, *Critique of Security* (Montreal: McGill-Queen's University Press, 2008), 118.

24 Walter Rostow, quoted in Michael A. Hennessy, *Strategy in Vietnam: The Marines and Revolutionary Warfare in I Corps, 1965–1972* (Westport, CT: Praeger, 1997), 18.

25 Colleen Bell, "Hybrid Warfare and Its Metaphors," *Humanity: An International Journal of Human Rights, Humanitarianism, and Development* 3.2 (Summer 2012): 226.

26 Ibid., 240.

27 David Kilcullen, *The Accidental Guerilla* (New York: Oxford University Press, 2009), 35–38.

28 Richard N. Haas, quoted in Ruth Mayer, "Virus Discourse: The Rhetoric of Threat and Terrorism in the Biothriller," *Cultural Critique* 66 (Spring 2007): 5.

29 Nick B. King, "Dangerous Fragments," *Grey Room* 7 (Spring 2002): 75.

30 Ibid., 77.

31 Yudhijit Bhattacharjee, "FBI to Request Scientific Review of Its Anthrax Investigation," *Science*, September 16, 2008, http://news.sciencemag.org/scientific-community/2008/09/fbi-request-scientific-review-its-anthrax-investigation.

32 William J. Broad, "Inquiry in Anthrax Mailings Had Gaps, Report Says," *New York Times*, December 19, 2014, http://www.nytimes.com/2014/12/20/science/inquiry-in-anthrax-mailings-had-gaps-report-says.html?ref=topics&_r=0.

33 King, "Dangerous Fragments," 77.

34 "You Are Either with Us or against Us," *CNN*, November 6, 2001, http://edition.cnn.com/2001/US/11/06/gen.attack.on.terror/.

35 Boaz Ganor, "Terrorism Networks: It Takes a Network to Beat a Network," in *The Network Challenge: Strategy, Profit, and Risk in an Interlinked World*, ed. Paul R. Kleindorfer, Yoram (Jerry) Wind, and Robert E. Gunther (Upper Saddle River, NJ: Wharton School Publishing, 2009), 454.

36 Walter Laqueur, "Postmodern Terrorism," *Foreign Affairs* 75.5 (Sept.–Oct. 1996): 34.

37 Ibid., 33, 28.

38 Gilles Deleuze, "Postscript on the Societies of Control," *October* 59 (Winter 1992): 3–7.

39 Alexander Galloway, *Protocol* (Cambridge, MA: MIT Press, 2004), 201, 204.

40 King, "Dangerous Fragments," 75.

41 Lynn Spigel, "Entertainment Wars: Television Culture after 9/11," *American Quarterly* 56.2 (June 2004): 244.

42 Stacy Takacs, *Terrorism TV: Popular Entertainment in Post-9/11 America* (Lawrence: University Press of Kansas, 2012), 61, 65.

43 Matthew B. Hill, "Tom Clancy, *24*, and the Language of Autocracy," in *The War on Terror and American Popular Culture*, ed. Andrew Schopp and Matthew B. Hill (Madison, NJ: Fairleigh Dickinson University Press, 2009), 127.

44 Laqueur, "Postmodern Terrorism," 34.

45 Hill, "Language of Autocracy," 128.

46 Silvio Waisbord, "Journalism, Risk, and Patriotism," in *Journalism after September 11*, ed. Barbie Zelizer and Stuart Allen (New York: Routledge, 2002), 213.

47 Takacs, *Terrorism TV*, 65.

48 Ibid., 66.

49 Ibid., 61.

50 James William Gibson, *The Perfect War: Technowar in Vietnam* (New York: Vintage, 1988), 200.

51 Takacs, *Terrorism TV*, 60.

52 Justin Lewis, Richard Maxwell, and Toby Miller, "9-11," *Television and New Media* 3.2 (2002): 126.

53 Takacs, *Terrorism TV*, 62.

54 Giorgio Agamben, *The State of Exception*, trans. Kevin Attell (Chicago: University of Chicago Press, 2005), 22.

55 Noah Feldman, "Our Presidential Era: Who Can Check the President?," *New York Times*, January 8, 2006, http://www.nytimes.com/2006/01/08/magazine/08court .html?pagewanted=print&_r=0.

56 "Bush Approval Falls to 33%, Congress Earns Rare Praise," Pew Research Center, March 15, 2006, http://www.people-press.org/2006/03/15/bush-approval-falls-to -33-congress-earns-rare-praise/.

57 Caroline Daniel, "Power Play: Why Bush Is Facing a Backlash against His 'Imperial' Presidency," *Financial Times*, July 6, 2006, http://www.ft.com/cms/s/0/148939e0 -0c8c-11db-8235-0000779e2340.html#axzz3wF2KU6Eh.

58 "Section 1: Trust in Government: 1958–2010," Pew Research Center, April 18, 2010, http://www.people-press.org/2010/04/18/section-1-trust-in-government-1958 -2010/.

59 Jennifer Gillan, *Television and New Media: Must Click TV* (New York: Routledge, 2011), 127.

60 Jane Mayer, "Whatever It Takes: The Politics of the Man Behind *24*," *New Yorker*, February 19, 2007, http://www.newyorker.com/magazine/2007/02/19/whatever-it -takes.

61 Bill Keveney, "Fictional *24* Brings Real Issue of Torture Home," *USA Today*, March 13, 2005, http://www.usatoday.com/life/television/news/2005-03-13-24 -torture_x.htm.

62 Torin Monahan, "Just-in-Time Security," in *Reading "24": TV against the Clock*, ed. Steven Peacock (London: I. B. Tauris, 2007), 114.

63 Anne Friedberg, *Virtual Window: From Alberti to Microsoft* (Cambridge, MA: MIT Press, 2006), 193–194.

64 Hill, "Language of Autocracy," 138.

65 Ibid., 136, 139.

66 Ibid., 139.

67 Bo Kampmann Walter "The Art of Staying Tuned in Real-Time. Remediation in *24*," *Contemporanea: Journal of Communication and Culture* 1.1 (2005): 30.

68 Christopher Gair, "*24* and Post-National American Identities," in *Reading "24": TV against the Clock*, ed. Steven Peacock (New York: I. B. Tauris, 2007), 202.

69 Hill, "Language of Autocracy," 134.

70 Ibid., 141.

71 Elwood Reid, e-mail message to author, November 3, 2015.

72 Mark Wheelis, "Biological Warfare at the 1346 Siege of Caffa," *Emerging Infectious Diseases* 8.9 (Sept. 2002): par. 2, http://wwwnc.cdc.gov/eid/article/8/9/01-0536 _article.

73 Dan Brown, *Inferno* (New York: Anchor Books, 2014), 60, 131.

74 Monahan, "Just-in-Time Security," 111.

75 Leger Grindon, "Cycles and Clusters," in *Film Genre Reader IV*, ed. Barry Keith Grant (Austin: University of Texas Press, 2012), 55.

76 Mayer, "Virus Discourse," 14–15.

77 "Apparent Suicide of Anthrax Suspect," *New York Times* video, August 1, 2008, http://www.nytimes.com/video/us/1194817108194/apparent-suicide-of-anthrax -suspect.html.

78 Mayer, "Virus Discourse," 5.

79 Jean Baudrillard, quoted in Ruth Mayer, "Virus Discourse: The Rhetoric of Threat and Terrorism in the Biothriller," *Cultural Critique* 66 (Spring 2007): 6.

80 Richard Haas, quoted in ibid.

81 Takacs, *Terrorism TV*, 75.

Chapter 4   The Postapocalypse Outbreak

1 John Knefel, "Apocalypse Soon: 9 Terrifying Signs of Environmental Doom and Gloom," *Rolling Stone*, August 18, 2015, http://www.rollingstone.com/culture/ news/apocalyse-soon-9-terrifying-signs-of-environmental-doom-and-gloom -20150818.

2 Cited in Roger Luckhurst, *Zombies: A Cultural History* (London: Reaktion Books, 2015), 30, 31.

3 Ibid., 81, 82.

4 Ibid., 109.

5 Ibid., 110.

6 Primo Levi, *If This Is a Man*, trans. Stuart Woolf (London: Orion Press, 1947), 96.

7 Luckhurst, *Zombies*, 119–120.

8 Ibid., 110–111.

9 Mariana McConnell, "Interview: George A. Romero on Diary of the Dead," *Cinemablend*, January 14, 2008, http://www.cinemablend.com/new/Interview-George -Romero-Diary-Dead-7818.html.

10 "Box Office History for George A. Romero's Dead Series Movies," The Numbers: Where Data and Box Office Meet, accessed May 18, 2017, http://www.the-numbers .com/movies/franchise/George-A-Romeros-Dead-Series#tab=summary.

11 Jamie Russell, *Book of the Dead: The Complete History of Zombie Cinema* (Godalming, Surrey: FAB Press, 2005), 151.

12 Luckhurst, *Zombies*, 169.

13 "Resident Evil," Box Office Mojo, accessed May 19, 2017, http://www.boxofficemojo .com/franchises/chart/?id=residentevil.htm.

14 Kyle William Bishop, *American Zombie Gothic* (Jefferson, NC: McFarland & Company, 2010), 10.

15 "Most Popular 'Zombie' Feature Films Released 2015-01-01 to 2015-12-31," IMDb, accessed May 18, 2017, http://www.imdb.com/search/title?at=0&keywords= zombie&sort=moviemeter,asc&title_type=feature&year=2015,2015.

16 James Berger, *After the End: Representations of Post-Apocalypse* (Minneapolis: University of Minnesota Press, 1999), 5.

17 Bishop, *American Zombie Gothic*, 18.

18 Alexander R. Galloway and Eugene Thacker, *The Exploit: A Theory of Networks* (Minneapolis: University of Minnesota Press, 2007), 9.

19 Steven Pokornowski, "Insecure Lives: Zombies, Global Health, and the Totalitarianism of Generalization," *Literature and Medicine* 31.2 (Fall 2013): 223.

20 Nick Muntean, "Nuclear Death and Radical Hope in *Dawn of the Dead* and *On the Beach*," *Better Off Dead: The Evolution of the Zombie as Post-Human*, ed.

Deborah Christie and Sarah Juliet Lauro (New York: Fordham University Press, 2011), 83.

21 Alexander Galloway, *Protocol* (Cambridge, MA: MIT Press, 2004), 31.

22 Stephanie Boluk and Wylie Lenz, "Introduction: Generation Z: The Age of Apocalypse," *Generation Zombie: Essays on the Living Dead in Modern Culture*, ed. Stephanie Boluk and Wylie Lenz (Jefferson, NC: McFarland & Company, 2011), 6.

23 Marina Warner, *Phantasmagoria: Spirit Visions, Metaphors, and Media into the Twenty-First Century* (Oxford: Oxford University Press, 2006), 357.

24 The movie *Warm Bodies* (Levine, 2013), with the tag line "He was dead inside until he met her," and the television show *iZombie* (CW, 2014–present) are two rare exceptions where the zombie has an actual point of view.

25 Kevin J. Wetmore, *Post-9/11 Horror in American Cinema* (London: Continuum, 2012), 2, 159–160.

26 Nick Muntean and Matthew Thomas Payne, "Attack of the Livid Dead: Recalibrating Terror in the Post–September 11 Zombie Film," in *The War on Terror and American Popular Culture: September 11 and Beyond*, ed. Andrew Schopp and Matthew B. Hill (Madison, NJ: Fairleigh Dickinson University Press, 2009), 246–247.

27 Robert Kirkman, quoted in David Peisner, "The Rise of *The Walking Dead*," *Rolling Stone*, October 31, 2013, http://www.rollingstone.com/movies/news/the-rise-of-the -walking-dead-20131031#ixzz3jyV383bD.

28 Kevin Voigt, "Hong Kong and SARS: A City under Siege," *CNN*, February 21, 2013, http://www.cnn.com/2013/02/21/world/asia/hong-kong-sars-anniversary/.

29 Bishop, *American Zombie Gothic*, 28.

30 Steven Pokornowski, "Burying the Living with the Dead: Security, Survival and the Sanction of Violence," in *We're All Infected*, ed. Dawn Keetley (Jefferson, NC: McFarland & Company, 2014), 53.

31 Ezra Klein, "Don't Be Afraid of Fast Zombies," *Washington Post*, November 15, 2015, https://www.washingtonpost.com/news/wonk/wp/2013/06/28/dont-be-afraid-of -fast-zombies/.

32 Wetmore, *Post-9/11 Horror*, 2.

33 Douglas Kellner, *Cinema Wars* (West Sussex: Wiley Blackwell, 2010), 81.

34 Susan Sontag, "The Imagination of Disaster," in *Film Theory and Criticism*, ed. Gerald Mast and Marshall Cohen (New York: Oxford University Press, 1974), 437.

35 Taffy Brodessor-Akner, "Max Brooks Is Not Kidding about the Zombie Apocalypse," *New York Times*, June 21, 2013, http://www.nytimes.com/2013/06/23/ magazine/max-brooks-is-not-kidding-about-the-zombie-apocalypse.html?ref= magazine&_r=1.

36 Terry Matalas, interview with author, July 29, 2015.

37 Andy Coghlan, quoted in Bishop, *American Zombie Gothic*, 27.

38 Pokornowski, "Insecure Lives," 200.

39 Luckhurst, *Zombies*, 181.

40 Luis P. Villarreal, "Are Viruses Alive?," *Scientific American* 291.6 (Dec. 2004): 104.

41 Wendell Stanley, quoted in Priscilla Wald, *Contagious: Cultures, Carriers, and the Outbreak Narrative* (Durham, NC: Duke University Press, 2008), 163.

42 Danny Boyle, quoted in Bishop, *American Zombie Gothic*, 28.

43 Richard Preston, *The Hot Zone* (New York: Anchor Books, 1995), 98.

44 Rob Thomas, e-mail message to author, October 18, 2016.

45 Gillian Bennett, *Bodies: Sex, Violence, Disease, and Death in Contemporary Legend* (Jackson: University Press of Mississippi, 2005), 105, 111.

46 Gwyneth Peaty, "Infected with Life: Neo-Supernaturalism and the Gothic Zombie," in *Gothic Science Fiction: 1980–2010*, ed. Sara Wasson and Emily Alder (Liverpool: Liverpool University Press, 2014), 108.

47 Josh Levin, "Dead Run," *Slate*, March 24, 2004, http://www.slate.com/articles/arts/culturebox/2004/03/dead_run.html.

48 Max Brooks, in his *Zombie Survival Guide*, describes a zombie's top speed as slower than a human's calm stride: "Zombies appear to be incapable of running. The fastest have been observed to move at a rate of barely one step per 1.5 seconds." Max Brooks, *The Zombie Survival Guide: Complete Protection from the Living Dead* (New York: Three Rivers Press, 2003), 13.

   The original book version of *World War Z*, written by Brooks, uses slow zombies, while the movie uses quick ones. Brooks himself cannot imagine how much more terrifying quick zombies would be. Brodessor-Akner, "Brooks Is Not Kidding."

   Simon Pegg, co-writer and star of *Shaun of the Dead* (Wright, 2004), argues that "Zombies don't run! I know it is absurd to debate the rules of a reality that does not exist, but this genuinely irks me. You cannot kill a vampire with an MDF stake; werewolves can't fly; zombies do not run. It's a misconception, a bastardisation that diminishes a classic movie monster." Simon Pegg, "The Dead and the Quick," *Guardian*, November 4, 2008, https://www.theguardian.com/media/2008/nov/04/television-simon-pegg-dead-set.

49 Keetley, "Introduction," in *We're All Infected*, ed. Dawn Keetley (Jefferson, NC: McFarland & Company, 2014), 4.

50 Ibid., 7, 10.

51 Steven Kane, e-mail message to author, August 6, 2015.

52 Natalie Abrams, "Syfy's *12 Monkeys* Changes the Rules of the Movie," *Entertainment Weekly*, January 6, 2015, http://www.ew.com/article/2015/01/16/12-monkeys-syfy.

53 Max Brooks, *World War Z: An Oral History of the Zombie War* (New York: Three Rivers Press, 2006), 53–54.

54 The reason they want the DC2 virus (codename "Project Terror") is complex. Rather than predictably wanting it to take over the world or conquer governments, like in *24*, these military thugs want it in order to prevent themselves from becoming zombies. As in *Covert One: The Hades Factor*, these men were originally infected with the virus while hunting Osama Bin Laden. The unique twist here is that in order to prevent themselves from turning into horrific monsters, they need to be exposed continually to low doses of DC2, which stops the infection from spreading. At the same time, if they continue to infect enough people, and then experiment on the survivors, they also increase the chance of finding a cure for themselves. So in this case, their agenda is both self-preservation, and destruction of anyone who gets in the way.

55 Brodessor-Akner, "Brooks Is Not Kidding."

56 Kim Paffenroth, "For Love Is Strong as Death," in *Triumph of "The Walking Dead": Robert Kirkman's Zombie Epic on Page and Screen*, ed. James Lowder (Dallas: Smart Pop Books, 2011), 222.

57 Mary Ann Doane, "Information, Crisis, Catastrophe," in *Logics of Television: Essays*

in Cultural Criticism, ed. Patricia Mellencamp (Bloomington: Indiana University Press, 1990), 229.

58 Fred Botting, "Zombie Death Drive: Between Gothic and Science Fiction," in *Gothic Science Fiction: 1980–2010*, ed. Sara Wasson and Emily Alder (Liverpool: Liverpool University Press, 2014), 42.

59 Steve Beard, "No Particular Place to Go," *Sight and Sound* 3.4 (1993): 30.

60 Sean Moreland, "Shambling towards Mount Improbable to Be Born: American Evolutionary Anxiety and the Hopeful Monsters of Matheson's *I Am Legend* and Romero's *Dead* Films," *Generation Zombie: Essays on the Living Dead in Modern Culture*, ed. Stephanie Boluk and Wylie Lenz (Jefferson, NC: McFarland and Company, 2011), 81.

61 Keetley, "Introduction," 1.

62 Robert Kirkman, Charlie Adlard, and Cliff Rathburn, *The Walking Dead*, vol. 4: *The Heart's Desire* (Berkeley: Image Comics, 2005), 129.

63 Xavier Aldana Reyes, "Nothing but the Meat: Posthuman Bodies and the Dying Undead," in *We're All Infected*, ed. Dawn Keetley (Jefferson, NC: McFarland & Company, 2014), 146.

64 Julia Kristeva, quoted in Laura Kremmel, "Rest in Pieces: Violence in Mourning the Un(Dead)," in *We're All Infected*, ed. Dawn Keetley (Jefferson, NC: McFarland & Company, 2014), 84.

65 Chris Schilling, *Body and Social Theory* (London: Sage Publications, 2005), 60.

66 Bishop, *American Zombie Gothic*, 21.

67 Eugene Thacker, "Necrologies; or the Death of the Body Politic," in *Beyond Biopolitics*, ed. Patricia Ticineto Clough and Craig Willse (Raleigh, NC: Duke University Press, 2011), 157.

68 Giorgio Agamben, *Moyens sans fins. Notes sur la politique* (Paris: Payot & Rivages, 1995), 50–51, quoted in J.-A. Mbembe and Libby Meintjes, "Necropolitics," *Public Culture* 15.1 (Winter 2003): 12.

69 Hannah Arendt, *The Origins of Totalitarianism* (New York: Harvest, 1966), 444.

70 Luckhurst, *Zombies*, 174–175, 178.

71 Boluk and Lenz, "Introduction: Generation Z," 7.

72 Lisa Morton, "*The Walking Dead* and Dance of Death," in *Triumph of "The Walking Dead": Robert Kirkman's Zombie Epic on Page and Screen*, ed. James Lowder (Dallas: Smart Pop Books, 2011), 177.

73 Michel Foucault, *Society Must Be Defended: Lectures at the College de France*, 1976–1976 (New York: Picador, 2003), 243.

74 James A. Tyner, *War, Violence, and Population: Making the Body Count* (New York: Guilford Press, 2009), 31, 32.

75 Timothy J. Reiss, "Calculating Humans: Mathematics, War, and the Colonial Calculus," in *Arts of Calculation: Quantifying Thought in Early Modern England*, ed. David Glimp and Michelle R. Warren (New York: Palgrave Macmillan, 2004), 137–138, 144, 145, 153 (original emphasis).

76 Volha Piotukh, *Biopolitics, Governmentality, and Humanitarianism: "Caring" for the Population in Afghanistan and Belarus* (New York: Routledge, 2015), 70, 73, 74.

77 Michel Foucault, *The History of Sexuality*, vol. 1: *An Introduction* (New York: Pantheon Books, 1978), 135.

78 The "disposability of the infected" plays out not only in zombie texts but also in other apocalyptic texts as well. In *Blindness* (Meirelles, 2008), the infected are the

abject other. All those infected are taken to an increasingly crowded makeshift quarantine zone in an abandoned asylum. As they enter the quarantine facility, a voice-over declares, "The isolation in which you find yourselves represents above any personal considerations an act of solidarity with the rest of the nation." Submitting to quarantine is an act of patriotism! Despite the increasing urgency, the government ignores the people in the quarantine zone, denying them anything but the barest essentials, forcing the sick to fight over food and allowing the asylum to become overrun with filth and feces. The soldiers outside the asylum are hostile and refuse to get close to any of the infected. By the end of the movie, the same space that was once white and clean has turned into total squalor. People are raped in exchange for food, and eventually the asylum burns down after riots break out among the infected.

79 J. A. Mbembe and Libby Meintjes, "Necropolitics," *Public Culture* 15.1 (2003): 11.

80 Brooks, *World War Z*, 107, 109.

81 The movie *Nerve* (Joost and Schulman, 2016) takes this competition and literalizes and commodifies it, as players compete in ever more challenging "dares" for money, for fame, and for their lives.

82 Carlo Rotella, "The American City in Literature," *American Urbanism*, ed. Joseph Heathcott, forthcoming from Routledge.

83 Luckhurst, *Zombies*, 186.

84 James Hibbard, "*The Walking Dead*: How to Comprehend Its Massive Ratings," *Entertainment Weekly*, January 17, 2015, http://www.ew.com/article/2013/11/11/the-walking-dead-ratings.

85 Alan Sepinwall, "Record-Setting *Fear the Walking Dead* Debut Proves Americans Still Love Zombies," *HitFix*, August 24, 2015, http://www.hitfix.com/the-dartboard/record-setting-fear-the-walking-dead-debut-proves-americans-still-love-zombies#cLXCa9zoHfBUmQ6L.99.

86 Ned Vizzini, "Rick and Rand," in *Triumph of "The Walking Dead": Robert Kirkman's Zombie Epic on Page and Screen*, ed. James Lowder (Dallas: Smart Pop Books, 2011), 129.

87 Robert Kirkman, Tony Moore, and Cliff Rathburn, *The Walking Dead*, vol. 1: *Days Gone Bye* (Berkeley: Image Comics, 2008), 7.

88 Keetley, "Introduction," 6.

89 Kirkman, *Days Gone Bye*.

90 Frank Darabont, quoted in Jeff Jensen, "*The Walking Dead*: TV's Best New Bloodbath," *Entertainment Weekly*, November 12, 2010, http://www.ew.com/article/2010/11/12/walking-dead-tvs-best-new-bloodbath.

91 Scott Kenemore, "Rick Grimes: A Zombie among Men," in *Triumph of "The Walking Dead": Robert Kirkman's Zombie Epic on Page and Screen*, ed. James Lowder (Dallas: Benbella Books, 2011), 193.

92 P. Ivan Young, "Walking Tall or Walking Dead? The American Cowboy in the Zombie Apocalypse," in *We're All Infected*, ed. Dawn Keetley (Jefferson, NC: McFarland & Company, 2014), 59.

93 Anna Froula, "Homeland Insecurity: *The Walking Dead* on the Postapocalyptic Frontier," paper presented at the annual conference of the Society for Cinema and Media Studies (SCMS), March 2014.

94 Philip L. Simpson, "The Zombie Apocalypse Is upon Us!," *We're All Infected*, ed. Dawn Keetley (Jefferson, NC: McFarland & Company, 2014), 36, 37.

95 Kay Steiger, "No Clean Slate: Unshakable Race and Gender Politics in *The Walking Dead*," *Triumph of "The Walking Dead": Robert Kirkman's Zombie Epic on Page and Screen*, ed. James Lowder (Dallas: Smart Pop Books, 2011), 107.

96 Froula, "Homeland Insecurity."

97 Susan Faludi, *Terror Dream: Fear and Fantasy in Post-9/11 America* (New York: Macmillan, 2007), 14.

98 Ina Rae Hark, "Today Is the Longest Day of My Life," in *Film and Television after 9/11*, ed. Wheeler Winston Dixon (Carbondale: Southern Illinois University Press, 2004), 126, 127.

99 Wetmore, *Post-9/11 Horror*, 15.

100 Brendan Riley, "Zombie People," in *Triumph of "The Walking Dead": Robert Kirkman's Zombie Epic on Page and Screen*, ed. James Lowder (Dallas: Smart Pop Books, 2011), 86.

101 Robert Kirkman, quoted in David Peisner, "The Rise of *The Walking Dead*," *Rolling Stone*, October 31, 2013, http://www.rollingstone.com/movies/news/the-rise-of-the-walking-dead-20131031.

102 Vizzini, "Rick and Rand," 128.

103 Ibid.

104 Kirkman, *Days Gone Bye*, back cover.

105 Camilla Fojas, *Zombies, Migrants, and Queers: Race and Crisis Capitalism in Pop Culture* (Urbana: University of Illinois Press, 2017), 68, 69.

106 Jeffrey Sconce, *Haunted Media: Electronic Presence from Telegraphy to Television* (Durham, NC: Duke University Press, 2000), 115.

107 Sarah Juliet Lauro and Karen Embry, "A Zombie Manifesto: The Nonhuman Condition in the Era of Advanced Capitalism," *Boundary 2* 35.1 (Spring 2008): 89.

108 Douglas Kellner, "Baudrillard, Globalization, and Terrorism," *International Journal of Baudrillard Studies* 2.1 (Jan. 2005).

Conclusion

1 Todd Haynes, quoted in Jason Tougaw, "We're Still Vulnerable: Todd Haynes's Safe in 2011," *Women's Studies Quarterly* 39.1&2 (Spring/Summer 2011): 44.

2 "Multiple Chemical Sensitivities," Occupational Health and Safety Administration, United States Department of Labor, accessed May 17, 2017, https://www.osha.gov/SLTC/multiplechemicalsensitivities.

3 Peter Knight, "ILOVEYOU: Viruses, Paranoia, and the Environment of Risk," in *The Age of Anxiety: Conspiracy Theory and the Human Sciences*, ed. Jane Parish and Martin Parker (Oxford: Blackwell/Sociological Review Monograph, 2001), 17–30.

4 Nick Harding, "Truth and Lies: Conspiracy Theories Are Running Rampant Thanks to Modern Technology," *Independent*, November 11, 2011, http://www.independent.co.uk/life-style/gadgets-and-tech/features/truth-and-lies-conspiracy-theories-are-running-rampant-thanks-to-modern-technology-6260128.html.

5 This line was a reference to the famous quotation "We have met the enemy and they are ours" from American Navy Commodore Oliver Hazard Perry after defeating a British naval squadron during the War of 1812.

6 Elaine Showalter, *Hystories: Hysterical Epidemics and Modern Media* (New York: Columbia University Press, 1997), 5.

7   Ruth Mayer, "Virus Discourse: The Rhetoric of Threat and Terrorism in the Bio-thriller," *Cultural Critique* 66 (Spring 2007): 2.

8   John L. Sherry, "Media Saturation and Entertainment-Education," *Communication Theory* 12.2 (May 2002): 219.

9   Kyle William Bishop, *American Zombie Gothic* (Jefferson, NC: McFarland & Company, 2010), 35.

10 Skye Cooley, "The Flood of 2016: Southeast Louisiana and the Consequences of Real Community," *Huffington Post*, August 18, 2016, http://www.huffingtonpost .com/entry/the-flood-of-2016-southeast-louisiana-the-consequences_us _57b47ffae4b0b3bb4b088bcd.

11 Lynn Spigel, "Entertainment Wars: Television Culture after 9/11," *American Quarterly* 56.2 (June 2004): 238, 240.

12 Kirsten Ostherr, *Cinematic Prophylaxis: Globalization and Contagion in the Discourse of World Health* (Durham, NC: Duke University Press, 2005), 178.

13 Jennifer Gillan, *Television and New Media: Must Click TV* (New York: Routledge, 2011), 77, 94–95.

14 Itay Hod and Anita Bennett, "Why TV Newscasters Are Hollywood's Latest Casting Obsession," *Wrap*, December 22, 2015, http://www.thewrap.com/why-tv -newscasters-are-hollywoods-latest-casting-obsession/.

15 Tricia Jenkins, *The CIA in Hollywood: How the Agency Shapes Film and Television* (Austin: University of Texas Press, 2012), 74–75.

16 Richard Lindhelm, interview by Bob Edwards, *Morning Edition*, NPR, October 15, 2007.

17 Mayer, "Virus Discourse," 2.

18 Gillan, *Television*, 102, 107.

19 John Gibson, *The Big Story*, Fox News, January 16, 2007.

20 Cal Thomas, "Aquarius Sunset," *Townhall*, January 30, 2007, http://townhall.com/ columnists/calthomas/2007/01/30/aquarius_sunset.

21 Mayer, "Virus Discourse," 2.

22 Matthew Biedlingermaier, "Dietl Tells Imam 'the Facts of Life': 'If You're on a Plane with Me . . . You'll Be Looked at a Little . . . More Carefully than Me,'" *Media Matters for America*, January 19, 2007, http://mediamatters.org/research/2007/01/19/ dietl-tells-imam-the-facts-of-life-if-youre-on/137791.

23 E. Ann Kaplan, *Trauma Culture* (New Brunswick, NJ: Rutgers University Press, 2005), 2.

24 Sarah Whitten, "Misinformation Spreads on Social Media following Paris Attacks," *CNBC*, November 16, 2015, http://www.nbcnews.com/tech/tech-news/ misinformation-spreads-social-media-following-paris-attacks-n464291.

25 Alison Bashford, "Panic's Past and Global Futures," in *Empires of Panic: Epidemics and Colonial Anxieties*, ed. Robert Peckham (Hong Kong: Hong Kong University Press, 2015), 206.

Index

About the Author

DAHLIA SCHWEITZER is an adjunct professor at ArtCenter College of Design in Pasadena, California. Her previous works include *Cindy Sherman's Office Killer: Another Kind of Monster* as well as essays in publications such as *Cinema Journal, Journal of Popular Film and Television*, and *Journal of Popular Culture*.